The
GOURMET
GAZELLE
Cookbook

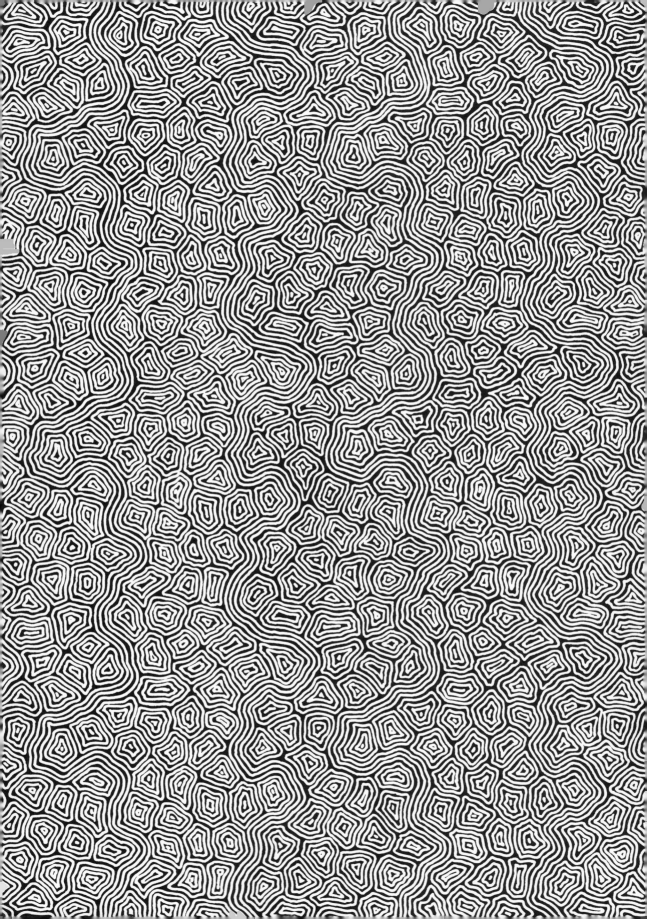

The GOURMET GAZELLE Cookbook

ELLEN BROWN

BANTAM BOOKS
NEW YORK • TORONTO • LONDON • SYDNEY • AUCKLAND

THE GOURMET GAZELLE COOKBOOK

A Bantam Book
Bantam hardcover edition / July 1989
Bantam trade paperback edition / June 1991

Book designed by Joel Avirom.

Library of Congress Catalog Card Number: 88-34234.

ISBN 0-553-35309-8

Published simultaneously in the United States and Canada

Bantam Books are published by Bantam Books, a division of
Bantam Doubleday Dell Publishing Group, Inc. Its trademark,
consisting of the words "Bantam Books" and the portrayal of a
rooster, is Registered in U.S. Patent and Trademark Office and in
other countries. Marca Registrada. Bantam Books, 666 Fifth Ave-
nue, New York, New York 10103.

PRINTED IN THE UNITED STATES OF AMERICA

KP   0 9 8 7 6 5 4 3 2 1

C O N T E N T S

Acknowledgments

While the actual writing of a book is a solitary effort, its completion is facilitated by the support and help of others. I would like to express my thanks:

To Suzanne and Michael Ainslie, my business partners, for their cherished friendship.

To Joe Printz, Gourmet Gazelle's first executive chef, who worked with me for hours developing recipes in a cramped New York apartment kitchen and who tastes food the same way I do.

To David Vaughan, for sharing his knowledge of wine and his choice of wines for these dishes.

To Coleen O'Shea, for her enthusiasm about the idea.

To Fran McCullough, not only for her superb editing skills, but also for her kindness and constant cheery encouragement.

To Gourmet Gazelle's investors, whose financial support allowed the concept of healthful eating on a retail level to briefly become reality.

To Lynne Hill of Hill Nutrition Associates, who analyzed all the recipes and has aided me so much over the years.

To my colleagues in the food world whose enthusiasm for the food, both verbally and in print, has been a source of pride and validation. My special thanks to Marian Burros, Ann Brody, Diane Worthington, Barbara Kafka, Carol Cutler, Barbara Tropp, John Mariani, and Jan Weimer.

To my friends, whose support, as always, was deeply felt and appreciated, with special thanks to Nancy Unger, Catherine Morrison, Barbara Walker, Meredith Whiting, Dick Earle, Helen Starr, and my sister, Nancy Dubler.

To Susan Preil, whose long hours in transcription made it possible to complete the manuscript.

To the many people who have tested the recipes to ensure they work in kitchens other than mine, especially to Val Sena, who mobilized all of Cincinnati to help in testing.

To Sam Cat the Magnificent and George Washington Park Cat, who kept me company in the kitchen and at the computer and ate all the mistakes.

Ellen Brown
Washington, D.C.

Introduction

This book is the result of one woman's lifelong battle with her hips. The battle has been waged since childhood and has certainly been exacerbated by the choice of profession as a food writer and consultant.

As the founding food editor of *USA Today*, I had what was perceived by my friends as a dream job. "Travel around the country and eat" was not the written job description; however, in reality that was how I spent my life. Between "research trips"—five to six meals a day—I would return to Washington and starve myself as penance for the most recent caloric transgressions.

I lived by a system of "calorie banking," which is the way most of us eat, whether or not we acknowledge the name. We save calories at lunch anticipating dinner, or we control lunch the next day, recalling the pastries ending the preceding dinner.

WHAT I WANTED TO DEVELOP WAS FOOD THAT WAS DELICIOUS, SATISFYING TO BOTH THE SENSES AND THE STOMACH, FOOD I WOULD NEVER SUSPECT WAS ACTUALLY GOOD FOR ME

I consider myself a walking calorie calculator, and I became increasingly concerned about cholesterol with every piece of *foie gras* I sampled. Although I enjoyed restaurant reviewing, I was becoming more and more convinced that healthy eating when at home had to become a way of life.

This philosophy was based on all the studies of the American Heart Association, the American Cancer Society, and the government concerning the relationship between sensible eating and longevity. In 1988, a comprehensive report by the U.S. Public Health Service was released linking diet to five of the top ten leading causes of death—heart disease, cancer, stroke, diabetes, and atherosclerosis.

Surgeon General C. Everett Koop wrote, "The report reveals clearly that the health of Americans could be improved by changing the diet to one that contains less fat."

I had already determined that it was necessary to control fat in order to control calories and, therefore, hip spread. However, the studies clearly showed that reducing fat to 30 percent of our caloric intake had far greater benefits.

Reducing salt intake in my diet also began with my extensive travels. In general, restaurant food is loaded with salt, and by cutting back in my own cooking I solved a frequent problem with water retention. Although I have never been plagued by high blood pressure, it is another physical problem that can be partially controlled through lower intake of sodium.

My need to eat more healthfully had to become reconciled,

however, with my rather jaded palate and demands that food be intellectually and emotionally satisfying.

The dishes in this book reflect my exuberance for ingredients. I love fresh herbs, start almost every dish with a few cloves of garlic, adore the gutsy spicing of southwestern cooking, and would rather eat at an Italian or a Chinese restaurant than any other.

I quickly discovered that bold flavors, vivid color combinations, contrasting textures, and a good nutritional profile were not mutually exclusive.

Many of these dishes are marinated, to add flavor while still cooking foods through dry heat methods such as grilling and broiling, which allow the saturated fat to be released.

While this was the way I was cooking at home, I became a professional practitioner of the style in 1987, when I designed the menu for The Portman San Francisco, a luxury hotel that wanted some nutritionally controlled items as an option.

This trend toward foods that are controlled in regard to calories, cholesterol, and sodium began decades ago at the country's top spas. It then spread to some restaurants, with New York's Four Seasons calling it "spa cuisine." Today, many luxury hotel chains, as well as independent restaurants, offer controlled options.

What I found at these spots, however, was a combination of elaborate presentation and portion control. I found neither approach acceptable. I was disappointed to realize how little innovation had been done commercially. Far more interesting dishes appeared on the pages of cookbooks than were being served at the restaurants featuring this genre of cooking.

As a home cook, I have always hated "fondled food" and assume most people agree with me. Six snow peas pointing in different directions around a portion of meat best observed through a magnifying glass is not what I consider a satisfying meal.

While there is a place for dramatic food, it is not the approach most cooks take to preparing dinner. At home, we are more likely to serve one platter than individual plates. Without the extra pairs of hands at our command to arrange those plates, which are available in restaurant kitchens, complicated presentation becomes a burden.

Portion control, the other popular approach, was also not a solution. Frankly, I left more meals hungry than I care to remember. Even a plate of calorie- and cholesterol-laden chocolate mousse can be calculated at fewer than 300 calories if it's the size of a quarter.

The problem, as I perceived it, was that the many talented restaurant chefs were applying the principles learned in classic, high-calorie restaurant cookery. They were merely cutting back on the portion size, perhaps eliminating some of the butter and cream, and emphasizing how food was presented rather than the food itself.

The foundation of my cooking is very different. By judiciously controlling the amount of fat and the use of egg yolks, and avoiding certain foods such as organ meats, both calories and cholesterol are harnessed. Nonfat yogurt and milk can convey a richness similar to that of heavy cream if pureed vegetables provide the texture. And dishes such as *soufflés* can be made successfully with just egg whites if the base is a fruit puree as thick as an emulsified custard.

In lieu of large quantities of salt, I use herbs, spices, and acids such as vinegar and citrus juices to perk the palate. In many cases, the balsamic vinegar or lemon juice is not detectable as a flavor; it is there to add vibrancy to the finished dish.

By adhering to this philosophy, I began to create dishes that were simultaneously healthy and hearty. This is not a book of "bunny food." Diets, to me, are synonymous with deprivation. They are for brief periods of time during which one suffers and pouts knowing they will be over soon, sort of like a case of the mumps.

What I wanted to develop was food that was delicious, satisfying to both the senses and the stomach, food I would never suspect was actually good for me.

My approach has certain idiosyncrasies. I use unsalted butter, albeit in small quantities, rather than soft margarine, which has a lower cholesterol count (but the same calories and fat content). Unfortunately, I have never tasted a margarine I like; to me they all taste oily and artificial. If you have a cholesterol problem, chances are you have switched to soft margarine, and the recipes specifying butter can be completed successfully with margarine as well. For a further discussion of which fats to use, see pages 284–285.

Other personal quirks include the use of no artificial sweeteners or salt substitutes. I think both categories of products leave a bitter, metallic taste on the tongue.

The Gourmet Gazelle Cookbook is not a diet book, although in "The Spa-at-Home Diet" chapter you will see how you can lose weight while following a planned eating program. This is a book for more healthful eating as part of everyday life.

In addition to exploring the potential range of ingredients, I want food to be sensual, in the most literal sense of the word, so our physiological responses to eating were factored into recipe concepts. The field of sensory perception is fascinating, and if our unconscious responses to eating are taken into account, almost any dish can be interpreted as satisfying by the brain.

We begin to alert our minds to whether or not we will like a food the moment we see it: we do eat first with our eyes. To our eyes, the stronger the color, the stronger the perceived flavor; that's why a leaf of iceberg lettuce is immediately termed "light," while a red bell pepper tells the brain "substantial."

Sight is also the tip-off to texture. That's why a thin sheet of browned phyllo dough, when we see light glistening on its crust, can produce a sense of satisfaction similar to a heavier, fat-laden egg roll wrapper.

Aroma is 80 to 90 percent of the tasting process, which is why ingredients such as garlic and fresh herbs are essential. The absence of aroma is why food tastes so bland when you have a cold and the nasal passages cannot function as part of this equation.

We experience aroma both through our nostrils and through the nasal cavity behind the mouth. Unless food is exactly body temperature, which is highly unlikely, cold food is warmed and hot food is cooled in the mouth. This process produces volatile compounds that are released through temperature changes while we chew.

The taste buds enter the picture only after sight and aroma have set the stage. Taste buds, which are located throughout the mouth and are concentrated on the top of the tongue, interpret only four sensations: sweet, located at the tip of the tongue; salty, on the front sides; sour, on the back sides; and bitter, at the back. Accenting vinegars and other sour flavors transmits the same signal to the brain as if the salt buds were more stimulated.

Another way foods are perceived is through the muscle structure. In the same way that your arm muscles send signals that an object you are picking up is either light or heavy, your facial muscles sense the force necessary to chew celery or a crust of bread. In the same way, the lack of pressure reinforces the creaminess of mashed potatoes.

The sense of hearing plays a role as well, both in anticipation and while eating. We begin to salivate at the sound of food grilling, hearing the sizzle as the juices drip onto the hot charcoal. And hearing the sound of hard food being chewed in the mouth validates the sensations being sent by the muscles.

The last reaction to monitor is the chemical sensations. Substances such as the potent oils of hot chili peppers induce chemical reactions, as do the bubbles in carbonated beverages, which cause mild pain in the mouth.

When all of these sensual reactions are taken into account, the experience of eating a food will have peaks and valleys rather than form a horizontal line. This undulating curve tells the brain the food is satisfying.

The joining of bold flavors and sensory perceptions produced the eclecticism of this book. There are also some pragmatic considerations. I limit the ingredient list mainly to those foods that can be purchased in any large supermarket, because there are few experiences more frustrating than deciding a dish sounds tantalizing only to discover the ingredients are available only in a specialty market in the Napa Valley.

Simplicity of preparation is also important. Dishes I originally planned for sale in the Gourmet Gazelle display case had to be cost-effective in terms of labor. If it took a cook three hours to cut vegetables for a certain salad, the cost per pound of that dish was extremely high. I've given total cooking times for each recipe, so you'll know when to start cooking, as well as hands-on work time, always under half an hour.

When I began revising those recipes for this book, I realized that this original approach made them quick and easy for the home cook as well, so the same economy of effort was considered with each new dish.

With each appropriate dish, wine recommendations are offered. Recent studies have shown that moderate alcohol consumption is not the evil it was once considered; in fact, it seems to be beneficial. But more important, this is a book for everyday eating, and part of my life is indulging my fondness for fine wines.

A glass of white or red wine (4 ounces) is merely 80 calories, and a glass of sweet dessert wine (3 ounces) is 138 calories, so I factor in those calories as part of my day. For a dinner party, you may want to serve a different wine with each course, so selections have been offered, acknowledging that most of us reserve a glass of wine to enjoy with our main dish. In the "Techniques" chapter, I explain how to freeze the wine remaining in a bottle to enjoy with a future dinner.

When asked to describe the dishes in this book, I've often said these are vibrant dishes with "added subtractions"—while they are low in calories, cholesterol, and sodium, they are high in flavor. I hope you enjoy them.

The History of
GOURMET GAZELLE

Many of the dishes in this book were initially developed for Gourmet Gazelle, the business Suzanne Ainslie and I co-founded on the Upper East Side of Manhattan in 1987; it closed in the spring of 1989. This short-lived critically acclaimed shop provided the opportunity for me to share my new style of cooking with the public.

While I had been cooking this way for myself, and had developed recipes professionally, I did not concentrate on the field until early 1987, when Suzanne and I determined to proceed.

Our rationale was that two of the fastest-growing trends in American food today—carryout for convenience and nutritionally controlled food for more healthful eating—had not previously been joined.

NO ONE LIKED THE WORD *DIET*

Suzanne and I had met in October 1986, prior to her marriage to my old friend Michael Ainslie.

Suzanne was a financial specialist working for a venture capital firm that funded small businesses. She, admittedly, did not know the difference at the time between a *soufflé* dish and a sauté pan. I had been professionally involved with food, and I, admittedly, at the time, did not know the difference between a Lotus program of financial projections and a page of hieroglyphics.

Theoretically, it was a front of the house, back of the house management team. The initial concept Suzanne and I discussed was my participation as a consultant to amass the inventory of a store called, as a working name, Diet Gourmet. She was frustrated that it took multiple stops to stock a pantry with low-calorie foods such as jams and salad dressings.

By April 1987, we had transformed the concept. We both realized that, especially in New York, gourmet carryout was an increasingly important alternative to eating in restaurants. After studying the future competition, we realized that while the cases at most shops looked attractive, none of the options were nutritionally sound. They were swimming in oil, or deep-fried, or the salads were glistening with mayonnaise.

I started developing recipes, and we began a series of focus groups to determine if those people we considered our target market liked the food and, more important, would buy it.

At these sessions we floated names and discovered that the selection of name was one of the most difficult problems facing us. Our market is both male and female, and there was no universal appeal to any word.

My first choice was Spa-to-Go, only to discover that men reacted to *spa* with the image of overweight women jumping around in sweat suits. Men didn't like anything including the word *lithe*; women didn't like the word *lean*. And no one liked the word *diet*.

It was at one of these sessions that I decided we had to abandon descriptive words and start thinking about imagery.

I then recalled a cartoon from my awkward adolescence that showed a gazelle standing on a hilltop, with another one flat on its back in the gully below. The caption was "for a gazelle, you're an awful klutz."

I had a positive feeling about gazelles, and I liked the alliteration of Gourmet Gazelle. The group approved of the gazelle. And so did the hundreds of people we then contacted to affirm the choice. After a name search determined that we could nationally register the mark, Gourmet Gazelle was incorporated.

We started working with Charles Morris Mount, an old friend whom I consider the best designer of food spaces in the country, and our logo and corporate identity became firmly based on this fleet-footed creature of the African plains.

I had a particular gazelle in mind—it's on a frieze of the Palm Court Bar of the Netherland Plaza Hotel in Cincinnati. It's an Art Deco gazelle, which was consistent with the postmodern design of the 1980s.

Where to cook the food was still a pressing problem. In this case, the lucky circumstance was Suzanne's acquaintance with Jean Christophe Le Picart, a young French caterer who, along with his partner, Emanuel du Chaunac, owned Tentation, an emerging force in New York's catering industry.

What began with our renting their Chelsea kitchen for a few weeks to cook lunch for prospective investors grew to a permanent relationship of integrated production with Tentation's executive chef also serving as our executive chef.

In August 1987, I moved two cats and a few boxes of kitchen equipment to New York. The shop was under construction, and we had a store manager, chef, and the chef's girlfriend all working out of my living room. Cases of jams and jellies were piled up to the ceiling in the Ainslies' kitchen. Cases of Gourmet Gazelle stainless-steel flatware to be used for promotion filled my closet. And we were touring the less-than-scenic sights of the South Bronx visiting paper distributors.

The store finally opened on October 19, 1987, known to most who follow Wall Street history as Black Monday. I remember walking into my apartment building and sharing an elevator with a man who kept shaking his head in disbelief and muttering, "I'm finished, wiped out." We had been so involved with living Murphy's Law that day—"If it can go wrong, it will"—with a deli case that froze the food and then died and a sales staff that couldn't make the cash register work, that neither of us had heard the news.

Five months after the shop opened on the Upper East Side, a boutique selling Gourmet Gazelle's dishes began in Macy's Cellar at Herald Square, a collection of gourmet counters in the basement of the world's largest department store.

In the same way that I maintained in my restaurant reviews that "you can't eat ambience," you also can't pay the rent with publicity. Gourmet Gazelle received rave notices in publications ranging from *Vogue* and *Bon Appétit* to *The New York Times* and *The Chicago Tribune,* but sales did not reach high enough levels to keep the business afloat once the initial capital was spent.

While the New York business no longer exists, the spirit of Gourmet Gazelle remains valid in the recipes contained in this book that can be made by people living in any city or state at any time.

Pairing Wine with Light Foods by David L. Vaughan

Classic French cooking relies to a great extent on rich ingredients—cream, eggs, and butter. Much of the wine produced in France, and elsewhere, has evolved to accompany this extravagantly rich cuisine, to cut through the richness and have its flavor register. Most of what we know in general about selecting wine is based on this equation. In contrast, Gourmet Gazelle cuisine relies on nonfat yogurt, pureed vegetables, fruits, egg whites, herbs, and spices. Not surprisingly, this change in basic ingredients affects the choice of wine to be served. The right wine for a salmon topped with a rich, buttery *hollandaise* sauce would be too intense for the Salmon with Basil Cream Sauce on page 143 of this book, for instance.

Gourmet Gazelle dishes are always light in calories, fat, sodium, and cholesterol and sometimes in texture and often pair well with light, mildly flavored wines. Don't automatically assume, however, that this is always the case. Many of these dishes have assertive, spicy flavors and call for a full-flavored wine to match. The key to selecting wines for these dishes is in matching the *intensity* of flavors.

Balance is the key to pairing wine and food. Neither the food nor the wine should overwhelm the other. Choose a savory, intensely flavored wine to accompany a dish of the same flavor characteristics and select a mildly flavored wine to accompany a mildly flavored dish. This rule may seem obvious, but it's often ignored.

An important aspect of choosing wine to accompany a meal is deciding whether you are going to emphasize the wine or the food. If the focus of the evening is the food, your wine should be less strongly flavored and less distinctive than the food. If, on the other hand, you wish to highlight your wines, you might select foods that are not complexly spiced so they won't compete with the wines for your guests' attention.

Needless to say, in deciding whether a dish is strongly flavored, you must also consider the sauce. For example, Alfred's Meat Loaf (page 158) served with the very mild Herbed Tomato Sauce (page 202) would require a much more mildly flavored wine than if it were served with the rich and spicy Smoked Tomato Sauce (page 203).

As with much of the accepted wisdom on wine, the maxim

"white wine with fish, red wine with meat" is not always true. Red wine and fish generally don't mix, particularly if the red wine is high in tannin. Tannin reacts with substances in the flesh of fish, causing an unpleasant flavor in the mouth. Also, the assertive flavor of most red wine will overpower the intrinsically delicate flavor of most fish. If you would prefer to have red wine with your fish, either serve a light, low tannin red such as Beaujolais or try cooking and serving the fish in a hearty tomato and red wine sauce. The classic example of a fish dish that can stand up to a red wine is a French *bouillabaisse* with a red wine, tomato and garlic sauce. You also might try a light, low tannin red wine with the Creole Swordfish (page 150) or Jambalaya (page 133).

Although fish usually tastes better with a white wine, meat is not always complemented by a red wine. Certainly a strong, heavily spiced red meat or savory game dish calls for a vigorous, intensely flavored red wine to match, but a lighter meat, such as the many veal dishes in this book, might find a better companion in a white Burgundy. Thus we revert back to our first principle—match the intensity of the wine's flavor to the flavor intensity of the food it will accompany.

THE KEY TO SELECTING WINES FOR THESE DISHES IS IN MATCHING THE INTENSITY OF FLAVORS

Another principle: Never serve a dry wine with a sweet dish. The sugar in the food will accentuate the acidity in the wine, making the wine taste sour. Thus, desserts should always be less sweet than the accompanying wine. Try a lush, sweet Sauternes from Bordeaux with the Strawberry Rhubarb Soufflé on page 253 for instance—a delightful combination. All the desserts are in the "less sweet" category and are therefore particularly tasty in the company of a sweet wine.

The order of service of wines is also important. In general you want to have lighter, more subtle, more delicate wines and dishes earlier in the meal while the palate can still appreciate them, and richer, heavier, more strongly flavored wines and foods later. If you want to serve wine with the salad course, choose a dressing made with lemon juice, not vinegar; the acidity of vinegar completely destroys the taste of wine.

I have listed below the major wine types by degree of flavor intensity to assist you in choosing a wine that will pair with the characteristics of the food you are preparing. There are also wine notes throughout the book with suggestions for individual dishes. A standard 4-ounce glass of wine contains about 80 calories. For a few recipes I recommend beer rather than wine; an 8-ounce glass of beer is about 100 calories.

WHITE WINES

LIGHT INTENSITY OF FLAVOR

Sylvaner or Pinot Blanc from Alsace; Muscadet and Gros Plant from the Loire; Entre-deux-Mers, Bordeaux, and Bordeaux Supérieur from Bordeaux; Vernaccia, Verdicchio, Orvieto, Frascati, Pinot Grigio, Trebbiano, and Soave from Italy; most jug white wines, foreign and domestic.

MEDIUM INTENSITY OF FLAVOR

Mild Riesling from Alsace; Vouvray, Bourgogne Blanc, Saint-Véran, Macon Blanc, Pouilly-Fuissé, Macon-Villages, Mercurey, Rully, and ordinary Chablis from Burgundy; mild-flavored Graves from Bordeaux; German Kabinett; certain Chenin Blancs and mildly flavored Sauvignon Blancs and Fumé Blancs from California.

INTENSELY FLAVORED/ASSERTIVE

Sancerre and Pouilly-Fumé from the Loire; strongly flavored Graves from Bordeaux; first and great growth white Burgundy (including *grand cru* Chablis) in superb years; white Châteauneuf-du-Pape, Hermitage, Crozes-Hermitage, and Condrieu from the Rhône; Gewürztraminer, Riesling, and Muscat from Alsace; Chardonnay and certain strongly flavored Sauvignon Blancs or Fumé Blancs from California.

RED WINES

LIGHT INTENSITY OF FLAVOR

Pinot Noir from Alsace; Saumur, Chinon, and Bourgueil, and St. Nicolas-de-Bourgueil from the Loire; Valpolicella and Bardolino from Italy; certain light Beaujolais, Beaujolais Supérieur, and Beaujolais-Villages; light Merlot from California; many light "jug" reds.

MEDIUM INTENSITY OF FLAVOR

Good Beaujolais, Beaujolais-Villages, and *grand cru* Beaujolais; Burgundy of ordinary quality (often labeled Côte de Nuits, Côte de Beaune, Fixin, Givrey-Chambertin, Morey-Saint-Denis, Chambolle-Musigny, Vosne-Romanée, Nuits-St.-Georges, Pernand-Vergelesses, Aloxe-Corton, Beaune, Pommard, Volnay, Santenay, Givry, Mercurey, or Rully); Bordeaux of ordinary quality (often labeled Médoc, Haut-Médoc, Graves, Saint-Julien, Moulis, Listrac, Côtes de Bourg, Blaye, Margaux, Saint-Emilion, or Pomerol); milder-flavored Côtes du Rhône and Côtes du Rhône–Villages; average Chianti, Barbera, Dolcetto, and Nebbiolo from Italy; Pinot Noir and richer Merlot from California, Rioja from Spain, Cabernet Sauvignon from South America and eastern Europe.

INTENSELY FLAVORED/ASSERTIVE

Châteauneuf-du-Pape, Côte Rotie, Hermitage, Crozes-Hermitage, and Cornas from the Rhône; wines from the great Bordeaux châteaux in good years; wines from the great Burgundy vineyards in good years; Barolo, Amarone, Brunello di Montalcino, and great Chianti from Italy; certain estates from Rioja in Spain; Cabernet Sauvignon and Zinfandel from California.

SWEET WINES

The desserts in this book offer a wonderful opportunity to enjoy a wide variety of sweet wines. Fortunately, the desserts in this book are low in sugar and will pair beautifully with most dessert wines. Look for wines labeled Sauternes or Barsac from France or late-harvest Riesling from California or Alsace or Essencia from California. Also, Tokaji from Hungary or Picolit from Italy will show well with the desserts here. Muscat Beaumes-de-Venise, a spicy sweet wine from the Rhône Valley in France, and Vin santo, a sweet wine from Italy with sherry overtones, also will match well with the desserts here. Sweet wines have on average about 138 calories for a 3-ounce glass.

Most wines improve the taste of most meals, so even with little familiarity with wine, it is likely that whatever wine you choose will improve your dining experience. However, working with the idea of pairing the basic wine types with food will enhance your chances for a superb match and enable you to avoid the occasional disaster that all too often results from the dart-throwing method of wine selection.

Soups

Honeydew Gazpacho
Chilled Cream of Zucchini Soup with Fresh Basil
Guacamole Soup
Vichyssoise
Golden Gazpacho
Cold Parsley Soup
Salsa Soup with Seafood
Dilled Cucumber Soup
Wild Mushroom Soup
Scallion Soup
Butternut Squash Soup
Curried Carrot Soup
Vegetable Soup with Roasted Garlic
Southwestern Vegetable Soup
Cream of Celery Soup with Tarragon
Lemon Egg Soup
Red Pepper Bisque with Seafood
Seafood Minestrone
Smoked Chicken and Seafood Gumbo
Italian Chicken Vegetable Soup

Soups are my favorite way to begin a meal. In summer, chilled soups cool the spirit as effectively as steaming bowls of soup take the chill from even the most blizzardy winter day. Another advantage to beginning a meal with soup is that it's filling, so the stomach begins to feel satisfied on just a few calories.

The pleasure of soup shouldn't be limited to seated meals. I fill thermos jugs with soups for picnics; at buffet dinners, I'll have trays of small plastic mugs of a hot or cold soup (pureed, so you don't need a spoon) passed as a signal that cocktail hour is over and dinner is beginning.

Some of the heartier soups, such as Seafood Minestrone (page 33) or Italian Chicken Vegetable Soup (page 37), can be served in a larger portion as a meal. However, most of the soups here are conceived as first courses.

The majority of the recipes in this chapter are quick and easy purees. In my experience there is a finite amount of time that most cooks will spend on *any* meal—even a formal party. I would rather put the effort into the main course and have the first course be memorable for its careful blending of flavors, not time-consuming presentation.

Cream soups belong here, too, but their creaminess has other sources. For the cold soups, most specify nonfat plain yogurt as the dairy product; hot soups list a small amount of light cream or milk. While working with these ingredients, I found that in addition to their handsome nutritional profile, they leave a much cleaner taste in the mouth—which allows the other elements to display their flavors more vividly than they would in a standard cream soup.

Most of the soups are vegetarian or include seafood as either a base or a garnish. In meal planning, I tend to reserve poultry and meat for the main course supported by a variety of vegetables; the soup can then introduce a different vegetable group to round out the meal.

You won't find a single *consommé*, that diet staple, among the group. I consider them boring, merely glorified stocks. Soups, like other courses of the meal, should have a complexity of flavor even if it's presented in a single texture.

COLD SOUPS

Honeydew Gazpacho

TOTAL TIME
2 hours, including chilling
WORK TIME
15 minutes

PER SERVING
60 calories
4 mg cholesterol
1 g fat
60 mg sodium

This quick puree has the same refreshing quality as the cucumber, mint, and yogurt *raita* used as a fire extinguisher for Indian curries. In this case, those flavors are joined with equally refreshing melon. The pale green color alone is a tonic for the hottest summer day.   *Serves 6*

1 ripe honeydew melon, peeled, seeded, and diced
⅓ cup white wine vinegar
¼ teaspoon freshly ground white pepper (or to taste)
3 tablespoons chopped fresh mint
2 cups sliced celery
1 medium onion, peeled and diced
2 cucumbers, peeled, seeded, and diced
1 cup plain low-fat yogurt
6 to 8 fresh mint sprigs for garnish

1. Combine all ingredients except the garnish in a blender or food processor fitted with the steel blade. Puree until smooth.

2. Refrigerate until cold, at least 2 hours, and serve in chilled bowls, each serving garnished with a sprig of mint.

NOTE: The soup can be prepared a day in advance; however, the flavor of the mint begins to fade after that time. Honeydew melons are available almost all year, and ripeness can be determined by a fruity aroma and slight softening at the blossom end. The rind should be waxy and have a uniform creamy color.

WINE NOTE
A Riesling from Alsace will match this unusual blending of flavors.

Chilled Cream of Zucchini Soup with Fresh Basil

This thick, fresh-tasting soup is a natural for summer, when both zucchini and fresh basil are plentiful in the markets, if not from your own garden. A little cream imparts added richness, and the texture comes from the base of pureed zucchini.   *Serves 6*

TOTAL TIME
3 hours, including chilling
WORK TIME
15 minutes

PER SERVING
120 calories
19 mg cholesterol
7 g fat
158 mg sodium

1 tablespoon unsalted butter
⅓ cup chopped onion
2 pounds (5 medium) zucchini, washed, trimmed, and sliced
3 cups chicken stock, preferably unsalted (page 266)
½ cup fresh basil leaves
½ cup light cream
1 cup plain nonfat yogurt
Pinch of freshly ground white pepper
¼ teaspoon salt (omit if using salted canned stock)
6 fresh basil sprigs for garnish

1. Heat the butter or margarine in a 4-quart saucepan over medium heat. Add the onion and sauté, stirring occasionally, for 5 minutes or until the onions are translucent.

2. Add the zucchini and stock and bring to a boil over high heat. Reduce the heat to low and simmer the mixture, uncovered, for 20 minutes.

3. Add the basil leaves and puree the soup in a blender or food processor fitted with the steel blade. Stir in the cream, yogurt, white pepper, and salt. Chill until ready to serve, at least 2 hours.

4. Serve in chilled soup bowls, each serving garnished with a sprig of basil.

WINE NOTE
The soft texture of a Vouvray from the Loire Valley in France will marry well with this soup, as will a grassy California Sauvignon Blanc.

Guacamole Soup

TOTAL TIME
2 hours, including chilling
WORK TIME
10 minutes

PER SERVING
104 calories
3 mg cholesterol
6 g fat
170 mg sodium

In the Gourmet Gazelle kitchen there are no "forbidden foods." The trick is using those ingredients high in calories or cholesterol only as flavoring agents, not as main ingredients. If you're a guacamole fan, you'll love this soup.   Serves 6

1 ripe avocado (the black-skinned Haas variety is particularly tasty)
⅓ cup chopped onion
¼ to ½ teaspoon Tabasco sauce (to taste)
¼ teaspoon salt (omit if using salted canned stock)
1 tablespoon chopped fresh cilantro or parsley
2 tablespoons drained canned chopped green chilies
1½ cups plain low-fat yogurt
2 cups chicken stock, preferably unsalted (page 266)
3 ripe plum tomatoes for garnish
2 corn tortillas for garnish

1. Peel and stone the avocado and cut into 1-inch cubes. Place in a blender or food processor fitted with the steel blade. Add remaining ingredients except tomatoes and tortillas and puree the soup until smooth.

2. Place in a stainless-steel or glass container and press plastic wrap directly onto the surface of the soup to prevent discoloration. Refrigerate until ready to serve, at least 2 hours.

3. Core and halve the tomatoes. Squeeze out the seeds and then chop the tomatoes into coarse dice, about ½ inch. Set aside until ready to serve.

4. Preheat the oven to 400 degrees. Cut the tortillas into strips ½ inch wide and arrange in a single layer on a cookie sheet. Bake for 10 minutes or until crisp. Set aside.

5. To serve, ladle the soup into chilled bowls. Top each serving with a few tortilla strips and a spoonful of diced tomato.

WINE NOTE
Try a Sauvignon Blanc or Fumé Blanc from California with this lightly spicy dish.

Vichyssoise

While the heavy cream used in classic Vichyssoise tends to coat the palate, using yogurt instead allows the delicacy of the leeks to emerge, and the potatoes provide a rich thickness. *Serves 6*

TOTAL TIME
3 hours, including chilling
WORK TIME
15 minutes

PER SERVING
137 calories
10 mg cholesterol
5 g fat
149 mg sodium

1½ tablespoons unsalted butter
6 leeks, including 2 inches of the green, trimmed, washed, and chopped (see page 271)
½ cup chopped onion
1 pound potatoes, peeled and thinly sliced
6 cups chicken stock, preferably unsalted (page 266)
¼ teaspoon freshly ground white pepper
¼ teaspoon salt (omit if using salted canned stock)
¾ cup plain nonfat yogurt
6 tablespoons chopped chives for garnish

1. Melt the butter in a 4-quart saucepan over medium heat. Add the leeks and onion and sauté over medium heat, stirring frequently, for 5 minutes or until the onions are translucent.

2. Add the potatoes, stock, white pepper, and salt and bring to a boil over high heat. Reduce the heat to low, partially cover the pan, and simmer the soup for 25 minutes or until the potatoes are tender.

3. Transfer the mixture to a blender or food processor fitted with the steel blade and puree. (This may have to be done in several batches.)

4. Refrigerate, covered, until cold, at least 2 hours, and then stir in the yogurt. Adjust seasoning, if necessary, and ladle soup into chilled bowls. Sprinkle with chives before serving.

NOTE: If leeks are unavailable, use an additional ½ cup onion plus ½ cup chopped scallions in their place.

WINE NOTE
The richness of a California Chardonnay will balance well with the rich textures of the mild soup.

Golden Gazpacho

TOTAL TIME
2 hours, including chilling
WORK TIME
10 minutes

PER SERVING
91 calories
0 cholesterol
.5 g fat
32 mg sodium

More than two thirds of the yearly cantaloupe crop comes to market during the summer, when this refreshing cold soup is most welcomed. Although it's a little more trouble than serving a wedge of fruit, this soup is an elegant first course for a summer brunch. The sweet-sharp flavor combination is reminiscent of that summer classic, *prosciutto e melone*. Serves 6

1 large *or* 2 small ripe cantaloupes, peeled, seeded, and diced (4 cups)
1 large carrot, peeled and sliced
2 cucumbers, peeled, seeded, and sliced
8 scallions, white part only
⅔ cup sherry vinegar
1 cup freshly squeezed orange juice
½ teaspoon freshly ground white pepper
2 tablespoons freshly squeezed lemon juice

1. Combine all ingredients in a blender or food processor fitted with the steel blade. Puree until smooth.

2. Serve in chilled soup bowls.

NOTE: The soup can be prepared up to two days in advance with no loss of flavor. Cantaloupes soften after picking; however, they do not ripen any further. To select a sweet, juicy fruit, look for a rough, well-netted surface and a smoothly rounded, depressed scar at the stem end. The pale orange color comes from carotene, which makes cantaloupe a good source of vitamin A. Half a cantaloupe provides 100 percent of the RDA of vitamin C and only 60 calories.

WINE NOTE
The sweet and sharp flavors in this soup make a wine match difficult; try a Gewürztraminer from Alsace.

Cold Parsley Soup

The fresh taste of parsley—without any of its inherent bitterness—is the dominant flavor in this bright green soup. There are no dairy products in the recipe; the potato cooked with the stock thickens the soup slightly and produces an almost creamy texture. This is an elegant soup, worthy of a dinner party.   *Serves 6*

TOTAL TIME
2½ hours, including chilling
WORK TIME
20 minutes

PER SERVING
100 calories
1 mg cholesterol
4 g fat
190 mg sodium

1 tablespoon vegetable oil
4 scallions, trimmed and sliced
1 medium onion, peeled and sliced
1 garlic clove, peeled and minced
¼ teaspoon salt (omit if using salted canned stock)
¼ teaspoon freshly ground black pepper
4 cups chicken stock, preferably unsalted (page 266)
1 medium potato, peeled and sliced
4 cups fresh parsley leaves
1 tablespoon freshly squeezed lemon juice
6 fresh parsley sprigs for garnish

1. In a 2-quart saucepan, heat the oil over medium heat. Add the scallions, onion, and garlic and sauté, stirring frequently, until the onion is translucent, about 5 minutes. Add the salt, pepper, stock, and potato to the pan and bring to a boil over high heat. Reduce the heat to low, cover the pan, and simmer the soup for 25 minutes.

2. While the soup base is simmering, bring 4 quarts of water to a boil. Have a bowl of ice water ready. Place the parsley leaves in a colander or strainer and blanch them in the boiling water for 15 seconds. Shake over the sink to remove excess water and then plunge them into ice water to stop the cooking. Drain well, pressing down to remove excess water.

3. Place the parsley and soup mixture in a blender or food processor fitted with the steel blade. Puree until smooth and then refrigerate until well chilled, at least 2 hours. Stir in the lemon juice and adjust seasoning if necessary.

4. Serve the soup in chilled bowls, each serving garnished with a sprig of parsley.

NOTE: For a variation on this soup, which gives it a decidedly southwestern flavor, substitute 1 cup cilantro leaves for a cup of the parsley. The soup can be prepared a day in advance. Blanching the parsley removes the bitterness from the herb, and quick chilling in ice water sets the vivid color of many green vegetables, such as broccoli, snow peas, and asparagus.

WINE NOTE
The pungent flavor of Pouilly-Fumé or Sancerre from the Loire Valley in France will match that of the parsley in this dish.

Salsa Soup with Seafood

TOTAL TIME
2½ hours, including chilling
WORK TIME
15 minutes

PER SERVING
65 calories
27 mg cholesterol
1 g fat
114 mg sodium

Mustard and vinegar make this cooling summer soup sparkle. The addition of cucumber to this attractive red soup lightens the tomato taste so you can appreciate the delicacy of the seafood; it also adds body, to make a simple bowl of soup seem far more filling.   *Serves 6*

1 tablespoon olive oil
½ cup chopped onion
½ teaspoon minced garlic
1 cucumber, peeled, seeded, and sliced
6 large ripe tomatoes, peeled, seeded, and chopped (see page 271)
2 cups chicken stock, preferably unsalted (page 266)
2 tablespoons salt-free tomato paste
¼ teaspoon freshly ground black pepper
¼ teaspoon salt (omit if using salted canned stock)
2 teaspoons Dijon mustard
3 tablespoons red wine vinegar
3 tablespoons chopped fresh parsley
½ pound baby shrimp, cooked, peeled, and chilled, or cooked and chilled bay scallops, lobster meat, or crab meat for garnish

1. Heat the olive oil in a 4-quart saucepan over medium heat. Add the onion and garlic and sauté, stirring frequently, for 5 to 7 minutes or until the onion is translucent.

2. Add the cucumber, tomatoes, chicken stock, tomato paste, pepper, and salt to the mixture and bring to a boil over medium heat, stirring well to dissolve the tomato paste into the soup. Reduce the heat and simmer the soup, uncovered, for 15 minutes.

3. Transfer the mixture to a blender or food processor fitted with the steel blade. Puree until smooth.

4. Chill the soup until cold, at least 2 hours. Stir in the mustard, vinegar, and parsley.

5. To serve, ladle into chilled soup bowls and divide the seafood among the bowls as a garnish.

NOTE: The flavor of the soup actually improves if it's made a day in advance.

WINE NOTE
The relatively strong flavors of the mustard, vinegar, and tomatoes dictate a red, such as a good Beaujolais from France.

Dilled Cucumber Soup

TOTAL TIME
3 hours, including chilling time
WORK TIME
20 minutes

PER SERVING
65 calories
4 mg cholesterol
3 g fat
171 mg sodium

Dill and cucumber are natural partners. While classic cream of cucumber soup is made with a rich *béchamel* base, the yogurt used here not only lowers the calories and fat but also speeds the cooking process.   *Serves 6*

2 teaspoons unsalted butter
1 leek, including 2 inches of the green, trimmed, washed, and chopped (see page 271), *or* ½ cup chopped onion
2 large *or* 3 small cucumbers, peeled, seeded, and sliced
2 tablespoons chopped fresh dill *or* 2 teaspoons dried
5 cups chicken stock, preferably unsalted (page 266)
1 cup plain low-fat yogurt
⅛ teaspoon freshly ground white pepper
¼ teaspoon salt (omit if using salted canned stock)
6 tablespoons finely chopped cucumber for garnish
6 fresh dill sprigs for garnish

1. In a 4-quart saucepan, melt the butter over medium heat. Add the leek, cucumber, and half the dill and sauté for 5 minutes.

2. Add the stock and bring to a boil over high heat. Reduce the heat to low, partially cover the pan, and simmer for 25 minutes.

3. Transfer the mixture to a blender or food processor fitted with the steel blade. Puree and refrigerate the soup until chilled, at least 2 hours.

4. Stir in the yogurt, white pepper, salt, and remaining dill. Serve in chilled soup bowls, each serving garnished with 1 tablespoon of chopped cucumber and a sprig of dill.

NOTE: The soup can be made two days in advance, but don't stir in the dill or garnish until ready to serve.

WINE NOTE
Try an equally light and refreshing Muscadet from the Loire Valley in France or a Fumé Blanc from California.

HOT SOUPS

Wild Mushroom Soup

Although wild mushrooms are part of many cuisines, there are Asian overtones to this elegant soup, imbued with the flavor of woodsy wild mushrooms, both fresh and dried.   *Serves 6*

TOTAL TIME
1 hour
WORK TIME
15 minutes

PER SERVING
126 calories
0 cholesterol
6 g fat
359 mg sodium

1 cup mixed dried wild mushrooms (*shiitake, morels, porcini, cèpes,* oyster mushrooms)
1 cup water
½ pound fresh *shiitake* mushrooms or *chanterelles*
½ pound fresh mushrooms
1 tablespoon dark sesame oil
1 tablespoon vegetable oil
6 scallions, white part only, coarsely chopped
6 cups chicken stock, preferably unsalted (page 266)
¼ teaspoon freshly ground black pepper
3 tablespoons reduced-sodium soy sauce
4 scallions for garnish

1. Bring the dried mushrooms and water to a boil, pushing the mushrooms down into the liquid. Remove from heat and set aside to soak for 20 minutes. Strain the dried mushrooms, reserving the soaking liquid. Rinse them under cold water, rubbing with your fingers to remove any elusive grit. Chop them finely. Strain the soaking liquid through a sieve lined with a coffee filter or cheesecloth.

2. While the dried mushrooms are soaking, clean the fresh *shiitake;* remove the stems and slice them into ¼-inch slices. Clean and slice the fresh mushrooms.

3. Heat the sesame and vegetable oils in a 4-quart saucepan over medium-high heat. Add the fresh *shiitake,* fresh mushrooms, and scallions; sauté, stirring constantly, for 5 minutes or until the wild mushrooms are almost soft.

4. Add the chicken stock, chopped dried mushrooms, soaking liquid, pepper, and soy. Bring to a boil, reduce heat to low, and simmer the soup, uncovered, for 15 minutes.

5. For the garnish, trim the scallions and wash under cold running water. Slice the white portion and separate into rings. Discard all but 2 inches of the green portion and cut into 1-inch lengths.

6. To serve, ladle the soup into heated bowls and garnish with scallions.

NOTE: The soup can be prepared up to three days in advance. Reheat slowly, stirring occasionally.

WINE NOTE
The spicy flavor of a Gewürztraminer from Alsace will blend well with the Asian flavors in this dish. For a different sensation, try some dry sherry.

Scallion Soup

This lighter version of onion soup owes its subtlety to the relative delicacy of the scallion, cooked with chicken stock instead of the heavier beef stock of the usual onion soup. It's both unusual and elegant.   *Serves 6*

TOTAL TIME
45 minutes

WORK TIME
15 minutes

PER SERVING
75 calories
2 mg cholesterol
3 g fat
150 mg sodium

3 bunches (about 24) scallions
1 tablespoon unsalted butter
7 cups chicken stock, preferably unsalted (page 266)
2 tablespoons chopped fresh marjoram *or* 1 teaspoon dried
2 tablespoons chopped fresh parsley
¼ teaspoon freshly ground white pepper
¼ teaspoon salt (omit if using salted canned stock)

1. Trim the scallions, reserving 4 inches of the green tops. Chop the white portion and slice the green portion into 1-inch lengths.

2. Melt the butter over medium heat in a 4-quart saucepan. Add the chopped white scallions, and sauté, stirring often, until the scallions are translucent, about 3 to 5 minutes.

3. Add the chicken stock, 1 tablespoon of the marjoram, 1 tablespoon of the parsley, the pepper and salt. Bring to a boil over high heat, reduce the heat to medium-low, and simmer the soup, uncovered, for 20 minutes.

4. Add the remaining marjoram and parsley along with the green scallion tops. When the soup returns to a boil, simmer 3 minutes.

5. To serve, ladle into heated soup bowls.

NOTE: You can make the recipe up to two days in advance through step 3. Reheat and, when it comes to a boil, continue with step 4.

WINE NOTE
The fullness of a good California Chardonnay will make a good companion to this soup.

Butternut Squash Soup

TOTAL TIME
2 hours
WORK TIME
15 minutes

PER SERVING
153 calories
6 mg cholesterol
2 g fat
138 mg sodium

Thick and velvety, this soup is a perfect prelude to any fall or winter dinner. It has a subtle sweet and spicy flavor and a glorious light orange tone. Its texture is derived from the squash, so it's rich-tasting without the concomitant calories.   *Serves 6*

3½ pounds (2 medium) butternut squash
2 cups chicken stock, preferably unsalted (page 266)
2 tablespoons chopped fresh parsley
¼ teaspoon freshly ground white pepper
1 tablespoon chopped fresh marjoram *or* ½ teaspoon dried
1 cup milk
2 tablespoons molasses
2 tablespoons bourbon
¼ teaspoon ground cinnamon
Pinch of freshly grated nutmeg
¼ teaspoon salt (omit if using salted canned stock)

1. Preheat the oven to 350 degrees. Bake the squash on a baking sheet for 1 hour or until the flesh is tender when probed with a sharp meat fork, turning occasionally during baking. Cut the squash in half, scrape out the seeds, and scrape the flesh from the shell. Cut the flesh into 2-inch chunks.

2. Combine the squash, chicken stock, parsley, pepper, and marjoram in a 4-quart saucepan. Bring to a boil over medium heat and simmer, partially covered, for 20 minutes.

3. Puree the soup in a blender or food processor fitted with the steel blade. Return soup to the pot and add the milk, molasses, bourbon, cinnamon, nutmeg, and salt. Bring to a boil over medium heat, stirring frequently, and simmer over low heat for 5 minutes. Serve immediately.

NOTE: Acorn squash can be substituted for the butternut. The soup can be made up to three days in advance and reheated over low heat.

WINE NOTE
The rich texture and sweet-spicy flavors of this soup require a big, full-flavored wine, such as one of the California Chardonnays, or a glass of dry Sherry.

Curried Carrot Soup

The sweetness of carrots and apples finds a perfect foil in the heady blend of spices called curry powder. This bright orange soup is not spicy but has a pleasing pungency.   *Serves 6*

1 tablespoon unsalted butter
6 carrots, peeled and sliced
1 medium onion, peeled and sliced
½ large apple, peeled and sliced
1½ to 2 tablespoons curry powder
6 cups chicken stock, preferably unsalted (page 266)
⅓ cup light cream
⅛ teaspoon freshly ground white pepper
¼ teaspoon salt (omit if using salted canned stock)

1. Melt the butter in a 4-quart saucepan over medium heat. Add the carrots, onion, and apple and sauté over medium heat, stirring frequently, for 10 minutes. Stir in the curry powder, reduce the heat to low, and stir constantly for 3 minutes to cook the curry powder.

2. Raise the heat to medium and slowly stir in the stock, reaching to all parts of the bottom to evenly release the curry powder. Bring to a boil and simmer, uncovered, for 20 minutes. Add the cream, pepper, and salt and simmer for 5 minutes.

3. Puree the soup in a blender or food processor fitted with the steel blade.

4. The soup can be served immediately or chilled for at least 2 hours and served cold.

NOTE: The soup can be made up to two days in advance and served either cold or reheated. The curry tends to get stronger, however, and this can be corrected by stirring in a few tablespoons of milk or adding less curry if made in advance.

WINE NOTE
Try a Pouilly-Fumé or Sancerre from the Loire Valley with this interestingly flavored soup.

TOTAL TIME
50 minutes, plus 2 hours if chilled
WORK TIME
20 minutes

PER SERVING
103 calories
12 mg cholesterol
5 g fat
123 mg sodium

Vegetable Soup with Roasted Garlic

TOTAL TIME
1 hour
WORK TIME
30 minutes

PER SERVING
117 calories
0 cholesterol
5 g fat
382 mg sodium

Slowly roasted garlic loses its bitterness and pungency and becomes a sweet, mild undertone in this pureed vegetable soup. The garnish of fresh herbs with lemon is reminiscent of the *gremolata* used to spark the flavor of long-simmered *osso buco.*   Serves 6

1 head garlic, unpeeled
2 tablespoons olive oil
2 large onions, peeled and chopped
1 small zucchini, trimmed and sliced
1 red bell pepper, seeds and ribs removed, chopped (page 269)
2 celery stalks, sliced
3 large tomatoes, peeled, seeded, and diced (page 271)
3 cups chicken stock, preferably unsalted (page 266)
2 tablespoons salt-free tomato paste
¼ teaspoon cayenne pepper
1 tablespoon freshly squeezed lemon juice
¼ teaspoon salt (omit if using salted canned stock)

FOR GARNISH

1 tablespoon finely chopped fresh parsley
1 tablespoon finely chopped fresh basil
1 tablespoon finely chopped fresh oregano
1 tablespoon finely chopped lemon zest

1. Preheat the oven to 350 degrees. Rub the head of garlic with oil and place on a baking sheet in the center of the oven for 15 minutes or until the cloves are very soft. When roasted, the soft pulp will pop out of its skins. Remove 8 cloves, reserving the others for another use.

2. Heat the olive oil in a 4-quart saucepan over medium-high heat. Add the onions, zucchini, red bell peppers, and celery and sauté, stirring often, for 7 to 10 minutes or until the onions are translucent.

3. Add the roasted garlic cloves, tomatoes, stock, tomato paste, and cayenne pepper, stirring well to dissolve the tomato paste. Bring the soup to a boil over medium-high heat. Reduce the heat to low and simmer the soup, uncovered, for 20 minutes.

4. Puree the soup in a blender or food processor fitted with the steel blade. Stir in the lemon juice and salt and adjust seasoning.

5. Mix the garnish ingredients together in a small bowl. To serve, ladle the soup into heated bowls and top each with 2 teaspoons of the garnish.

NOTE: The soup can be prepared up to two days in advance. Do not stir in the lemon juice or prepare the herb garnish until just before serving.

WINE NOTE
A richer Beaujolais-Villages or *grand cru* Beaujolais from France, or a California Cabernet Sauvignon, will stand up to this full-flavored soup.

Southwestern Vegetable Soup

TOTAL TIME
45 minutes
WORK TIME
20 minutes

PER SERVING
170 calories
5 mg cholesterol
8 g fat
126 mg sodium

My travels have served as the basis for many dishes, including this one, inspired by the *Sopa Azteca* that is part of traditional southwestern cooking. It is the specialty of El Mirador in San Antonio, Texas. It's spicy, and while it's cooking the kitchen is filled with glorious anticipatory aromas. With a salad, this could be a meal in itself.

1 tablespoon olive oil
1 medium onion, peeled and chopped
2 garlic cloves, peeled and minced
1 pound (3 to 4) ripe tomatoes, cored, seeded, and diced
2 tablespoons chopped fresh oregano *or* 2 teaspoons dried
2 tablespoons chopped fresh basil *or* 2 teaspoons dried
1 teaspoon ground cumin
4 cups chicken stock, preferably unsalted (page 266)
3 tablespoons salt-free tomato paste
2 celery stalks
¼ red bell pepper
1 medium zucchini
½ carrot
1 large boiling potato

FOR GARNISH

2 corn tortillas
1 tablespoon vegetable oil
½ cup shredded low-fat (part-skim milk) mozzarella cheese

1. Heat the oil over medium heat in a 4-quart saucepan. Add the onion and garlic and sauté, stirring frequently, until the onion is translucent, about 5 minutes. Add the tomatoes, oregano, basil, and cumin. Cook the mixture for 10 minutes over medium heat, stirring frequently.

2. Transfer the vegetable mixture to a blender or food processor fitted with the steel blade and puree. Return it to the pot and add the chicken stock and tomato paste, stirring well to dissolve the tomato paste. Bring to a boil over medium heat.

3. While the soup is coming to a boil, wash and trim the celery, bell pepper, zucchini, carrot, and potato. Cut all the vegetables into ½-inch dice. Add the vegetables to the soup and simmer, uncovered, for 15 minutes or until the vegetables are cooked through but retain their texture.

4. For the garnish, preheat the oven to 375 degrees. Cut each tortilla into 8 to 10 triangles and brush the wedges lightly with oil. Place in the oven for 5 minutes, turning once, or until the tortilla wedges are crisp.

5. To serve, ladle the soup into shallow heated bowls and top each serving with tortilla wedges and a heaped tablespoon of cheese.

NOTE: The soup can be made up to three days in advance. Reheat it slowly and don't allow it to simmer, or the vegetables will overcook.

WINE NOTE
A Beaujolais from France will work with this richly flavored dish. If you prefer a white, choose a full-flavored one such as Gewürztraminer from Alsace.

Cream of Celery Soup with Tarragon

TOTAL TIME
45 minutes
WORK TIME
15 minutes

PER SERVING
83 calories
3 mg cholesterol
2 g fat
207 mg sodium

The natural fiber of the celery and the rice thicken this elegant, pale green soup. While most appropriate for a dinner party, this is also comfort food, with tarragon adding zest to the fresh celery flavor.   *Serves 6*

4 cups sliced celery (about ⅔ bunch)
4 cups chicken stock, preferably unsalted (page 266)
⅓ cup white rice
¼ teaspoon salt (omit if using salted canned stock)
Pinch of freshly ground white pepper
1 teaspoon chopped fresh tarragon *or* ¼ teaspoon dried
1 tablespoon freshly squeezed lemon juice
½ cup milk

1. In a 4-quart saucepan, combine the celery, stock, rice, salt, pepper, and tarragon. Bring to a boil over high heat, partially cover the pan, and simmer the soup over low heat for 30 minutes.

2. Place the soup in a blender or food processor fitted with the steel blade and puree until smooth. Return the soup to the pot, stir in the lemon juice and milk, and simmer 2 minutes. Serve immediately in heated bowls.

NOTE: The soup can be made up to three days in advance and reheated over low heat, stirring frequently.

WINE NOTE
A California Sauvignon Blanc will match the herbaceous flavor of the tarragon nicely.

Lemon Egg Soup

Greek *avgolemono* is one of my favorite winter soups—rich and velvety from the eggs and simultaneously refreshing from the lemon juice. In this version, most of the eggs of the traditional soup have been replaced by egg whites to lower the cholesterol count without sacrificing the comforting qualities.   *Serves 8*

TOTAL TIME
30 minutes
WORK TIME
10 minutes

PER SERVING
76 calories
68 mg cholesterol
2 g fat
102 mg sodium

7 cups chicken stock, preferably unsalted (page 266)
¼ cup long-grain white rice
½ cup freshly squeezed lemon juice
2 eggs
3 egg whites
¼ teaspoon freshly ground white pepper
Pinch of salt (omit if using salted canned stock)

1. Bring the stock to a boil in a large covered saucepan over high heat. Add the rice, reduce the heat to low, and simmer, covered, for 20 minutes or until the rice is soft.

2. While the soup is simmering, whisk the lemon juice with the eggs and egg whites. Set aside.

3. When the rice is cooked, turn off the heat and wait until the bubbling has stopped. If you are using an electric stove, remove the pot from the burner. Whisk the lemon-egg mixture into the hot soup and immediately cover the pot. Allow the soup to sit undisturbed for 5 minutes.

4. Season with pepper and salt. Serve immediately.

NOTE: This soup can be made up to two days in advance. Be very careful when reheating it, so that it does not come to a boil, or the eggs will curdle.

WINE NOTE
Try a tart Muscadet from France with this rich yet refreshing dish.

Red Pepper Bisque with Seafood

TOTAL TIME
1 hour
WORK TIME
15 minutes

PER SERVING
64 calories
5 mg cholesterol
2 g fat
91 mg sodium

Sweet red peppers are a perfect foil for the delicate seafood. While satisfying, the soup remains light, with an underlying sweet and sour flavor and a luscious vivid red color.   Serves 6

1 tablespoon vegetable oil
4 red bell peppers, seeds and ribs removed (page 269), chopped
½ cup chopped onion
¼ cup chopped peeled apple
½ cup chopped peeled carrot
4 cups chicken stock, preferably unsalted (page 266)
½ cup fresh corn kernels
Pinch of crushed red pepper
¼ cup tarragon vinegar
1 tablespoon freshly squeezed lime juice
2 tablespoons chopped fresh parsley or cilantro
Pinch of freshly ground white pepper
¼ teaspoon salt (omit if using salted canned stock)
¼ cup baby shrimp, peeled and deveined
¼ cup bay scallops, halved

1. Heat the oil in a 4-quart saucepan over medium heat. Add the red bell pepper, onion, apple, and carrot. Sauté, stirring frequently, for 5 to 7 minutes or until the onions are translucent.

2. Add the chicken stock and bring to a boil over high heat. Reduce the heat and simmer the soup, partially covered, for 25 minutes. Puree the soup in a blender or food processor fitted with the steel blade; return it to the saucepan.

3. Stir in the corn, crushed red pepper, tarragon vinegar, parsley, white pepper, and salt. Bring to a boil over medium heat, stirring occasionally, and simmer, uncovered, for 7 minutes.

4. Add the shrimp and scallops to the simmering soup, turn off the heat, and cover the pot. Allow it to sit for 5 minutes. Serve immediately in heated soup bowls.

NOTE: The soup can be prepared up to step 4 two days in advance. Bring it slowly back to a boil and then add the raw seafood just before serving.

WINE NOTE
A California Sauvignon Blanc will have the intensity of flavor to match this full-flavored soup.

Seafood Minestrone

This hearty fish soup can be your entree if served in a larger portion, accompanied by crusty Italian bread and a green salad. The soup is gently spiced, so the flavors of the various species of fish are enhanced without being overwhelmed.   Serves 6

TOTAL TIME
2 hours, including shell-fish soaking
WORK TIME
20 minutes

PER SERVING
180 calories
54 mg cholesterol
4 g fat
248 mg sodium

1 dozen mussels
1 dozen small hard-shelled clams
2 tablespoons cornmeal
1 tablespoon olive oil
1 leek, cleaned and chopped (page 271)
½ cup chopped onion
1 garlic clove, peeled and minced
¼ cup chopped celery
¼ cup sliced fresh mushrooms
4 large ripe tomatoes, peeled, seeded, and diced (page 271)
1¾ cups chicken stock, preferably unsalted (page 266)
1 cup clam juice
2 tablespoons chopped fresh basil or 2 teaspoons dried
¼ teaspoon freshly ground pepper
1 cup chopped washed kale
¼ cup macaroni
¼ pound shrimp, peeled and deveined
¼ pound fillet of sole, cut into ½-inch pieces
¼ pound bay scallops
3 tablespoons freshly grated Parmesan cheese

1. Scrub the mussels and clams under cold running water with a stiff brush, discarding any that are not firmly shut. Scrape off the mussels' beards with a sharp paring knife. Place the mollusks in a bowl of cold water and sprinkle the cornmeal on the top. Place in the refrigerator for at least 2 hours.

2. Heat the olive oil in a large stockpot over medium heat. Add the leek, onion, garlic, celery, and mushrooms. Sauté over medium heat, stirring frequently, for 5 minutes or until the onions are translucent. Add the tomatoes, stock, clam juice, basil, and pepper. Bring to a boil, reduce the heat to low, and simmer the soup, uncovered, for 15 minutes. Add the kale and macaroni and simmer for 5 minutes.

3. Drain the mussels and clams, then wash again. Raise the heat to high, add the shellfish, and cover the pot. Steam the mussels and clams, with the pot tightly covered, for 5 to 7 minutes, depending on the size of the seafood. Shake the pot occasionally to redistribute the clams and mussels.

4. Remove the clams and mussels with a slotted spoon, discarding any that did not open. Set aside.

5. Return the soup to a boil and add the shrimp, sole, and scallops. Cover the pot and turn off the heat. Let the pot sit undisturbed for 5 minutes.

6. To serve, ladle the soup into shallow flat soup bowls, arrange the clams and mussels on top, and sprinkle with Parmesan cheese.

NOTE: As with most seafood chowders and stews, substitutions can be made liberally, and the proportion of one species to others can be changed. Any firm, white fish such as snapper, grouper, whitefish, halibut, or swordfish can be used in lieu of sole, and crab meat could take the place of shrimp or scallops. The soup can be made up to step 4 in advance and reheated slowly before the mussels and clams are added.

WINE NOTE
Try a Vouvray from the Loire Valley or a Macon-Villages from France with this soup.

Smoked Chicken and Seafood Gumbo

Gumbo, one of the Cajun contributions to American cooking, is a spicy salvation on a cold night. This version cuts back on the fat, adding a smoky undertaste through smoked poultry, not ham. *Serves 8 as a soup course, 6 as an entree*

1 large whole chicken breast, boned and skinned (½ pound commercially prepared smoked chicken or turkey can be substituted—however, the sodium content will be much higher)

2 tablespoons vegetable oil

1½ cups chopped onion

1½ cups chopped celery

1½ cups chopped green bell pepper

2 garlic cloves, peeled and minced

2 tablespoons gumbo filé powder

1 teaspoon cayenne pepper

1 teaspoon paprika

¼ teaspoon freshly ground white pepper

¼ teaspoon salt (omit if using salted canned stock)

1 bay leaf

1 tablespoon chopped fresh oregano *or* ½ teaspoon dried

1 cup salt-free tomato sauce

2 cups fish stock or clam juice (see note)

2 cups chicken stock, preferably unsalted (page 266)

¾ pound medium shrimp, peeled and deveined, with the shells reserved if using clam juice

½ pound crab meat, picked over

1. If you're using a raw chicken breast, light a covered grill or smoker. Smoke the breast, using either mesquite, hickory, or a combination of woods, until cooked through. The amount of time depends on which method you're using; follow manufacturer's instructions. Remove the skin and bones, saving them for stock, and cut the meat into ½-inch cubes. Set aside.

2. Heat the oil in a heavy-bottomed 4-quart saucepan over medium heat. Add the onion, celery, green pepper, and garlic; sauté, stirring frequently, for 5 minutes. Stir in the gumbo filé

TOTAL TIME
1½ hours, including smoking the chicken
WORK TIME
20 minutes

PER SERVING
(ASSUMING 8 SOUP-COURSE PORTIONS)
185 calories
105 mg cholesterol
6 g fat
455 mg sodium

powder, cayenne, paprika, pepper, salt, bay leaf, and oregano. Raise the heat to high and cook the mixture, stirring constantly, for 5 minutes. The vegetables will have reduced, and the mixture will have darkened.

3. Whisk in the tomato sauce, seafood stock, and chicken stock. When the mixture comes to a boil, reduce the heat to low and simmer the soup, uncovered, for 45 minutes, stirring occasionally.

4. Stir in the chicken, shrimp, and crab. Cover the pot, turn off the heat, and allow the soup to sit undisturbed for 5 minutes. Serve immediately, either over ½ cup cooked rice as an entree, or in heated soup bowls as an appetizer.

NOTE: If seafood stock is not available, use 3 cups of bottled clam juice, and cook it with the shrimp shells, ½ cup chopped onion, ½ cup chopped celery, and 6 peppercorns until the mixture has reduced to 2 cups. The soup can be made up to two days in advance and slowly reheated either on top of the stove or in a microwave. Do not allow it to boil, or the shrimp will toughen.

WINE NOTE
You will need a very full-flavored white, such as one of the richest of the California Chardonnays or a Gewürztraminer from Alsace, or a light red such as a *grand cru* Beaujolais or an Italian Chianti.

Italian Chicken Vegetable Soup

There is a smoky nuance to the flavor of this *minestrone* variation from the crumbled bacon, and the cornmeal thickens it to a wonderful, hearty consistency. It's the perfect Sunday supper with a tossed salad.   *Serves 6*

TOTAL TIME
1 hour, plus 1 to 8 hours soaking (depending on soaking method)
WORK TIME
25 minutes

PER SERVING
166 calories
9 mg cholesterol
4 g fat
135 mg sodium

¼ pound dried navy beans
3 slices bacon
1 tablespoon olive oil
1 medium (⅓ pound) zucchini, trimmed and sliced
1 medium carrot, peeled and sliced
½ cup chopped onion
½ pound (½ medium) eggplant cut into ½-inch dice
¼ pound fresh mushrooms, washed and sliced
2 garlic cloves, peeled and minced
1 large ripe tomato, peeled, seeded, and diced (page 271)
½ cup chopped cooked chicken
4 cups chicken stock, preferably unsalted (page 266)
¼ cup dry white wine
2 teaspoons chopped fresh rosemary *or* ½ teaspoon dried
¼ teaspoon freshly ground black pepper
¼ cup yellow cornmeal
Pinch of salt (omit if using salted canned stock)

1. Wash the beans in a sieve and place in a 2-quart saucepan. Soak them overnight—or, bring them to a boil, allow to simmer for 3 minutes, then remove from heat and allow to sit, covered, for 1 hour. Cook the beans for 20 minutes or until cooked but still crisp.

2. Fry the bacon slices in a skillet until crisp. Remove with a slotted spatula and drain on paper towels. Crumble the bacon and set aside.

3. Heat the olive oil in a 4-quart saucepan over medium heat. Add the zucchini, carrot, onion, eggplant, mushrooms, and garlic. Sauté over medium heat, stirring frequently, for 5 minutes.

4. Add the tomato, cooked chicken, stock, wine, rosemary, navy beans, bacon bits, and pepper to the pot and bring to a boil over medium heat. Reduce the heat to medium-low and cook the soup, uncovered, for 15 minutes or until the vegetables are cooked but retain their texture.

5. Slowly stir in the cornmeal, and salt, if used, stirring well to ensure that no lumps are forming, and reduce the heat so that the soup is barely simmering. Cook for 5 minutes to thicken it slightly. Serve immediately in heated bowls.

NOTE: The soup is best if served right after cooking; however, it can be made up to two days in advance. Reheat it slowly, stirring it frequently and gently to make sure the cornmeal doesn't stick to the bottom of the pan.

WINE NOTE
Serve a white Burgundy or a California Chardonnay to match the chicken and herbs in this dish.

Appetizers

Phyllo Egg Rolls
Grilled Vegetable Pizza
Herbed Quesadillas
Grilled Vegetable Kabobs
Zucchini Mousse with Salsa
Chinese Eggplant Spread
Mushrooms Stuffed with Spinach and Chèvre
Spinach and Carrot Loaf
Herbed Turkey Sausage
Southwestern Turkey Sausage with Yogurt Dill Dressing
Chicken Yakitori
Chinese Chicken Tacos
Shrimp-Stuffed Wild Mushrooms
Scallop Kabobs with Fresh Rosemary
Salmon Tartare
Garlic Steamed Clams
Salmon Bundles with Vegetables
Japanese Pork Balls on Wilted Spinach
Grilled Sirloin Kabobs

Appetizers should tantalize the taste buds and satisfy the senses with their textures, colors, and flavors. But they should be light, not filling, or the main dish will not be eagerly anticipated. These appetizers fit all the requirements for such "little dishes."

They meet another criterion too: flexibility. All of these dishes are indeed appetizers, but most of them can also be served in other contexts.

The rationale is that recipes are like old friends; you feel comfortable once you've gotten to know them. After you've made a recipe a few times, chances are you rarely refer to the text and innately know what to do. In this case, your appetizer from one dinner, such as Shrimp-Stuffed Wild Mushrooms (page 60), becomes your hors d'oeuvre for a party; another appetizer, such as Grilled Vegetable Kabobs (page 47), can become the vegetable accompaniment to an entree on another evening; a larger portion of a dish, such as Garlic Steamed Clams (page 65) or Salmon Tartare (page 63), can become an entree.

In eating healthfully, one of the most difficult habits to overcome—for both shedding pounds and maintaining weight—is "mindless munching." It seems this is hardest to do at parties, when we're presented with hors d'oeuvres loaded with calories—we know dinner is coming, yet we usually eat them anyway. Except for a large buffet or cocktail party, I serve *no* hors d'oeuvres. My guests know that the cocktail hour is limited, and after a glass of wine they will be seated for dinner.

For the cocktail party, there are many options from which to choose, and all of them can be ready in the kitchen hours before your guests arrive. Everything from crispy and crunchy Phyllo Egg Rolls (page 42) to triangles of Herbed Quesadillas (page 46), stuffed with a creamy herbed mozzarella, to hearty Sirloin Kabobs (page 70) makes wonderful finger food.

You can also create an entire meal with the appetizers, selecting the recipes for a variety of ingredients and flavors. While the term "grazing" offends me, I adore a combination of small dishes in lieu of a traditional entree. From this chapter, for example, you could select a group of dishes unified by Asian seasonings—Chinese Eggplant Spread (page 49), Chicken Yakitori (page 57), and Japanese Pork Balls on Wilted Spinach (page 68)—or you could select a vegetable, meat, and fish recipe representing a panoply of flavors.

Phyllo Egg Rolls

TOTAL TIME
35 minutes
WORK TIME
25 minutes

PER SERVING
92 calories
0 cholesterol
1 g fat
110 mg sodium

These crispy, delicate rolls have all the textural qualities of a traditional egg roll—a crunchy vegetable filling flavored with Asian tidbits—yet the thin phyllo dough creates a crispy wrapper with virtually no fat.   *Makes 6*

1 celery stalk, cut into fine julienne
2 stalks bok choy cabbage, cut into fine julienne
¼ medium red onion, cut into fine julienne
4 snow peas, cut into fine julienne
2 scallions, cut into fine julienne
¾ cup shredded green cabbage
2 tablespoons chopped red bell pepper
1 tablespoon reduced-sodium soy sauce
2 teaspoons Sherry
1 teaspoon rice wine vinegar
1 teaspoon plum wine
¼ teaspoon cayenne pepper
¼ teaspoon ground coriander
2 tablespoons vegetable oil
1 teaspoon grated fresh gingerroot
½ teaspoon minced garlic
2 tablespoons chopped fresh cilantro or parsley
¼ cup bean sprouts
1 teaspoon dark sesame oil
6 sheets phyllo dough
Vegetable oil spray

1. Combine all the vegetables except the bean sprouts. In a small bowl, combine the liquid seasonings, cayenne pepper, and coriander.

2. Heat the oil in a wok or large skillet over high heat. Add the ginger and garlic and stir-fry, stirring constantly, for 30 seconds or until fragrant. Add the vegetables and stir-fry for 2 minutes or until slightly cooked but still crisp. Add the liquids and stir-fry for 1 minute.

3. Remove from the heat and stir in the cilantro, bean sprouts, and sesame oil. Set aside.

4. Preheat the oven to 375 degrees. Carefully separate a sheet of phyllo and place about ¾ cup of the vegetable filling in the center of one of the shorter ends of the rectangle. Fold the sides around the filling to enclose it and then roll the phyllo into an egg roll. Place on a baking sheet seam side down.

5. Spray the rolls lightly with vegetable oil spray and bake for 10 to 12 minutes in the center of the oven or until the rolls are golden brown.

NOTE: The filling can be prepared up to two days in advance and kept tightly covered with plastic wrap in the refrigerator. Or the rolls can be baked and reheated in a 350-degree oven for five to seven minutes. If baking in advance, it is advisable to slightly underbake them. Do not reheat in a microwave oven.

WINE NOTE
You will enjoy a Pouilly-Fumé or Sancerre from the Loire Valley in France with this dish.

Grilled Vegetable Pizza

TOTAL TIME
1½ hours
WORK TIME
30 minutes

PER SLICE
169 calories
5 mg cholesterol
5 g fat
138 mg sodium

Pizza can be healthful if you watch the fat of the topping. While this chewy, easy-to-prepare crust is topped with grilled vegetables, you can augment the topping with Herbed Turkey Sausage (page 54) or vary the vegetables used.
Makes 12 slices (2 pizzas)

FOR THE CRUST

3 cups whole-wheat flour
1 package active dry or fresh yeast
¼ teaspoon salt
1 tablespoon honey
2 tablespoons olive oil
¾ cup warm water

FOR THE TOPPING

1 medium zucchini, trimmed and sliced
1 red bell pepper, seeds and ribs removed (page 269), cut into 1-inch slices
1 yellow bell pepper, seeds and ribs removed (page 269), cut into 1-inch slices
½ small red onion, peeled and thickly sliced
½ small eggplant, trimmed and cut into ¼-inch slices
18 fresh mushrooms, washed and halved
1 cup grated low-fat (part skim milk) mozzarella cheese
2 teaspoons finely minced garlic
4 tablespoons fresh oregano leaves *or* 1 teaspoon dried
¼ teaspoon freshly ground black pepper
¼ teaspoon salt

1. Preheat a grill or broiler. For the crust, combine the ingredients in a mixing bowl or the bowl of an electric mixer fitted with a dough hook. Mix until a soft ball forms, then transfer the dough to a lightly floured surface and knead it until smooth. Place in a lightly greased bowl and allow it to rest, covered with a dry towel, for 30 minutes.

2. While the dough is rising, grill the vegetables for 2 to 3 minutes on each side. Set aside.

3. Preheat the oven to 450 degrees. Divide the dough in half and form each half into a ball. Roll into a thin circle to fit a 14-inch pizza pan, with the edges slightly thicker than the center. Arrange the grilled vegetables on top of the dough. Sprinkle with the remaining ingredients and bake the pizzas for 12 to 15 minutes. Cut each into 6 wedges and serve immediately.

NOTE: The pizza dough can be prepared up to six hours in advance and refrigerated, tightly covered with plastic wrap. Allow it to sit at room temperature for one hour before rolling.

WINE NOTE
A crisp, dry wine such as an Italian Soave, California Fumé Blanc, or white wine from the Loire Valley will go nicely with the clean taste of the vegetables. Or, have a glass of beer as you might with other pizzas.

Herbed Quesadillas

TOTAL TIME
20 minutes
WORK TIME
15 minutes

PER WEDGE
43 calories
4 mg cholesterol
1 g fat
33 mg sodium

These are one of my favorite party hors d'oeuvres since they are so easy and fast to make for a crowd. The fresh herbs with the creamy cheese contrast wonderfully with the slight grilled taste of the vegetables. They need no garnish, but look most attractive presented on colorful paper napkins. *Makes 16 pieces*

½ red onion, peeled and cut into ¾-inch slices
2 tablespoons vegetable oil
8 8-inch flour tortillas
1 red bell pepper, roasted, peeled, seeded (page 269), and cut into ½-inch strips
½ pound low-fat (part skim milk) mozzarella cheese, grated
2 garlic cloves, peeled and minced
2 tablespoons chopped fresh marjoram *or* 1 teaspoon dried
2 tablespoons chopped fresh oregano *or* 1 teaspoon dried
Pinch of freshly ground black pepper

1. Preheat a grill or broiler. Brush the onion slices with 1 tablespoon of the oil and grill or broil 6 inches from the heat for 4 minutes on each side. Separate into rings and set aside.

2. Heat a skillet over high heat. Soften the tortillas by grilling for 30 seconds on each side.

3. Mix the onion, red pepper strips, mozzarella, garlic, marjoram, oregano, and pepper. Divide evenly over 4 tortillas and top with the remaining 4, pressing them down gently. Brush both sides lightly with oil.

4. Preheat the oven to 400 degrees. Bake the quesadillas for 3 to 5 minutes or until lightly browned and the cheese is melted. Cut into quarters and serve immediately.

NOTE: The quesadillas can be prepared through step 3 up to two days in advance. Stack them, separated with plastic wrap and covered with plastic wrap, in the refrigerator.

WINE NOTE
One of the richer white Burgundies from France or a California Chardonnay or Sauvignon Blanc will balance the textures and flavors of this appetizer.

Grilled Vegetable Kabobs

Colorful and savory with a spicy mustard flavor, the kabobs can be served as a side dish with a simple grilled or broiled entree or as an appetizer. The vinaigrette marinade becomes a simple sauce to moisten them once they are grilled.   *Serves 6*

3 small red potatoes, unpeeled
2 small zucchini, trimmed and cut into 1-inch chunks
1 red bell pepper, seeds and ribs removed (page 269), cut into 1-inch slices
1 yellow bell pepper, seeds and ribs removed (page 269), cut into 2-inch squares
1 large onion, peeled, halved, and cut into ½-inch wedges
2 tablespoons grainy mustard
1 tablespoon chopped fresh rosemary *or* 1 teaspoon dried
½ cup white wine vinegar
3 garlic cloves, peeled and minced
2 shallots, peeled and minced
¼ teaspoon freshly ground black pepper

1. Scrub and quarter the potatoes. Parboil until almost tender, about 7 minutes. Drain and set aside.

2. Combine the potatoes in a glass or stainless-steel bowl with the zucchini, red bell pepper, yellow bell pepper, and onion. Whisk together the remaining ingredients. Pour the marinade over the vegetables and marinate for 4 to 6 hours at room temperature, or overnight in the refrigerator, covered with plastic wrap.

3. Soak 6 bamboo skewers in water for at least 20 minutes. Preheat a grill or broiler. Thread the vegetables onto the skewers, reserving the marinade, and grill or broil for 10 to 12 minutes, basting and turning twice.

4. Serve on small plates and spoon the marinade over the hot kabobs as a sauce.

WINE NOTE
With the vinegar, a spicy Gewürztraminer from Alsace or a white Zinfandel from California is the best match.

TOTAL TIME
5 hours, including marinating
WORK TIME
15 minutes

PER SERVING
51 calories
0 cholesterol
.5 g fat
99 mg sodium

Zucchini Mousse with Salsa

TOTAL TIME
5 hours, including chilling
WORK TIME
20 minutes

PER SERVING
117 calories
1 mg cholesterol
5 g fat
161 mg sodium

Most vegetable mousses have a delicate flavor as a corollary to the light and silky texture. Don't let the pale green tone of this one fool you; there is a hint of hot chilies and fresh cilantro to enliven the dish. Those flavors are complemented by the spicy *salsa*, which provides a bright red contrast to the pale pastel mousse.   *Serves 6*

2 envelopes unflavored gelatin
¾ cup cold water
1 tablespoon olive oil
3 medium (about 1 pound) zucchini, trimmed and thinly sliced
2 teaspoons minced *jalapeño* and *serrano* chili pepper (page 269)
2 scallions, including 3 inches of the green, trimmed and sliced
1 cup plain nonfat yogurt
2 tablespoons freshly squeezed lime juice
2 tablespoons chopped fresh cilantro or parsley
¼ teaspoon salt
2 cups Fresh Tomato Salsa (page 207)

1. Sprinkle the gelatin over ½ cup of the water to soften for 10 minutes.

2. Heat the olive oil over medium-high heat in a 12-inch skillet. Add the zucchini, chili pepper, and scallions. Sauté for 7 to 10 minutes, stirring frequently, until the zucchini has softened and the scallions are translucent. Cool for 10 minutes.

3. Heat the remaining ¼ cup water in a small saucepan and add the softened gelatin. Stir until the granules are dissolved.

4. Puree the zucchini mixture, along with the yogurt, lime juice, cilantro, salt, and gelatin. Pour into a lightly oiled mold and chill, covered with plastic wrap, until set and firm, at least 4 hours.

5. To serve, dip the mold into hot water, place a platter over the mold, and invert, rapping on the counter to dislodge. To serve, place ⅓ cup Fresh Tomato Salsa on each plate and cover it with a slice of the mousse.

NOTE: The mousse can be made up two days in advance and kept, covered with plastic wrap, in the refrigerator. Unmold just before serving.

WINE NOTE
Although this dish is creamy, the *jalapeños* dictate a spicy wine, such as Gewürztraminer from Alsace or white Zinfandel from California.

Chinese Eggplant Spread

This method of baking the eggplant eliminates the need for the large amounts of salt and oil specified in most recipes. The Szechwan spicing, inspired by a dish enjoyed at my friend Barbara Tropp's wonderful China Moon Cafe in San Francisco, sparks the mild natural flavor of the vegetable. It can also be served as an hors d'oeuvre, spread on crackers.   Serves 6

2 medium (1-pound) eggplants
4 scallions, including 2 inches of the green, trimmed and chopped
2 teaspoons minced garlic
¼ to ½ teaspoon hot chili oil (to taste)
2 tablespoons reduced-sodium soy sauce
1 tablespoon balsamic vinegar
1 tablespoon sugar
1 tablespoon dark sesame oil
Colorful lettuce leaves, such as *radicchio* or red leaf, for serving

1. Preheat the oven to 400 degrees. Prick the eggplants with a sharp meat fork and place on a baking dish in the center of the oven. Bake the eggplants for 40 to 50 minutes, turning after 20 minutes, or until they are uniformly soft.

2. Remove the eggplants from the oven. They will look brown and will deflate as if you punctured a balloon. When cool enough to handle easily, cut off the top and peel away the skin with your fingers. Drain any liquid that seeps out by shaking the pulp in a sieve and chop the flesh either by hand or in a food processor fitted with the steel blade, pulsing it on and off.

TOTAL TIME
3 hours, including chilling
WORK TIME
10 minutes

PER SERVING
70 calories
0 cholesterol
3 g fat
205 mg sodium

3. Mix the scallions with the remaining ingredients except lettuce. Stir into the chopped eggplant and chill well, at least 2 hours.

4. To serve, arrange some lettuce leaves on a small plate and mound the eggplant in the center.

NOTE: The dish is even better if made a day in advance, to allow the flavors to blend.

WINE NOTE
The Asian flavors here make a Fumé Blanc or Sauvignon Blanc from California a good choice.

Mushrooms Stuffed with Spinach and Chèvre

TOTAL TIME
30 minutes
WORK TIME
20 minutes

PER SERVING
141 calories
23 mg cholesterol
10 g fat
178 mg sodium

Stuffed mushrooms never go out of style. Mellow goat cheese becomes the flavor secret in the bright green spinach filling. These are not only the perfect cocktail party hors d'oeuvre, you can also serve them as a vegetable to glamorize simple entrees.

18 large fresh mushrooms
1 tablespoon olive oil
1 tablespoon unsalted butter
2 garlic cloves, peeled and minced
¼ cup finely chopped shallots
1 10-ounce package frozen chopped spinach, defrosted
2 tablespoons chopped fresh parsley
1 teaspoon chopped fresh thyme *or* ¼ teaspoon dried
½ teaspoon chopped fresh rosemary *or* pinch of dried
1 tablespoon freshly squeezed lemon juice
Pinch of freshly ground white pepper
Pinch of salt
¼ pound goat cheese

1. Wash the mushrooms and twist out the stems. Set aside the caps and finely chop the stems.

2. Heat the olive oil and butter in a 12-inch skillet over medium heat. Sauté the chopped mushroom stems, garlic, and shallots, stirring frequently, for 7 to 10 minutes or until the vegetables are soft.

3. Place the defrosted spinach in a colander and press to remove excess liquid. Add to the pan and cook for 3 minutes. Add the parsley, thyme, rosemary, lemon juice, pepper, salt, and goat cheese. Mix until smooth and remove from heat.

4. Preheat the oven to 350 degrees. Stuff the mushroom caps with the mixture and place on a baking sheet. Bake in the center of the oven for 8 to 10 minutes or until the mushrooms are cooked. Serve warm or at room temperature.

NOTE: You can fill the mushrooms a day in advance, keep them refrigerated, tightly covered with plastic wrap, and bake just prior to serving. Or, you can bake them up to four hours in advance and keep them at room temperature. They are much better if not reheated.

WINE NOTE
One cannot think of goat cheese without thinking of a Pouilly-Fumé or Sancerre from the Loire Valley in France, and they work well here.

Spinach and Carrot Loaf

TOTAL TIME
2 hours (4 hours if served chilled)
WORK TIME
25 minutes

PER SERVING
113 calories
52 mg cholesterol
4 g fat
255 mg sodium

This pureed vegetable terrine is extremely easy to make and very elegant to serve. It's subtly seasoned, so what you taste is the pure flavors of the sweet carrots and the fresh taste of the spinach. Their vivid orange and green colors create a dramatic presentation.   Serves 6

1 pound carrots, peeled and sliced
1 pound frozen chopped spinach, defrosted
1 tablespoon unsalted butter
1 garlic clove, peeled and minced
1½ cups chopped onion
1 egg
5 egg whites
Vegetable oil for greasing loaf pan
2 tablespoons freshly grated Parmesan cheese
¼ teaspoon salt
¼ teaspoon freshly ground white pepper

1. Steam the carrots in a vegetable steamer for 10 to 15 minutes or until tender. Allow to cool for 10 minutes. Place the spinach in a colander and squeeze it over the sink with the back of a large spoon to extract all the liquid.

2. Melt the butter in a 12-inch skillet over medium heat. Add the garlic and onions and sauté, stirring frequently, for 7 minutes or until the onions are translucent. Allow to cool slightly. Beat the egg with the egg whites lightly and divide the mixture into 2 equal parts.

3. Preheat the oven to 350 degrees. Oil the inside of a 1-quart loaf pan, line the bottom with wax paper or parchment, and grease the paper.

4. Place the carrots, along with half the onions and garlic, half the egg mixture, half the Parmesan, and half the salt and pepper in a blender or food processor fitted with the steel blade. Puree until smooth and scrape the puree into the loaf pan, smoothing the top with a spatula. Repeat with the spinach, using the remaining ingredients.

5. Smooth the top and place the loaf pan in a 9- by 13-inch pan. Pour boiling water halfway up the sides of the loaf pan and bake for 1 hour. Remove from the oven and allow to stand for 20 minutes in the water before unmolding. Serve hot, at room temperature, or chilled.

NOTE: The loaf can be made to the point of baking up to a day in advance; allow it to reach room temperature before baking. Or, it can be totally cooked up to three days in advance, to serve cold.

WINE NOTE
Try a Vouvray from the Loire Valley in France or an Italian Vernaccia or Pinot Grigio with this light dish.

Herbed Turkey Sausage

TOTAL TIME
30 minutes
WORK TIME
20 minutes

PER SERVING
181 calories
47 mg cholesterol
7 g fat
312 mg sodium

These sausages are savory and redolent of fresh herbs without being spicy. You can make the mixture into sausage balls and serve them with more tomato sauce on top of pasta or use them as an hors d'oeuvre; you can also serve the patties (minus the sauce, perhaps) at breakfast.   Serves 6

2 tablespoons olive oil
1 cup finely chopped shallot
1 garlic clove, peeled and minced
1 pound turkey breast meat, ground or finely chopped* (page 272)
2 teaspoons finely chopped fresh sage *or* ½ teaspoon dried
2 teaspoons finely chopped fresh oregano *or* ½ teaspoon dried
2 teaspoons finely chopped fresh basil *or* ½ teaspoon dried
2 teaspoons finely chopped fresh marjoram *or* ½ teaspoon dried
2 teaspoons finely chopped fresh thyme *or* ½ teaspoon dried
¼ teaspoon freshly ground white pepper
¼ teaspoon salt
1 tablespoon freshly squeezed lemon juice
¾ cup Herbed Tomato Sauce (page 202)
Fresh herb flowers or fresh herb sprigs for garnish

*Commercially packaged ground turkey breast often contains a substantial amount of fat-laden turkey skin, so it's best to grind your own.

1. Heat 1½ tablespoons of the oil in a 12-inch skillet over medium heat. Add the shallots and garlic; sauté, stirring frequently, for 7 minutes or until the shallots are soft.

2. Combine the shallots and garlic with the remaining ingredients, except sauce and garnish.

3. Preheat a grill or broiler. Form the turkey mixture into 12 sausage-shaped cylinders and brush with the remaining oil. Grill or broil for a total of 8 minutes, turning a quarter turn every 2 minutes. To serve, place 2 tablespoons of the tomato sauce on each plate and top with 2 sausages.

NOTE: The sausage mixture can be made a day in advance and kept, covered with plastic wrap, in the refrigerator. Grill or broil the sausages just before serving.

WINE NOTE
Try a red Beaujolais from France or a richer white such as a white Burgundy from France or a California Chardonnay.

Southwestern Turkey Sausage with Yogurt Dill Dressing

The spiciness of the sausage, with its decidedly southwestern accent, is cooled by the creamy, light dressing. The dish can also be made into miniatures and skewered on toothpicks for cocktail parties.   *Serves 6*

TOTAL TIME
20 minutes
WORK TIME
15 minutes

2 tablespoons vegetable oil
1 cup finely chopped onion
2 garlic cloves, peeled and minced
1 *jalapeño* chili pepper, seeded and finely chopped (page 269)
1 pound turkey breast meat, ground or finely chopped*
¼ pound ground veal
2 tablespoons white wine vinegar
½ cup chopped fresh cilantro or parsley
½ teaspoon freshly ground white pepper
¼ teaspoon salt
12 leaves *radicchio*
½ cup Yogurt Dill Dressing (page 210)

PER SERVING
180 calories
60 mg cholesterol
8 g fat
159 mg sodium

*Commercially packaged ground turkey breast often contains a substantial amount of fat-laden turkey skin, so it's best to grind your own.

1. Heat 1½ tablespoons of the oil in a skillet over medium heat; add the onions, garlic, and chili pepper. Sauté, stirring often, for 5 to 7 minutes or until the onions are translucent.

2. Mix the sautéed vegetables with the remaining ingredients except *radicchio* and dressing.

3. Preheat a grill or broiler. Form the mixture into 12 patties, about ½ inch thick, and brush with the remaining oil. Grill or broil the patties for 3 minutes on each side; they should be cooked through but not well done.

4. To serve, place each patty in a leaf of *radicchio* and top with a dollop of dressing. They can be served with a fork or rolled up and eaten as finger food.

NOTE: The sausage mixture can be prepared a day in advance. Grill the patties just before serving.

WINE NOTE
You will need a wine with some intensity of flavor, such as a *grand cru* Beaujolais or a red Burgundy from France or one of the richer Chardonnays from California.

Chicken Yakitori

This variation on the Japanese classic can be made in smaller versions as hors d'oeuvres and can also be eaten at room temperature for picnics. The chewy mushrooms and crunchy jicama add textural diversity, and all ingredients absorb the vibrant marinade.   *Serves 6*

TOTAL TIME
3½ hours, including marinating
WORK TIME
20 minutes

PER SERVING
120 calories
32 mg cholesterol
3 g fat
640 mg sodium

¾ pound boneless, skinless chicken breast, trimmed (page 272)
1 cup reduced-sodium soy sauce
1 cup Sherry
2 tablespoons grated fresh ginger
2 tablespoons dark sesame oil
1 tablespoon minced garlic
6 large fresh mushrooms, washed and halved
3 scallions, trimmed and cut into 1-inch lengths, including 2 inches of the green
¼ pound jicama, peeled and cut into 1-inch cubes
1 bunch of watercress for garnish
2 tablespoons sesame seed

1. Pound the chicken breasts to an even ¼-inch thickness (or get the butcher to do it) and then cut them into 1-inch squares.

2. Mix the soy sauce, Sherry, ginger, sesame oil, and garlic. Soak 6 bamboo skewers in water for at least 20 minutes. Thread the skewers with chicken cubes, alternating with mushrooms, scallions, and jicama.

3. Place the skewers in a shallow dish large enough to accommodate them and pour the marinade over the top. Refrigerate the skewers, covered with plastic wrap, for 3 hours, turning occasionally.

4. Wash and dry the watercress, removing the tough stems. Refrigerate until ready to serve.

5. Preheat a grill or broiler. Remove the skewers from the marinade and shake over the sink. Sprinkle the skewers with sesame seeds and grill them for 8 minutes, turning them a quarter turn every 2 minutes.

6. To serve, place a bed of watercress on each plate and place a skewer on the top.

NOTE: If jicama cannot be found, you can substitute canned water chestnuts. Pour boiling water over them to remove the tinned taste.

WINE NOTE
The Asian flavors make a Gewürztraminer from Alsace or a Fumé Blanc or Sauvignon Blanc from California the right choice.

Chinese Chicken Tacos

TOTAL TIME
30 minutes
WORK TIME
20 minutes

PER SERVING
91 calories
21 mg cholesterol
3 g fat
132 mg sodium

Think of these as healthful Chinese tacos. Based on the traditional Chinese appetizer of minced squab in lettuce leaves, the quickly stir-fried filling is presented in a leaf of crispy lettuce. The way to eat it is to roll it up and use your fingers.   Serves 6

½ cup water
12 dried *shiitake* mushrooms
¼ cup chicken stock, preferably unsalted (page 266)
1 tablespoon reduced-sodium soy sauce
1 tablespoon dry Sherry
½ pound boneless, skinless chicken breast, finely minced
3 scallions, including 2 inches of the green, finely chopped
¼ medium (about ½ pound) jicama, peeled and chopped
2 teaspoons vegetable oil
2 teaspoons dark sesame oil
1½ teaspoons grated fresh ginger
½ teaspoon minced garlic
Pinch of freshly ground black pepper
1 teaspoon cornstarch mixed with 1 tablespoon cold water
6 large iceberg lettuce leaves

1. Bring the water to a boil over high heat. Remove pan from heat and add the dried *shiitake* mushrooms, pushing them into the water with a spoon so they will begin to soften. Allow them to soak for 20 minutes, then drain them, squeezing well to extract the liquid; reserve the soaking liquid. Remove and discard the stems and cut the mushrooms in half if large. Strain the soaking liquid through a sieve lined with a coffee filter or cheesecloth.

2. Combine the chicken stock, soy sauce, Sherry, and reserved mushroom soaking liquid. Set aside. Combine the chicken, scallions, and jicama. Set aside.

3. Heat the vegetable and sesame oils in a wok or skillet over high heat. Add the ginger and garlic and stir-fry, stirring constantly, for 30 seconds. Add the chicken mixture, sprinkle with pepper, and stir-fry for 3 minutes or until the chicken is no longer pink. Add the liquid mixture, stir well, and cook for 3 minutes.

4. Stir the cornstarch mixture into the chicken mixture and cook briefly until it thickens slightly.

5. To serve, place an equal portion of the chicken mixture in the center of each lettuce leaf.

NOTE: The chicken mixture can be made up to two days in advance. Reheat it over low heat, stirring often.

WINE NOTE
As with many dishes flavored with Asian seasonings, a fruity wine such as a Riesling or Gewürztraminer from Alsace or California will work nicely with this dish. Another option is a glass of warm *sake*.

Shrimp-Stuffed Wild Mushrooms

TOTAL TIME
45 minutes
WORK TIME
20 minutes

PER SERVING
112 calories
78 mg cholesterol
4 g fat
135 mg sodium

While the success of stuffed cultivated mushrooms depends on the ingredients of the filling, baking wild mushrooms brings out their woodsy flavor, blended here with the creamy shrimp filling. These are worthy of a special party—serve them at room temperature in that case.   *Serves 6*

18 large fresh *shiitake* or Italian brown wild mushrooms (about 1 pound)
¾ pound medium shrimp, peeled, deveined, and coarsely chopped
   (save the shells)
1½ cups water
¼ cup dry white wine
¼ cup chopped celery
¼ cup chopped onion
1 teaspoon chopped fresh thyme *or* ¼ teaspoon dried
4 black peppercorns
1 tablespoon unsalted butter
2 tablespoons flour
¼ cup milk
Pinch of salt
Pinch of freshly ground white pepper
2 tablespoons freshly grated Parmesan cheese
1 tablespoon chopped fresh parsley

1. Wash the mushrooms and remove the stems. In a 2-quart saucepan, combine the shrimp shells, water, wine, celery, onion, thyme, and peppercorns. Bring to a boil over high heat and cook the stock until only ¼ cup of liquid remains. This should take about 25 minutes. Strain, pushing with a spoon to extract the liquid from the solids. Set aside.

2. In a small saucepan, melt the butter over medium heat. Stir in the flour and cook over low heat, stirring constantly, for 2 minutes. Whisk in the milk, reserved seafood stock, salt, pepper, cheese, and parsley. Bring to a boil, stirring constantly, and cook over low heat for 1 minute. Add the chopped shrimp and cook over low heat for 2 minutes, until the shrimp are pink.

3. Preheat the oven to 375 degrees. Fill the mushroom caps with the mixture and bake for 8 to 10 minutes or until the mushrooms are cooked but still slightly firm. Serve either hot or at room temperature.

NOTE: The recipe can be completed through step 2 a day in advance, keeping the filling refrigerated, covered with plastic wrap. Heat it slowly in a small saucepan before baking the mushrooms.

WINE NOTE
A white Burgundy from France or a California Chardonnay matches both the shrimp and mushrooms.

Scallop Kabobs with Fresh Rosemary

TOTAL TIME
4 to 6 hours, including marinating
WORK TIME
10 minutes

PER SERVING
132 calories
41 mg cholesterol
3 g fat
183 mg sodium

Tender, silky sea scallops are one of the most elegant forms of seafood, and these grilled kabobs enhance their natural sweetness with fresh rosemary. Halved scallops can be served as hors d'oeuvres.   *Serves 6*

1½ pounds sea scallops
3 tablespoons freshly squeezed lemon juice
2 teaspoons grated lemon zest
¼ cup fresh rosemary leaves, bruised, *or* **1 tablespoon dried**
1 tablespoon extra-virgin olive oil
¼ teaspoon freshly ground white pepper
Seaweed (available at seafood markets that sell live lobsters) for serving

1. Wash and dry the scallops. Make the marinade: Whisk the lemon juice, lemon zest, rosemary, olive oil, and pepper together in a glass or stainless-steel bowl.

2. Marinate the scallops for 4 to 6 hours, refrigerated and covered with plastic wrap. Soak 6 bamboo skewers in water to cover for at least 20 minutes.

3. Preheat a grill or broiler. Thread the scallops onto the skewers, tucking rosemary leaves in between them. Grill or broil for a total of 5 minutes, turning them a quarter turn every few minutes. Be careful not to overcook them, or they will toughen. Serve immediately, placing a kabob on a bed of washed seaweed.

NOTE: The scallops can be served hot or at room temperature, and the same treatment is delicious with jumbo shrimp.

WINE NOTE
A French Chablis, white Burgundy, or Macon-Villages will be the perfect companion for these grilled scallops.

Salmon Tartare

While I've never been a fan of *sashimi*, I adore the fresh parsley and spicy flavors blended into this raw salmon dish, inspired by Michael Roberts of Trumps in Los Angeles. For a cocktail party, I buy the ready-to-serve canapé shells and fill them with the *tartare*, reserving the capers to sprinkle on top as a garnish. *Serves 6*

TOTAL TIME
45 minutes
WORK TIME
15 minutes

PER SERVING
210 calories
63 mg cholesterol
10 g fat
446 mg sodium

1½ pounds salmon fillet (any species, preferably a bright orange one)
1 bunch of fresh parsley, tough stems removed, washed and chopped
4 shallots, peeled and chopped
1 garlic clove, peeled and minced
1 tablespoon drained capers
2 tablespoons prepared horseradish
1 teaspoon anchovy paste
3 tablespoons Dijon mustard
1 tablespoon fruity olive oil
4 tablespoons freshly squeezed lemon juice
¼ teaspoon Tabasco sauce
Pinch of freshly ground white pepper
¼ teaspoon salt
Canapé shells, toast points, or colorful lettuces for serving

1. Remove the skin from the salmon, if necessary, and go over it carefully to pull out any hidden bones. Wash the salmon and pat dry. Cut the salmon into 1-inch pieces and set aside.

2. Place the salmon and parsley in a food processor fitted with the steel blade. Chop it, using on-and-off pulsing motions, until it is coarsely chopped. Be careful not to puree it.

3. Combine the remaining ingredients except canapé shells until well blended.

4. Combine the fish mixture with the seasonings and refrigerate for 30 minutes to blend the flavors.

5. To serve, divide the salmon among the lettuce cups in the center of an appetizer plate and serve with toast points, if desired. Or scoop into canapé shells and decorate with additional capers.

NOTE: The dish can be made up to six hours in advance; however, do not combine the fish with the seasonings more than one hour in advance. Any leftovers can become broiled "salmon burgers" the next day.

WINE NOTE
A Riesling from Alsace or a Sancerre or Pouilly-Fumé from the Loire Valley balances the salmon oils and spices.

Garlic Steamed Clams

Based on the Portuguese way of cooking clams, this dish is a combination appetizer and soup and should be served with a seafood fork and a soup spoon. The broth resulting from the clam juices mingling with the garlic, wine, and parsley is as good as any fish soup I've ever eaten. Better yet, it comes to the table within minutes.   Serves 6

3 dozen small hard-shelled clams
1 tablespoon cornmeal
2 tablespoons olive oil
6 garlic cloves, peeled and minced
¼ cup water
¼ cup white wine
¼ cup chopped fresh parsley
Pinch of freshly ground white pepper

TOTAL TIME
2 hours, including soaking the clams
WORK TIME
15 minutes

PER SERVING
90 calories
18 mg cholesterol
5 g fat
32 mg sodium

1. Scrub the clams with a stiff brush under cold running water, discarding any that are not firmly closed. Place them in a bowl of cold water and sprinkle the cornmeal on top. Place them in the refrigerator for at least 1½ hours. Then drain and scrub them again.

2. Heat the olive oil in a Dutch oven over medium heat. Add the garlic and sauté, stirring frequently, for 5 minutes.

3. Raise the heat to high and add the water, wine, and clams. Cover the pot and steam the clams for 3 to 8 minutes, depending on the size of the clams. Shake the pan a few times, without opening it, to redistribute the clams.

4. Remove the clams with a slotted spoon, discarding any that did not open. Stir the parsley and pepper into the broth.

5. To serve, place the clams in a shallow bowl and ladle the broth on top.

NOTE: Mussels can be substituted for clams. Trim the beards with a sharp paring knife and then soak as you would clams.

WINE NOTE
A French white Burgundy, such as a Macon-Villages, will enhance the flavors of this dish.

Salmon Bundles with Vegetables

TOTAL TIME
30 minutes
WORK TIME
30 minutes

PER SERVING
228 calories
59 mg cholesterol
6 g fat
80 mg sodium

This is one of the most elegant and dramatic appetizers to serve. The pasta bundles are filled with a subtly seasoned salmon mousse, tied with chives into little bundles, then sauced with a lightly herbed reduction of chicken stock and white wine, along with some colorful vegetables.   *Serves 6*

FOR THE PASTA BUNDLES

¾ pound salmon fillets, skinned and cut into 1-inch pieces
1 tablespoon freshly squeezed lemon juice
1 egg white
1 tablespoon light cream
Pinch of salt
Pinch of freshly ground white pepper
1 tablespoon chopped fresh basil *or* ½ teaspoon dried
1 tablespoon chopped fresh parsley
½ pound wonton wrappers
Chives for tying the bundles

FOR THE SAUCE

2 cups chicken stock, preferably unsalted (page 266)
½ cup dry white wine
½ teaspoon minced garlic
2 shallots, peeled and chopped
2 tablespoons chopped fresh parsley
1 tablespoon chopped fresh oregano *or* ½ teaspoon dried
1 tablespoon chopped fresh marjoram *or* ½ teaspoon dried
1 tablespoon chopped fresh basil *or* ½ teaspoon dried
¼ pound fresh wild mushrooms (*shiitake,* oyster mushrooms, *chanterelles,* morels), cleaned and sliced
18 snow peas, stringed
¼ pound *haricots verts,* stringed (or string beans, stringed and halved lengthwise)

1. For the fish mousse, chill the fish well. In a blender or food processor fitted with the steel blade, puree the salmon, lemon juice, egg white, cream, salt, and pepper. Scrape down the sides of the bowl as necessary. Place the mixture in a mixing bowl and stir in the basil and parsley.

2. Cut the wonton wrappers into rounds with a cookie cutter of the same dimensions, or follow the outline of a glass or cup. To make the bundles, place 1½ teaspoons of the fish mixture in the center of a wrapper. Rub the exposed dough with water, and close the filling around the top, pressing it to adhere. It will resemble a little bundle. Tie each one with a chive, and trim the ends of the chives. Place the bundles on a sheet of waxed paper on a cookie sheet. Repeat until all filling is used. Refrigerate until ready to cook.

3. For the sauce, combine the chicken stock and wine in a 12-inch skillet and place over high heat. Add the garlic and shallots and boil until the mixture is reduced by two thirds. Add the parsley, oregano, marjoram, and basil; simmer 2 minutes. Set aside until ready to finish the dish.

4. Bring 6 quarts of water to a boil. Add the bundles and cook for 3 minutes, at which time they should have floated to the top. As the water is coming to a boil, bring the sauce back to a simmer and add the mushrooms. Cook 2 minutes, then add the snow peas and *haricots verts*. Cover the pan and steam the vegetables for 2 minutes.

5. To serve, remove the bundles quickly but gently with a slotted spoon and place on a platter to drain briefly. Divide them among six heated appetizer plates and spoon the sauce and vegetables around them.

NOTE: The bundles and sauce can be prepared up to six hours in advance and kept refrigerated. Do not cook or assemble the dish until just before serving.

WINE NOTE
Try a French Muscadet or Chablis or a Tokaji from Alsace with the delicate flavors here.

Japanese Pork Balls on Wilted Spinach

TOTAL TIME
40 minutes

WORK TIME
15 minutes

PER SERVING
170 calories
49 mg cholesterol
5 g fat
283 mg sodium

This moist, succulent appetizer is lightly seasoned with Asian overtones to allow the flavors of the sweet red pepper and woodsy mushrooms to emerge. The pork balls can be served on plates or passed as hors d'oeuvres on toothpicks, omitting the spinach.   Serves 6

⅓ cup long-grain white rice
½ pound fresh *shiitake* mushrooms
3 scallions
1 tablespoon dark sesame oil
½ red bell pepper, seeds and ribs removed (page 269), finely chopped
1 pound pork tenderloin, trimmed of silver skin and chopped
2 tablespoons reduced-sodium soy sauce
Pinch of freshly ground white pepper
1 pound fresh spinach, washed and stemmed
1 tablespoon rice wine vinegar

1. Bring 2 cups of water to a boil over high heat. Add the rice, lower the heat to a simmer, and cook the rice, uncovered, for 15 minutes, or until cooked but not mushy. Drain in a sieve, rinse with cold water, and set aside.

2. While the rice is cooking, wash the *shiitake*. Remove and discard the stems. Trim the scallions, discarding all but 2 inches of the green stems. Chop the mushrooms and scallions finely by hand or in a food processor fitted with the steel blade, using on-and-off pulsing motions.

3. Heat the sesame oil in a 12-inch skillet over medium heat. Add the mushrooms, scallions, and red pepper. Sauté, stirring frequently, for 5 minutes or until the mushrooms are soft.

4. Preheat the oven to 375 degrees. Remove the skillet from the heat and stir in the rice to cool the mixture. Stir in the pork, soy sauce, and pepper.

5. Form the mixture into 24 balls and place on a lightly oiled or nonstick baking sheet. Bake in the center of the oven for 20 minutes.

6. While the pork balls are baking, heat a skillet over medium-high heat. Add the spinach and sauté for 1 minute or until the spinach is wilted and bright green. Drain if necessary and sprinkle with the rice wine vinegar.

7. To serve, divide the spinach among small plates and place 4 pork balls on top.

NOTE: The meat mixture can be made a day in advance and kept covered with plastic wrap in the refrigerator. Bake the balls and wilt the spinach just before serving.

WINE NOTE
A Gewürztraminer from Alsace or a Sancerre or Pouilly-Fumé from the Loire Valley will marry well with the delicate Asian flavors.

Grilled Sirloin Kabobs

TOTAL TIME
2½ hours, including marinating
WORK TIME
15 minutes

PER SERVING
131 calories
33 mg cholesterol
7 g fat
35 mg sodium

Omitting fragile tomatoes and using large mushrooms and small scallions together ensures that all the foods on these skewers cook properly in the same amount of time. The zesty, herbed red wine marinade adds a pungent flavor to this robust dish.   *Serves 6*

1 pound boneless sirloin, trimmed of all fat and cut into 2-inch cubes
1 cup red wine
1 tablespoon olive oil
1 teaspoon minced garlic
1 tablespoon chopped fresh rosemary *or* ½ teaspoon dried
1 tablespoon chopped fresh basil *or* ½ teaspoon dried
2 shallots, peeled and chopped
¼ teaspoon freshly ground pepper
1 green bell pepper, seeds and ribs removed (page 269), cut into 2-inch cubes
12 scallions, white part only, trimmed
6 large fresh mushrooms, washed and halved

1. Place the meat in a glass or stainless-steel bowl. Combine the wine, olive oil, garlic, rosemary, basil, shallots, and pepper in a jar with a tight-fitting lid. Shake well and pour the marinade over the meat. Marinate for at least 2 hours at room temperature or up to a day refrigerated, covered with plastic wrap.

2. Soak 6 bamboo skewers in water for at least 20 minutes and preheat a grill or broiler. Thread the meat onto the skewers, alternating with cubes of green pepper, scallions, and mushrooms. Grill or broil for 8 minutes for medium-rare meat, turning a quarter turn every 2 minutes. Serve immediately, or at room temperature, or chilled.

NOTE: You can make this dish up to two days in advance if it is to be served at room temperature or chilled and keep it tightly covered with plastic wrap in the refrigerator.

WINE NOTE
This full-flavored dish provides you an opportunity to open some bigger reds, such as an Hermitage or Côte Rotie from the Rhône, a California Zinfandel, or an Italian Barolo or Barbera.

Salads

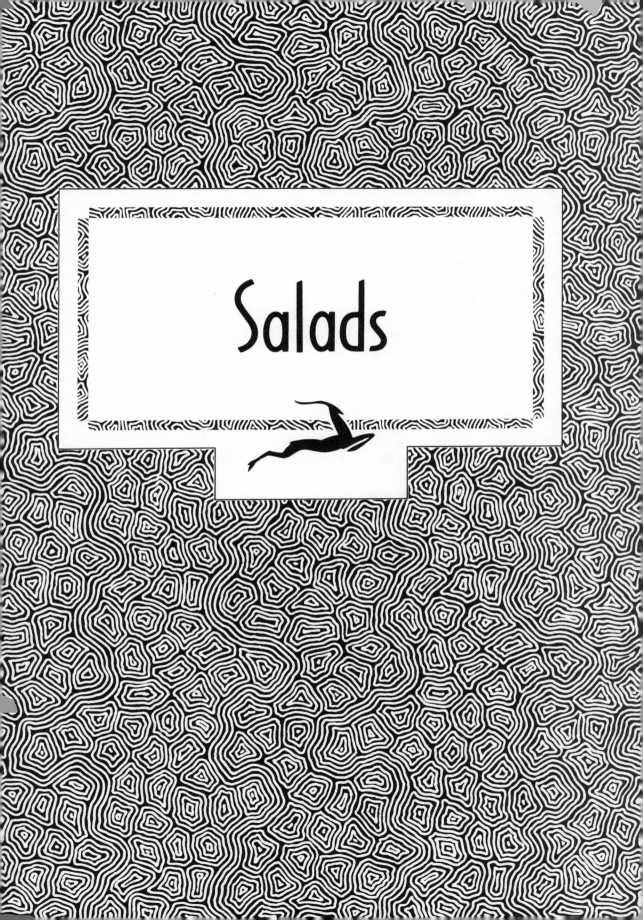

Mixed Grilled Vegetable Salad with Rosemary Vinaigrette
Radicchio Salad with Balsamic Vinaigrette
Green Bean and Tomato Salad
Pickled Celery Salad
Dilled Cucumbers
Three-Pepper Gazpacho Salad
Gingered Red Cabbage
Celery Root Rémoulade
Mexican Cilantro Slaw
Asian Cabbage Salad
Southwestern Salad
Potato Salad Vinaigrette
Mushrooms à la Grecque
Confetti Rice Salad
Wild Rice Salad
Grilled Chicken and Red Pepper Salad
Curried Chicken Salad
Asian Chicken Salad
Grilled Chicken and Tropical Fruit Salad
Cajun Chicken Salad
Salmon and Cucumber Salad
Shrimp and Snow Pea Salad
Scallop and Asparagus Salad
Seviche Salad
Tuna Salad Niçoise
Red Pepper Pasta
Pasta Salad Provençal
Pasta Salad with Carrot Sauce
Chinese Chicken and Pasta Salad
Mediterranean Lamb Salad with Barley
Spicy Beef, Pasta, and Fresh Shiitake Mushroom Salad
Sesame Pork, Pasta, and Vegetable Salad

old salads command an increasingly important position in our culinary culture. Always the stalwarts for casual outdoor entertaining, their portability and durability have given salads a larger role in our peripatetic society.

Salads have also been viewed, perhaps somewhat erroneously, as the dieter's best friend. A salad tossed with lemon juice or a chef's salad (turkey only) was the standard lunchtime penance for nocturnal caloric transgressions. In reality, however, any salad dressed with mayonnaise or a classic vinaigrette should not be perceived as healthful. Both contain hundreds of hidden fat calories, and in the case of mayonnaise, cholesterol-laden egg yolks.

You will find in this chapter a wide selection of easy-to-prepare salads that derive their interest from color, flavor, and textural contrasts. They are lightly dressed to allow the ingredients to retain their integrity, not counteract their inherent healthfulness with exorbitant amounts of oil.

While Radicchio Salad with Balsamic Vinaigrette (page 75) is a variation on a tossed salad, the vegetable salads are conceived to present interesting alternatives to greens and are intended to complement and elevate simple entrees to a more interesting meal.

The Dilled Cucumbers (page 78) are a crisp and light, refreshing side dish to serve with poached or grilled fish, while the Mixed Grilled Vegetable Salad with Rosemary Vinaigrette (page 74) is a flavorful *antipasto*.

The main dish salads focus on poultry and fish. Among the chicken salads, you'll find a fiery, bright orange Cajun Chicken Salad (page 97), tempered with the delicate sweetness of fresh papaya, and an Asian Chicken Salad (page 93), a stir-fried dish dressed with a light rice wine vinaigrette.

Much has been written in the last few years on the benefits of eating pasta and other complex carbohydrates, and the pasta salads in this chapter—the vegetarian ones and those with poultry or meat—are consistent with our general approach to eating. The somewhat caloric pasta is balanced by a large percentage of vegetables in the dish to improve the nutritional profile.

These salads are used for many of the buffet menus listed in "Menus for Entertaining." I find that cold or room-temperature food is best for large parties. Serving salads means that all dishes can be on platters and decorated before the first guest arrives.

Mixed Grilled Vegetable Salad with Rosemary Vinaigrette

TOTAL TIME
2 hours, including chilling
WORK TIME
10 minutes

PER SERVING
138 calories
0 cholesterol
12 g fat
67 mg sodium

There are endless variations on the vegetables that take well to grilling—the one essential is a firm texture. When you're assembling a grilled vegetable salad, keep an eye for contrasts of color and texture as well as flavor. While this salad is intended to accompany a meal, a larger portion can be served as a vegetarian entree.   *Serves 6*

2 tablespoons vegetable oil
6 ¼-inch slices of eggplant
1 red bell pepper, seeds and ribs removed (page 269), cut into sixths
1 medium zucchini, trimmed, cut in half across the width, each half cut lengthwise into 3 slices
6 ¼-inch slices of red onion
6 large fresh mushrooms, washed and halved
1 cup Rosemary Vinaigrette (page 212)

1. Preheat a grill or broiler. Using a pastry brush, lightly oil all of the vegetable slices. Place the vegetable slices on the hot grill for 4 to 5 minutes on each side, turning once. Watch closely so that the vegetables cook and brown but do not burn.

2. Arrange the vegetables decoratively on a serving platter or individual plates and chill well, at least 2 hours. Drizzle a few tablespoons of Rosemary Vinaigrette on the salad just before serving.

NOTE: The dish can be made up two days in advance and kept refrigerated, tightly covered with plastic wrap. The dressing can be kept for up to a week.

Radicchio Salad with Balsamic Vinaigrette

This salad is as festive as a bowl of confetti, and it is one of the few tossed salads you can make in a large batch to keep for a few days. The ingredients are sturdier than most fragile salad greens, and the chick-peas add richness.   Serves 6

10 scallions, including 3 inches of the green, trimmed and sliced
12 cherry tomatoes, halved
2 cucumbers, peeled, seeded, and sliced
1 ¼-pound head of radicchio, quartered, cored, and sliced
6 radishes, trimmed and sliced
¼ cup cooked chick-peas, drained and rinsed
¼ cup chopped fresh parsley
3 tablespoons fresh marjoram leaves *or* 1 teaspoon dried
½ cup Balsamic Vinaigrette (page 213)

1. In a large mixing bowl or salad bowl, combine all ingredients except the dressing. If you are using dried marjoram, add it to the dressing, not the salad. Toss the vegetables with the dressing just before serving.

NOTE: Yellow cherry tomatoes can be substituted for red, and if you're making the salad in advance, leave the tomatoes whole.

TOTAL TIME
10 minutes
WORK TIME
10 minutes

PER SERVING
65 calories
0 cholesterol
5 g fat
127 mg sodium

Green Bean and Tomato Salad

TOTAL TIME
15 minutes
WORK TIME
10 minutes

PER SERVING
49 calories
0 cholesterol
5 g fat
112 mg sodium

The creamy yogurt dressing, sparked with mustard and a hint of garlic, is the perfect foil for the delicate flavors of the green beans and tomatoes. This is a stunning salad; it can take the place of a tossed salad at a buffet dinner and is far easier to eat. *Serves 6*

1 pound green beans, trimmed and cut into 2-inch lengths
24 cherry tomatoes, washed and halved
2 garlic cloves, peeled and minced
1 tablespoon dry mustard
½ cup plain nonfat yogurt
2 tablespoons freshly squeezed lemon juice
1 teaspoon sugar
¼ teaspoon freshly ground white pepper
¼ teaspoon salt

1. Have a bowl of ice water handy. Place the green beans in a vegetable steamer and place them in a deep pot with water in the bottom. Bring to a boil over high heat, covered, and steam the beans for 5 minutes. Remove the steamer from the pot and plunge the beans into the ice water to stop the cooking action and set the color.

2. Place the green beans in a mixing bowl and combine with the cherry tomatoes.

3. Whisk the remaining ingredients together until smooth and well blended. Toss the dressing with the beans and tomatoes and serve immediately.

NOTE: You can achieve an even more colorful look if you use half red and half yellow cherry tomatoes. You can make the salad up to six hours in advance and keep it refrigerated, tightly covered with plastic wrap. The beans can be steamed up to a day in advance; however, do not add the cherry tomatoes or dress the salad longer than six hours before serving.

Pickled Celery Salad

Celery absorbs the flavors of a pickling brine as effectively as cucumber. This crunchy salad is perfect for that casual meal where you want the vibrant taste of a pickle to complement a mildly flavored salad or even a turkey sandwich.   Serves 6

6 cups sliced celery
1 cup water
2 tablespoons sugar
½ cup rice wine vinegar
Pinch of cayenne pepper
¼ teaspoon salt
½ cup finely chopped red bell pepper
¼ cup finely chopped scallion, white and green parts

1. Combine the celery and water in a large covered skillet. Bring to a boil over high heat and cook, partially covered, for 5 minutes.

2. Stir the sugar into the rice wine vinegar until dissolved. Add the cayenne pepper and salt and shake well. Pour the dressing over the celery and add the red bell pepper and scallion. Refrigerate until well chilled, at least 2 hours.

NOTE: The celery will lose its vivid green color from the vinegar, the same process that takes place in pickling.

TOTAL TIME
3 hours, including chilling
WORK TIME
15 minutes

PER SERVING
41 calories
0 cholesterol
.2 g fat
199 mg sodium

Dilled Cucumbers

TOTAL TIME
12 hours, including
marinating
WORK TIME
10 minutes

PER SERVING
32 calories
0 cholesterol
.1 g fat
53 mg sodium

The cucumbers are a refreshing, crispy tonic on a hot day; they cleanse the palate with their fresh taste. Inspired by a Danish dish, this salad is best as an accompaniment to grilled or broiled seafood.   Serves 6

3 cucumbers, peeled, seeded, and thinly sliced
½ large onion, peeled and thinly sliced
1 cup rice wine vinegar
1 cup water
2 tablespoons chopped fresh dill
1 tablespoon sugar
Pinch of salt
Pinch of freshly ground white pepper

1. Place the cucumbers and onion in a glass or stainless-steel bowl. Combine the remaining ingredients in a jar with a tight-fitting lid. Shake well to combine.

2. Pour the marinade over the vegetables, cover with plastic wrap, and refrigerate overnight. Drain before serving well chilled.

NOTE: The cucumbers can marinate for up to three days, or, once drained, the salad will keep for two days.

Three-Pepper Gazpacho Salad

This crispy salad contains the repertoire of *gazpacho*. The difference is that the vegetables are carefully cut rather than pureed. It does take some time to cut everything up; however, the dramatic presentation and blending of colors and flavors makes it worth the trouble.   *Serves 6*

TOTAL TIME
1½ hours, including chilling
WORK TIME
25 minutes

PER SERVING
62 calories
0 cholesterol
4 g fat
151 mg sodium

FOR THE SALAD

2 red bell peppers, seeds and ribs removed (page 269), cut into fine julienne

2 yellow bell peppers, seeds and ribs removed (page 269), cut into fine julienne

1 green bell pepper, seeds and ribs removed (page 269), cut into fine julienne

⅓ cup chopped red onion

2 cucumbers, peeled, seeded, and thinly sliced

2 celery stalks, washed and cut into fine julienne

1 pint cherry tomatoes, washed and halved

FOR THE DRESSING

2 garlic cloves, peeled and minced

¼ cup chopped fresh cilantro or parsley

3 tablespoons freshly squeezed lime juice

2 tablespoons white wine vinegar

1 tablespoon olive oil

¼ teaspoon salt

Pinch of cayenne pepper

1. Combine the vegetables in a glass or stainless-steel bowl.

2. Whisk together the dressing ingredients. Toss the dressing with the salad and refrigerate for 1 hour, tossing occasionally. Serve well chilled.

NOTE: The salad can be made a day in advance.

Gingered Red Cabbage

TOTAL TIME
3 hours, including marinating
WORK TIME
20 minutes

PER SERVING
126 calories
0 cholesterol
3 g fat
112 mg sodium

This brightly colored salad is a cold version of braised red cabbage, with the same sweet-and-sour taste. The ginger makes a lively contrast with the sweet raisins. The dish is hearty and pairs well with grilled meats and poultry. *Serves 6*

6 cups (about 1½ pounds) shredded red cabbage
1 cup coarsely grated carrot
½ red onion, peeled and thinly sliced
2 tablespoons grated fresh ginger
¾ cup cider vinegar
2 tablespoons honey
1 tablespoon oil
¼ teaspoon salt
Pinch of freshly ground white pepper
½ cup golden raisins, plumped in 1 cup boiling water for 15 minutes
3 scallions, including 2 inches of the green, trimmed and thinly sliced

1. Place the cabbage, carrot, and onion in a vegetable steamer over boiling water. Steam for 5 minutes, drain, and place in a glass or stainless-steel bowl.

2. Combine the ginger, vinegar, honey, oil, salt, and pepper in a jar with a tight-fitting lid. Shake to combine and then pour the mixture over the steamed vegetables. Marinate at room temperature for at least 2 hours, stirring occasionally, or in the refrigerator overnight.

3. Place the mixture in a colander over another mixing bowl. Drain the vegetables, pressing with the back of a spoon to extract as much liquid as possible. Boil down the juices until only ½ cup of liquid remains. Stir the dressing back into the salad, along with the raisins and scallions. Chill for 1 hour before serving.

NOTE: The salad keeps for up to three days in the refrigerator, tightly covered with plastic wrap.

Celery Root Rémoulade

Simultaneously creamy and spicy, *rémoulade* sauce is part of the Creole contribution to American cooking. While retaining the innate flavor sensations, a perfect complement to the sharp, fresh taste of celery root, this yogurt version is healthful. Serves 6

1 (about 1 pound) celery root
1 cup plain nonfat yogurt
¼ cup grainy mustard
¼ teaspoon freshly ground white pepper
¼ teaspoon freshly ground black pepper
1 tablespoon freshly squeezed lime juice

1. Peel the tough brown skin from the celery root and grate it coarsely. This can be done with a hand grater or with the grating blade of a food processor.

2. Immediately mix the celery root with the remaining ingredients. The acidity in the ingredients will prevent the celery root from discoloring. Refrigerate for 2 hours, and serve well chilled.

NOTE: The salad can be made up to three days in advance and kept covered with plastic wrap in the refrigerator.

TOTAL TIME
2 hours, including chilling
WORK TIME
10 minutes

PER SERVING
62 calories
2 mg cholesterol
1 g fat
226 mg sodium

Mexican Cilantro Slaw

TOTAL TIME
12 hours, including
marinating
WORK TIME
15 minutes

PER SERVING
39 calories
0 cholesterol
.2 g fat
120 mg sodium

This marinated cabbage salad is piquant without being spicy, with the mellow flavor of the chilies balancing the crisp, clean tastes of the cabbage and cilantro.   *Serves 6*

FOR THE SLAW

6 cups shredded green cabbage (about 1½ pounds)
3 tablespoons chopped fresh cilantro or parsley
1 red bell pepper, seeds and ribs removed (page 269), cut into fine
    julienne
1 red onion, peeled, halved, and thinly sliced
1 4-ounce can chopped mild green chilies, drained

FOR THE DRESSING

Juice of 2 limes
2 garlic cloves, peeled and minced
¼ cup white wine vinegar
1 tablespoon sugar
¼ teaspoon Tabasco sauce
½ cup water

1. Place the cabbage, cilantro, red pepper, onion, and chilies in a glass or stainless-steel bowl. In a jar with a tight-fitting lid, combine the remaining ingredients. Shake well.

2. Pour the dressing over the slaw and toss to coat well. Marinate refrigerated, tightly covered with plastic wrap, for at least 12 hours, tossing frequently. Drain and serve well chilled.

NOTE: The salad can be made up to three days in advance. Drain it after two days and keep it tightly covered.

Asian Cabbage Salad

The gentle flavor of rice wine vinegar is the secret to this subtly flavored cabbage salad, milder than most slaws since some of the cabbage taste is removed by blanching. The Asian influence is restrained, so it can be served with any entree.   *Serves 6*

TOTAL TIME
6 hours, including marinating
WORK TIME
10 minutes

PER SERVING
35 calories
0 cholesterol
.2 g fat
105 mg sodium

6 cups shredded green cabbage (about 1½ pounds)
1 cup sliced scallion, including 2 inches of the green
1 red bell pepper, ribs and seeds removed (page 269), chopped
⅔ cup rice wine vinegar
¼ cup water
1 tablespoon reduced-sodium soy sauce
1 tablespoon sugar
¼ teaspoon freshly ground white pepper

1. Place the cabbage in a colander in the sink. Pour boiling water over it for 30 seconds. Shake to drain and then press it with the back of a spoon to extract moisture.

2. Place the cabbage in a glass or stainless-steel bowl along with the scallions and red pepper. In a jar with a tight-fitting lid, combine the remaining ingredients. Shake well and pour over the cabbage, tossing to coat it.

3. Refrigerate the salad, tightly covered with plastic wrap, for at least 6 hours, tossing occasionally. Drain and serve well chilled.

NOTE: The salad can be made up to three days in advance. Drain it after one day and keep tightly covered with plastic wrap in the refrigerator.

Southwestern Salad

TOTAL TIME
3 hours
WORK TIME
20 minutes

PER SERVING
104 calories
0 cholesterol
3 g fat
7 mg sodium

This refreshing salad is a visual stunner—small cubes of pale white jicama contrasted with brilliant orange papaya and purple black beans. It can be an appetizer as well as a side dish and pairs well with any grilled poultry or fish. *Serves 6*

FOR THE BEANS

⅓ cup dried black beans
1 stick cinnamon
2 garlic cloves
4 peppercorns

FOR THE SALAD

1 ripe papaya, peeled, seeded, and cut into ½-inch dice
1 medium jicama, peeled and cut into ½-inch dice (3½ cups)

FOR THE DRESSING

2 garlic cloves, peeled and minced
3 shallots, peeled and chopped
¼ teaspoon ground cumin
2 tablespoons freshly squeezed lime juice
3 tablespoons sherry vinegar
⅓ cup freshly squeezed orange juice
2 tablespoons olive oil
Pinch of cayenne pepper

1. Place the beans in a sieve and wash them well under cold running water, picking through them to remove any pebbles or broken beans. Either soak them in cold water to cover overnight or bring them to a boil, boil for 1 minute, then remove from heat and allow them to stand, covered, for 1 hour. Either tie the cinnamon stick, garlic, and peppercorns in cheesecloth or break the cinnamon stick into small pieces and place all the flavoring agents in a tea ball.

2. Bring the beans to a boil and simmer, covered, for 30 minutes or until cooked but still slightly crunchy. Drain and chill well.

3. Combine the beans with the papaya and jicama. For the dressing, combine the remaining ingredients in a small bowl.

4. Combine the dressing with the jicama, papaya, and beans. Allow the salad to sit refrigerated for at least 20 minutes before serving.

NOTE: If you can't find jicama, you can use peeled apple. Toss it with the dressing first to prevent discoloration. This salad can be made a day in advance.

Potato Salad Vinaigrette

Potatoes vinaigrette, with the tart flavor of the tarragon vinegar and savory mustard part of every bite, make a delicious salad as part of a cold buffet or as an accompanying starch for simple grilled entrees.   *Serves 6*

TOTAL TIME
2½ hours, including marinating
WORK TIME
15 minutes

1½ pounds small red potatoes
2 tablespoons freshly squeezed orange juice
4 tablespoons tarragon vinegar
2 tablespoons safflower oil
2 tablespoons grainy mustard
¼ teaspoon freshly ground pepper
1 tablespoon chopped fresh rosemary *or* ½ teaspoon dried

PER SERVING
127 calories
0 cholesterol
4 g fat
45 mg sodium

1. Scrub the potatoes and place in a deep pot; add water to cover. Bring to a boil over high heat and boil until tender, about 10 to 12 minutes, depending on the size. Drain and, when cool enough to handle, slice into ¼-inch slices.

2. Whisk together the remaining ingredients. Toss with the warm potatoes and let them marinate for at least 2 hours at room temperature or overnight in the refrigerator. Toss occasionally and gently so as not to break the potatoes. Serve chilled or at room temperature.

NOTE: The potato salad can be made up to three days in advance and kept tightly covered in the refrigerator.

Mushrooms à la Grecque

TOTAL TIME
3 hours, including chilling
WORK TIME
15 minutes

PER SERVING
60 calories
0 cholesterol
3 g fat
103 mg sodium

Since mushrooms and onions are inherently low in calories, this salad can become a first course to be followed by a more indulgent entree. The vegetables absorb the vibrant flavors of the herbs and spices. This is a perfect make-ahead dish, since it tastes even better the next day.   *Serves 6*

2 cups water
3 tablespoons freshly squeezed lemon juice
1 tablespoon olive oil
2 shallots, peeled and chopped
2 garlic cloves, peeled and chopped
¼ teaspoon salt
10 black peppercorns
1 celery stalk, washed and sliced
¼ teaspoon fennel seed
1 teaspoon fresh thyme *or* pinch of dried
6 parsley sprigs
½ pound pearl onions
1 pound small fresh mushrooms, washed and trimmed

1. Combine the water, lemon juice, olive oil, shallots, garlic, and salt in a stainless-steel or enamel saucepan. Tie the peppercorns, celery, fennel, thyme, and parsley in cheesecloth and add to the pot. Bring to a boil over high heat and simmer, uncovered, for 15 minutes.

2. While the mixture is simmering, blanch the pearl onions in boiling water for 1 minute. Drain; when cool enough to handle, trim the root end and pop the onions out of their skins. Set aside.

3. Add the onions and mushrooms to the simmering liquid and simmer, covered, for 10 minutes. Remove the vegetables with a slotted spoon and set aside. Boil the poaching liquid until only ½ cup remains. Pour over the vegetables and refrigerate until well chilled, at least 2 hours. Drain before serving.

NOTE: The salad can be kept refrigerated, tightly covered, for up to three days.

Confetti Rice Salad

Bright, colorful, and light, this rice and mixed vegetable salad is the perfect accompaniment for any summer meal. It pairs well with poultry, seafood, or grilled meat. *Serves 6*

⅔ cup long-grain white rice
1 quart water
⅓ cup finely diced carrot
⅓ cup diced red bell pepper
⅓ cup finely diced celery
⅓ cup finely diced green bell pepper
½ cup Rosemary Vinaigrette (page 212)

TOTAL TIME
3 hours, including chilling
WORK TIME
15 minutes

PER SERVING
118 calories
0 cholesterol
4 g fat
42 mg sodium

1. Place the rice in a strainer and wash well under cold running water. Place in a saucepan with the water and bring to a boil over high heat. Lower the heat and simmer the rice for 15 to 18 minutes, stirring occasionally, until cooked but still slightly resilient. Drain the rice and wash under cold water to remove any remaining starch; chill.

2. Have a bowl of ice water handy. While the rice is simmering, place the carrots in a vegetable steamer and steam over boiling water for 4 to 6 minutes or until the carrots are cooked but still slightly firm. Remove the steamer from the pot and place the carrots in the ice water to stop the cooking action.

3. Combine the rice, carrots, red bell pepper, celery, and green pepper in a large mixing bowl. Toss with Rosemary Vinaigrette and chill the salad until cold, at least 2 hours.

NOTE: The salad can be prepared up to two days in advance and kept refrigerated, tightly covered with plastic wrap.

Wild Rice Salad

TOTAL TIME
4 hours, including chilling
WORK TIME
15 minutes

PER SERVING
207 calories
0 cholesterol
5 g fat
109 mg sodium

Wild rice, the quintessentially American starch, makes an elegant, hearty, nutty salad. The vegetables add both textural and visual interest, and the dressing with citrus juice and heady balsamic vinegar enhances the natural flavors.   Serves 6

FOR THE SALAD

1⅓ cups wild rice
½ cup finely diced carrot
½ cup sliced asparagus
¾ cup peeled, seeded, and diced tomato (page 271)
½ cup chopped celery
½ cup chopped red onion

FOR THE DRESSING

¼ cup golden raisins
1 garlic clove, peeled and minced
3 tablespoons chopped scallion, white part only
3 tablespoons freshly squeezed orange juice
2 tablespoons balsamic vinegar
2 tablespoons oil
¼ teaspoon salt
¼ teaspoon freshly ground black pepper

1. Place the wild rice in a strainer and place under cold running water for 2 minutes, rubbing with your hands to remove any starch. Place the wild rice in a heavy saucepan with water to cover by 2 inches and bring to a boil over high heat. Cook the wild rice, covered, over low heat for 45 minutes to 1 hour or until the water is absorbed and the rice is tender. Check after 30 minutes and add more water if necessary.

2. Have a bowl of ice water handy. Place the carrot and asparagus in a vegetable steamer and steam over boiling water for 4 minutes or until the asparagus is cooked but still slightly crunchy. Remove the steamer from the pot and plunge the vegetables into ice water to stop the cooking action.

3. In a large mixing bowl, combine the wild rice, carrot, asparagus, tomato, celery, and red onion. Place the raisins in a bowl along with the remaining ingredients. Allow the dressing to sit for 15 minutes.

4. Combine the dressing with the wild rice and vegetable mixture, tossing to coat the grains well, and refrigerate until cold, at least 2 hours.

NOTE: The salad can be prepared up to two days in advance. Do not combine the salad with the dressing more than a day in advance, however, or the asparagus will lose its color.

Grilled Chicken and Red Pepper Salad

TOTAL TIME
2½ hours, including
chilling
WORK TIME
20 minutes

PER SERVING
237 calories
68 mg cholesterol
10 g fat
172 mg sodium

This chicken salad is southwestern in origin. The smoky grilled taste of the chicken meat combines well with the light seasoning in the vinaigrette dressing.   *Serves 6*

FOR THE SALAD

1½ pounds boneless, skinless chicken breasts, trimmed (page 272)
2 red bell peppers, roasted and peeled (page 269), cut into strips
1 cucumber, peeled, seeded, and thinly sliced
1 small red onion, peeled and thinly sliced

FOR THE DRESSING

¼ cup balsamic vinegar
¼ cup vegetable oil
¼ cup freshly squeezed orange juice
¼ cup freshly squeezed lime juice
2 garlic cloves, peeled and minced
1 teaspoon ground coriander
½ teaspoon freshly ground black pepper
¼ teaspoon salt

1. Preheat a gas or charcoal grill or a broiler. Pound the chicken breast fillets to a uniform thickness of ¼ inch (or have your butcher do it); do not pound the tenderloins. Grill the chicken breasts on a hot grill for 2 minutes on each side. Be careful not to overcook, or they will dry out.

2. Cut the chicken breasts into strips ½ inch wide and 2 inches long. In a mixing bowl, combine the chicken with the red peppers, cucumber, and onion.

3. In a jar with a tight-fitting lid, combine the remaining ingredients. Shake well to emulsify the dressing and toss the dressing with the salad. Refrigerate the salad until well chilled, at least 2 hours.

NOTE: The salad can be prepared up to two days in advance and refrigerated, tightly covered with plastic wrap. You can substitute one roasted peeled poblano chili for one of the red peppers, if desired, for a spicier salad.

WINE NOTE
The smoky, spicy flavors here call for a red Côtes du Rhône or *grand cru* Beaujolais from France.

Curried Chicken Salad

This tangy, refreshing chicken salad is as appropriate for a formal lunch as it is packed in a pita for a picnic. The grapes add the sweetness of fresh fruit as a contrast to the lightly spicy curry in the creamy yogurt dressing.   *Serves 6*

TOTAL TIME
2 hours, including chilling
WORK TIME
15 minutes

PER SERVING
142 calories
46 mg cholesterol
2 g fat
85 mg sodium

FOR THE SALAD

1 pound boneless, skinless chicken breasts, trimmed (page 272)
2 cups chicken stock, preferably unsalted (page 266), or water
2 cucumbers, peeled, seeded, and thinly sliced
3 celery stalks, washed and thinly sliced
1 cup green or red seedless grapes, halved
4 scallions, trimmed and sliced, including 2 inches of the green
1 tablespoon dried currants

FOR THE DRESSING

1 cup plain nonfat yogurt
2 tablespoons curry powder
1 tablespoon white wine vinegar
2 teaspoons freshly squeezed lime juice
Pinch of freshly ground white pepper

1. Pound the chicken breast fillets to an even thickness of ¼ inch (or have your butcher do this); do not pound the tenderloins. Bring the stock or water to a boil in a large skillet over high heat. Poach the chicken breasts for 5 to 6 minutes, until cooked through but not dried out. Remove with a slotted spoon and,

when cool enough to handle, cut the chicken breast meat into 1-inch cubes. Place in a mixing bowl and add the cucumber, celery, grapes, scallions, and currants.

2. In a mixing bowl, whisk together the remaining ingredients. Gently fold the dressing into the salad and refrigerate, tightly covered with plastic wrap, until well chilled, at least 2 hours.

NOTE: You can vary the sort of grapes used in the salad. Tiny Champagne grapes, available at gourmet grocery stores, have a different visual appeal from the usual Thompson seedless grapes, for example. The salad can be prepared up to two days in advance and refrigerated, tightly covered with plastic wrap.

WINE NOTE
The curry flavors will pair well with a spicy Gewürztraminer from Alsace or a Pouilly-Fumé or Sancerre from the Loire Valley in France.

Asian Chicken Salad

Cold Asian food is a welcome relief from the all-American theme of most summer entertaining. This main-dish salad, colorful with a variety of crisply steamed vegetables, and flavored with the elements of *ponzu* sauce—soy, ginger, vinegar, and sesame—is a crunchy centerpiece for any meal.   *Serves 6*

FOR THE SALAD

1¼ pounds boneless, skinless chicken breasts, trimmed (page 272)
3 tablespoons dark sesame oil
¼ pound snow peas, stringed
2 carrots, peeled and cut into fine julienne
2 celery stalks, washed and cut into fine julienne
1 cup peeled and julienned jicama

FOR THE DRESSING

⅔ cup rice wine vinegar
½ cup reduced-sodium soy sauce
2 tablespoons sugar
3 tablespoons grated fresh ginger
½ to 1 teaspoon freshly ground white pepper

1. Pound the chicken breasts to an even thickness of ¼ inch (or have the butcher do it) and cut into strips 4 inches long and 1 inch wide. Heat 2 tablespoons of the sesame oil in a skillet over high heat and stir-fry the chicken for 2 minutes or until cooked through. Set aside. Have a bowl of ice water handy.

2. Place the snow peas, carrots, and celery in a vegetable steamer and steam for 4 minutes. Plunge the vegetables into ice water to stop the cooking action and then drain. Combine the vegetables with the jicama and chicken. Chill well, at least 1 hour.

TOTAL TIME
1½ hours, including chilling
WORK TIME
20 minutes

PER SERVING
175 calories
53 mg cholesterol
6 g fat
416 mg sodium

3. In a jar with a tight-fitting lid, combine the remaining ingredients, including the remaining tablespoon of sesame oil. Shake well. Just before serving, toss the dressing with the salad.

NOTE: The salad and dressing can be made up to two days in advance and kept refrigerated, tightly covered with plastic wrap. Do not toss until just before serving, or the snow peas will lose their color, as is the case with most salads containing steamed green vegetables.

WINE NOTE
Gewürztraminer from Alsace is a frequent companion to food with Asian flavors and will work nicely with this dish.

Grilled Chicken and Tropical Fruit Salad

This is a perfect summer lunch or supper dish. It's a contrast of pale and vivid tones, all of which have different flavor and texture nuances. It's crunchy and creamy and satisfyingly filling.   *Serves 6*

TOTAL TIME
2 hours, including chilling
WORK TIME
30 minutes

PER SERVING
280 calories
65 mg cholesterol
6 g fat
97 mg sodium

FOR THE SALAD

1½ pounds boneless, skinless chicken breasts, trimmed (page 272)
1 ripe papaya, peeled, seeded, and cut into ½-inch dice
1 ripe mango, peeled, flesh cut away from the pit and cut into ½-inch dice
2 navel oranges, peeled and sectioned, with all white membranes cut away
2 bananas, sliced
2 tablespoons freshly squeezed lemon juice
2 celery stalks, washed and sliced
1 cucumber, peeled, seeded, and sliced

FOR THE DRESSING

2 shallots, peeled and chopped
4 tablespoons freshly squeezed orange juice
2 tablespoons freshly squeezed lime juice
2 tablespoons white wine vinegar
2 tablespoons fruity olive oil
¼ teaspoon freshly ground white pepper
¼ teaspoon celery seed
1 tablespoon finely minced chives

1. Preheat a grill or broiler. Grill the chicken breasts on both sides until the juices run clear, about 3 to 5 minutes per side, depending on the thickness of the chicken. Remove from the grill and chill.

2. Place the remaining salad ingredients in a large bowl.

3. Whisk together the dressing ingredients. Combine with the fruits and vegetables and refrigerate for 30 minutes, tossing occasionally.

4. Cut the chilled chicken breasts into thin slices across the grain.

5. To serve, arrange the fruits on chilled salad plates using a slotted spoon and divide the chicken across the top. Drizzle the chicken with any dressing and fruit juices that remain in the bowl.

NOTE: The fruit can be marinated up to six hours before serving.

WINE NOTE
Try some Champagne or a California sparkling wine with this refreshing dish.

Cajun Chicken Salad

Bright red and bursting with the spicy flavors of traditional Cajun cookery, this salad balances the fires of peppers with the refreshing coolness of tropical papaya. The intensity of flavor makes this a most unusual chicken salad. *Serves 6*

TOTAL TIME
2 hours, including chilling
WORK TIME
15 minutes

PER SERVING
204 calories
49 mg cholesterol
2 g fat
79 mg sodium

1½ pounds boneless, skinless chicken breasts, trimmed (page 272)

FOR THE SPICE MIXTURE

1 teaspoon garlic powder
1 teaspoon onion powder
½ teaspoon cayenne pepper
1 teaspoon chili powder
2½ teaspoons dried thyme
2 teaspoons dried oregano
¼ teaspoon freshly ground white pepper
½ teaspoon freshly ground black pepper
½ teaspoon ground cumin
½ teaspoon paprika

FOR THE SALAD

2 ripe fresh papayas
10 scallions, including 2 inches of the green, trimmed and sliced
½ cup finely chopped red bell pepper, seeds and ribs removed (page 269), finely chopped
¼ cup chopped fresh cilantro
6 tablespoons freshly squeezed lime juice

1. Pound the chicken breast fillets to an even thickness of ¼ inch (or have your butcher do this); pound the tenderloins to the same thickness. Cut the chicken breasts into strips ½ inch wide by 2 inches long. Set aside.

2. In a small bowl, combine the spice mixture.

3. Preheat the oven to 350 degrees. Place the spice mixture on a plate and roll the chicken strips in it to coat them evenly. Arrange the chicken strips in a single layer on a nonstick or lightly greased cookie sheet. Bake in the center of the oven for 10 to 12 minutes. Remove from the oven and place the chicken strips in a mixing bowl.

4. While the chicken is baking, peel the papayas, discard the seeds, and cut into 1-inch dice. Place the papaya in the mixing bowl along with the chicken strips, scallion, red bell pepper, and cilantro. Drizzle the salad with lime juice and toss to coat evenly. Refrigerate until well chilled, at least 1½ hours.

NOTE: The salad can be prepared up to two days in advance and kept refrigerated, tightly covered with plastic wrap. If you want to tone down the spice level, reduce the amount of cayenne pepper.

WINE NOTE
A cold beer tastes refreshing with the extremely hot spices in this dish. If you wish to serve wine, however, try a California Zinfandel or an Italian Barolo or Barbera.

Salmon and Cucumber Salad

A pastiche of pastels, the pale pink salmon and light green cucumbers are a perfect combination for the tangy yogurt dressing. This is an elegant dish, perfect for a spring or summer luncheon.   *Serves 6*

2 cups water or fish stock
1½ pounds salmon fillets, skinned (page 272)
3 cucumbers, peeled, seeded, and cut into ¼-inch slices
1 cup Yogurt Dill Dressing (page 210)

1. Bring the water or fish stock to a boil in a large skillet. Add the salmon fillets, reduce the heat to a simmer, and poach the fillets for 7 to 10 minutes, depending on size. Remove the fillets from the pan with a slotted spatula and break the fillets with a fork into 1-inch chunks. Place in a mixing bowl and chill until cold, at least 1½ hours.

2. Before serving, gently toss the salmon with the cucumbers and dressing. Serve immediately.

NOTE: For a different presentation of the salad, toss half of the dressing with the cucumbers, creating a bed on each plate; top with a piece of salmon fillet, rather than flaking the salmon. The salad can be prepared up to a day in advance and refrigerated, tightly covered with plastic wrap. Do not dress it until just before serving.

WINE NOTE
A crisp Chablis from France, Champagne, or a California sparkling wine will enhance this subtle, elegant dish.

TOTAL TIME
2 hours, including chilling
WORK TIME
20 minutes

PER SERVING
270 calories
42 mg cholesterol
15 g fat
72 mg sodium

Shrimp and Snow Pea Salad

TOTAL TIME
1½ hours, including chilling
WORK TIME
15 minutes

PER SERVING
100 calories
57 mg cholesterol
3 g fat
190 mg sodium

Crunchy snow peas, delicate shrimp, and a light Asian-inspired dressing make this a refreshing, elegant entree. The color and flavor contrast is enlivened with touches of fresh sharp ginger and cilantro in the dressing. *Serves 6*

FOR THE SALAD

1 pound jumbo shrimp
Water or fish stock
½ pound snow peas, washed and stemmed
6 ounces *enoki* mushrooms, washed and trimmed
6 scallions, including 2 inches of the green, trimmed and sliced

FOR THE DRESSING

3 garlic cloves, peeled and minced
3 tablespoons freshly squeezed lime juice
1 tablespoon grated fresh ginger
3 tablespoons chopped fresh cilantro
1 tablespoon dark sesame oil
1 tablespoon reduced-sodium soy sauce
1 tablespoon freshly squeezed orange juice
2 teaspoons sesame seed, toasted in a dry skillet until brown

1. Wash the shrimp and place in a saucepan with water or fish stock to cover. Bring to a boil over high heat, cover the pan, and remove from the heat. Allow the shrimp to sit undisturbed for 5 minutes. Drain; when cool enough to handle, peel, devein, and cut in half lengthwise.

2. Have a bowl of ice water handy. Place the snow peas in a vegetable steamer in a large pot with water at the bottom. Bring to a boil over high heat and steam the snow peas for 3 minutes. Remove the steamer from the pot and plunge the snow peas into ice water to stop the cooking action and set the color. Drain and set aside.

3. Place the shrimp, snow peas, *enoki* mushrooms, and scallions in a mixing bowl and refrigerate until well chilled, at least 1 hour. In a jar with a tight-fitting lid, combine the dressing ingredients. Shake well and refrigerate until ready to serve.

NOTE: The snow peas will lose color within a few hours once tossed with the dressing. You can prepare the salad up to a day in advance and keep it refrigerated, tightly covered with plastic wrap. Do not dress the salad until just before serving.

WINE NOTE
A Riesling from Alsace or a Pouilly-Fumé or Sancerre from the Loire Valley will marry well with the Asian accents.

Scallop and Asparagus Salad

Succulent scallops and crunchy asparagus create a delicious salad when dressed with a very light citrus dressing, which makes the disparate flavors sparkle.   Serves 6

TOTAL TIME
2 hours, including chilling
WORK TIME
20 minutes

PER SERVING
200 calories
31 mg cholesterol
11 g fat
210 mg sodium

FOR THE SALAD

1 pound bay scallops, or sea scallops cut into eighths
Water or fish stock
1½ pounds asparagus
¼ cup finely chopped red onion

FOR THE DRESSING

½ cup freshly squeezed orange juice
2 tablespoons white wine vinegar
½ teaspoon sugar
1 teaspoon chopped fresh thyme *or* ¼ teaspoon dried
2 tablespoons chopped fresh parsley
1 tablespoon grated lemon zest
2 tablespoons grated orange zest
2 tablespoons extra-virgin olive oil

1. Place the scallops in a small saucepan with water or fish stock to cover. Bring to a boil over high heat, cover the pan, then remove from heat, allowing the scallops to sit undisturbed in the covered pan for 2 minutes. Remove the scallops with a slotted spoon and place in a mixing bowl to chill.

2. Soak the asparagus in cold water for 20 minutes, changing the water frequently and rubbing the stalks gently with your fingers to remove any grit clinging to the tips. Trim the tough ends from the asparagus and peel as necessary. Roll-cut the asparagus by holding your knife at an angle and slicing off the tip. Holding your knife in the same position, turn the asparagus stalks a quarter turn in between slices. Your slices will be more attractive if cut in this manner.

3. Have a bowl of ice water handy. Place the asparagus in a vegetable steamer and place in a large pot with water at the bottom. Bring to a boil and steam the asparagus, covered, for 5 minutes or until the asparagus is cooked but still slightly crunchy. Remove the steamer from the pot and plunge the asparagus into the ice water to stop the cooking action and set the color. Drain and add the asparagus to the mixing bowl with the scallops along with the red onion. Refrigerate, covered with plastic wrap, until chilled, at least 1 hour.

4. In a jar with a tight-fitting lid, combine the remaining ingredients. Shake well to emulsify. Ten minutes before serving, toss the dressing with the salad to allow the flavors to blend.

NOTE: The salad can be made up to a day in advance and kept refrigerated, tightly covered with plastic wrap. Do not dress the salad until just before serving, or the asparagus will lose its color.

WINE NOTE
Try a California Sauvignon Blanc or Chardonnay to match the diverse flavors and textures of this dish.

Seviche Salad

Unlike the classic seviche, this salad of acidulated seafood tempers the hot chilies and lime juice with the slightly sweeter flavor of orange juice. The salad creates a dramatic visual presentation, with the white seafood arranged on a bed of colorful vegetables.   *Serves 6*

TOTAL TIME
At least 12 to 24 hours, including marinating
WORK TIME
15 minutes

PER SERVING
180 calories
40 mg cholesterol
1 g fat
180 mg sodium

FOR THE SEAFOOD

¾ pound bay scallops, or sea scallops cut into quarters
¾ pound fish fillet, such as snapper, sole, halibut, or grouper, cut into 1-inch cubes

FOR THE MARINADE

Juice of 5 limes
Juice of 2 oranges
½ red onion, peeled and sliced into thin rings
2 garlic cloves, peeled and minced
2 tablespoons chopped fresh cilantro
½ teaspoon Tabasco sauce
1 tablespoon finely grated orange zest
2 teaspoons finely grated lime zest
¼ teaspoon salt

FOR THE VEGETABLES

2 cucumbers, peeled, seeded, and thinly sliced
1 green bell pepper, seeds and ribs removed (page 269), cut into julienne
1 red bell pepper, seeds and ribs removed (page 269), cut into julienne
1 pint red or yellow cherry tomatoes, halved

1. Rinse the scallops and fish fillet and pat dry. Combine the marinade ingredients in a glass or stainless-steel mixing bowl. Add the seafood, cover the bowl with plastic wrap, and refrigerate for at least 12 hours, turning occasionally.

2. Arrange the vegetables in a decorative pattern on individual plates or a serving platter. Remove the seafood from the marinade with a slotted spoon and arrange the scallops and fish on top of the vegetables. Serve chilled.

NOTE: The salad can marinate for up to a day. Remove from the marinade at that time and keep the seafood refrigerated, tightly covered with plastic wrap.

WINE NOTE
The spicy, acidic nature of this dish makes it difficult to pair with a wine. I suggest you do as they do in Mexico: drink beer.

Tuna Salad Niçoise

TOTAL TIME
1½ hours, including chilling
WORK TIME
15 minutes

PER SERVING
236 calories
22 mg cholesterol
11 g fat
285 mg sodium

Artfully arranged, this variation on the French *provençal* prototype is a complete summer lunch. The dressing can be used in lieu of mayonnaise for any tuna or fish salad, and its tangy flavor and bright taste also enhance the vegetables.   *Serves 6*

¾ pound small red potatoes

FOR THE DRESSING

¼ cup olive oil
¼ cup chicken stock, preferably unsalted (page 266)
¼ cup freshly squeezed lemon juice
¼ cup white wine vinegar
2 tablespoons chopped fresh oregano *or* ½ teaspoon dried
2 tablespoons chopped fresh parsley
¼ teaspoon freshly ground white pepper

FOR THE VEGETABLES

1 pound green beans, trimmed
12 leaves romaine or head lettuce
1 red bell pepper, roasted, peeled (page 269), and sliced
12 ounces water-packed tuna, drained and broken into chunks
3 celery stalks, washed and sliced
¼ cup sliced black olives

1. Scrub the potatoes and boil until tender, about 10 to 15 minutes, depending on size. Drain and slice. Combine the dressing ingredients in a jar with a tight-fitting lid. Shake well and pour over the warm potatoes. Refrigerate for at least 1 hour or until chilled.

2. Have ready a bowl of ice water. Steam the beans in a vegetable steamer over boiling water for 5 minutes. Remove from the steamer and plunge into the ice water to stop the cooking action. Drain and set aside.

3. To serve, arrange the romaine on a large platter or place 2 leaves on individual platters. Mix the red pepper, tuna, celery, and olives together gently and place the mixture in the center of the platter. Ring the tuna with the green beans on one side and the potatoes on the other, removing the potatoes from the dressing with a slotted spoon. Drizzle the dressing over the tuna and green beans and serve immediately.

NOTE: The salad components can be made a day in advance; however, do not arrange the salad or dress it until just before serving, or the green beans will lose their color.

WINE NOTE
A California Chardonnay or a white Burgundy from France will balance the full flavors of this dish.

Red Pepper Pasta

TOTAL TIME
2 hours, including chilling
WORK TIME
20 minutes

PER SERVING
198 calories
0 cholesterol
5 g fat
94 mg sodium

This sweet flavor of roasted red bell peppers creates a very mild yet vividly colored pasta salad. This dish has a slight southwestern accent; if you substitute chopped basil or oregano for the cilantro, the salad will be compatible with Italian entrees. *Serves 6*

½ **pound fresh angel hair pasta**
3 **tablespoons chopped fresh cilantro**
4 **red bell peppers, roasted and peeled (page 269)**
3 **tablespoons chicken stock, preferably unsalted (page 266)**
2 **tablespoons vegetable oil**
4 **tablespoons white wine vinegar**
2 **garlic cloves, peeled and minced**
1 **tablespoon freshly squeezed lime juice**
1 **tablespoon freshly squeezed orange juice**
Pinch of cayenne pepper
¼ **teaspoon salt**

1. Bring a large pot of water to a boil and add the pasta. When the water returns to a boil, drain the pasta and place in a mixing bowl. Toss with the cilantro and refrigerate.

2. Combine the remaining ingredients in a blender or food processor fitted with the steel blade and puree until smooth. Toss the dressing with the pasta and refrigerate, covered with plastic wrap, until chilled, at least 1½ hours.

NOTE: The pasta salad can be made up to three days in advance and refrigerated, tightly covered with plastic wrap. Yellow bell peppers can be substituted for the red bell peppers and will produce a dish that looks entirely different.

Pasta Salad Provençal

The vegetable sauce on the pasta shells is so hearty that this could be a cold vegetarian lunch or light supper. The mélange of vegetables is similar to those in *ratatouille*, and this is a most colorful dish to place on a buffet.   Serves 6

TOTAL TIME
1½ hours (room temperature) or 3 hours (chilled)
WORK TIME
20 minutes

PER SERVING
179 calories
0 cholesterol
4 g fat
151 mg sodium

⅓ pound small pasta shells
1½ tablespoons olive oil
4 garlic cloves, peeled and minced
1 small red onion, peeled and chopped
1 medium (about 1 pound) eggplant, stemmed, trimmed, and cut into ¾-inch cubes
3 small zucchini, trimmed and cut into ¾-inch cubes
1 red bell pepper, seeds and ribs removed (page 269), cut into strips
1 green bell pepper, seeds and ribs removed (page 269), cut into thin strips
¼ cup chopped fresh parsley
1 tablespoon chopped fresh oregano *or* ½ teaspoon dried
1 teaspoon chopped fresh rosemary *or* pinch of dried
2 teaspoons chopped fresh thyme *or* ½ teaspoon dried
1 cup chicken stock, preferably unsalted (page 266)
1 cup salt-free tomato sauce
1 tablespoon capers, rinsed
1 tablespoon freshly squeezed lemon juice
2 tablespoons tarragon vinegar
¼ teaspoon freshly ground black pepper
¼ teaspoon salt (omit if using salted canned stock)

1. Bring a large pot of water to a boil. Add the pasta shells and cook *al dente* according to manufacturer's instructions. Drain and place in a mixing bowl. Refrigerate, covered with plastic wrap.

2. Heat the oil in a large skillet over medium-high heat. Add the garlic and onion and sauté for 3 minutes, stirring frequently. Add the eggplant, zucchini, red pepper, and green pepper and sauté, stirring frequently, for 5 minutes. Add the remaining ingredients, bring to a boil over high heat, and cook for about 10 minutes, stirring occasionally, until the vegetables are tender but still slightly resilient.

3. Toss the vegetable mixture with the pasta and serve either at room temperature or chilled.

NOTE: The salad can be prepared up to two days in advance and refrigerated, tightly covered with plastic wrap.

Pasta Salad with Carrot Sauce

TOTAL TIME
3 hours, including chilling
WORK TIME
20 minutes

PER SERVING
164 calories
2 mg cholesterol
4 g fat
175 mg sodium

Crunchy vegetables, chewy pasta, and a mildly flavored, vivid orange sauce create a stunning and unusual pasta salad. Serve this with any of the chicken salads or as a side dish to accompany a simple piece of grilled poultry or fish.   *Serves 6*

FOR THE SALAD

⅓ pound dried small pasta shells
1 cup broccoli flowerets (about ½ bunch)
1 cup diced zucchini (about 1 medium), cut into ¾-inch dice
1 green bell pepper, seeds and ribs removed (page 269), cut into fine julienne

FOR THE SAUCE

½ pound carrots (about 6 to 8), peeled and thinly sliced
4 garlic cloves, peeled and minced
1 teaspoon chopped fresh thyme *or* ¼ teaspoon dried
2 tablespoons chopped fresh basil *or* 1 teaspoon dried
1 cup chicken stock, preferably unsalted (page 266)
¼ cup tarragon vinegar
1 tablespoon olive oil
Pinch of freshly ground white pepper
¼ teaspoon salt (omit if using salted canned stock)
3 tablespoons freshly grated Parmesan cheese

1. Bring a large pot of water to a boil and cook the pasta shells *al dente,* according to manufacturer's directions. Drain and place in a mixing bowl.

2. Have a bowl of ice water handy. Place the broccoli and zucchini in a vegetable steamer and place the steamer in a large pot with water at the bottom. Bring to a boil over high heat and steam the vegetables, covered, for 5 minutes. Remove the steamer from the pot and plunge the vegetables into the ice water to stop the cooking action. Combine the broccoli and zucchini with the pasta shells and green bell pepper. Refrigerate, covered with plastic wrap.

3. Combine the remaining ingredients in a saucepan and bring to a boil over medium heat, stirring occasionally. Lower the heat and simmer the mixture, uncovered, for 15 minutes or until the carrots are very tender. Place the mixture in a blender or food processor fitted with the steel blade and puree until smooth. Toss the sauce with the pasta and vegetables and refrigerate until chilled, at least 2 hours.

NOTE: The pasta salad can be made up to two days in advance and refrigerated, tightly covered with plastic wrap. Cauliflower flowerets and yellow squash can be substituted for the broccoli and zucchini.

Chinese Chicken and Pasta Salad

TOTAL TIME
3 hours, including chilling
WORK TIME
20 minutes

PER SERVING
265 calories
44 mg cholesterol
8 g fat
478 mg sodium

By substituting French Dijon mustard for the more bitter Chinese variety, you achieve a dressing for this succulent main-course salad that is both mellow and slightly hot. The red pepper and snow peas add color and texture to the dish, which serves well for a large buffet party since it's little more work to make it for a crowd.   Serves 6

FOR THE SALAD

⅓ **pound fresh angel hair pasta**
1 **pound boneless, skinless chicken breasts, trimmed (page 272)**
1 **red bell pepper, ribs and seeds removed (page 269), cut into fine julienne**
¼ **pound snow peas, stringed and cut into fine julienne**
1 **tablespoon vegetable oil**

FOR THE DRESSING

¼ **cup rice wine vinegar**
1 **tablespoon dark sesame oil**
3 **tablespoons Dijon mustard**
2 **teaspoons sugar**
2 **tablespoons reduced-sodium soy sauce**
2 **garlic cloves, peeled and minced**
1 **teaspoon grated fresh ginger**
Pinch of freshly ground white pepper
2 **tablespoons sesame seed, toasted in a dry frying pan over low heat until lightly browned**
⅓ **cup chopped fresh cilantro**

1. Bring a large pot of water to a boil and add the pasta. When the water returns to a boil, drain the pasta and place in a large mixing bowl.

2. Cut the chicken breasts into very fine shreds and mix with the red pepper and snow peas. Heat the oil in a heavy wok or skillet over high heat. Add the chicken and vegetable mixture and stir-fry for 3 minutes or until the chicken shreds are cooked through. Combine the chicken/vegetable mixture with the pasta.

3. Combine the dressing ingredients in a jar with a tight-fitting lid and shake well until blended. Toss the dressing with the pasta and chicken mixture and refrigerate, tightly covered with plastic wrap, until well chilled, at least 2 hours.

NOTE: The salad can be prepared up to two days in advance and kept refrigerated, tightly covered with plastic wrap.

WINE NOTE
A red French Côtes du Rhône, an Italian Chianti, or a Spanish Rioja will match the spices in the dish, as will a Gewürztraminer from Alsace.

Mediterranean Lamb Salad with Barley

This is a most satisfying salad, with the soft, grainy barley absorbing the herbed flavor of the quickly sautéed lamb. The combination of the rosemary, garlic, and lemon zest is an excellent rub for any grilled or baked lamb.   *Serves 6*

TOTAL TIME
2 hours (room temperature) or 3 hours (chilled)
WORK TIME
20 minutes

PER SERVING
118 calories
0 cholesterol
4 g fat
123 mg sodium

1 pound lean lamb, trimmed of all visible fat and gristle, cut into thin
    slices, and then cut into pieces ½ inch wide by 2 inches long
2 tablespoons chopped fresh rosemary *or* 1 teaspoon dried
2 teaspoons minced garlic
1 tablespoon grated lemon zest
1½ tablespoons olive oil
¼ teaspoon freshly ground black pepper
¼ teaspoon salt (omit if using salted canned stock)
½ cup pearl barley
3 cups chicken stock, preferably unsalted (page 266)
1 large tomato, cored, seeded, and diced
½ small red onion, peeled and diced
½ cucumber, peeled, seeded, and diced
4 tablespoons red wine vinegar
3 tablespoons freshly squeezed lemon juice
1 tablespoon chopped fresh basil *or* ½ teaspoon dried

1. Place the lamb in a glass or stainless-steel bowl and toss it with half the rosemary, the garlic, lemon zest, olive oil, pepper, and salt. Allow it to marinate for 30 minutes.

2. Rinse the barley in a sieve under cold running water for 2 minutes. Place in a covered saucepan with the chicken stock, bring to a boil over high heat, and simmer the barley, covered, for 40 to 50 minutes or until the barley is tender. Drain and place in a mixing bowl.

3. Heat a skillet over high heat and stir-fry the lamb for 2 minutes or until lightly browned. Combine the lamb and any pan juices with the barley and add the tomato, red onion, and cucumber. Whisk together the vinegar, lemon juice, basil, and remaining rosemary. Toss with the salad and serve either at room temperature or chilled.

NOTE: The salad can be made up to a day in advance and kept refrigerated, tightly covered with plastic wrap. You can also substitute leftover roast leg of lamb for the freshly sautéed. Add the lamb marinade ingredients to the salad.

WINE NOTE
Red Bordeaux is the classic companion for lamb and will work well here. A California Cabernet is another good choice.

Spicy Beef, Pasta, and Fresh Shiitake Mushroom Salad

The fresh *shiitake* mushrooms now widely available in supermarkets add a more delicate yet woodsy taste than their dried counterparts, used in much of traditional Chinese cooking. The spicy dressing for this hearty pasta salad is derived from currently popular Szechwan regional cooking.   *Serves 6*

TOTAL TIME
2 hours, including chilling
WORK TIME
20 minutes

PER SERVING
295 calories
24 mg cholesterol
11 g fat
350 mg sodium

FOR THE SALAD

½ **pound very thin dried spaghetti**
8 **scallions**
1 **tablespoon vegetable oil**
½ **pound beef tenderloin, trimmed and cut into ¼-inch cubes**
½ **pound fresh** *shiitake* **mushrooms, washed, stemmed, and cut into ¼-inch slices**
1 **cucumber, peeled, seeded, and cut into ¼-inch slices**

FOR THE DRESSING

3 **tablespoons reduced-sodium soy sauce**
3 **tablespoons balsamic vinegar**
3 **tablespoons rice wine vinegar**
½ **teaspoon crushed red pepper**
2 **teaspoons finely minced garlic**
1 **teaspoon finely minced fresh ginger**
½ **teaspoon sugar**
2 **tablespoons dark sesame oil**
2 **tablespoons sesame seeds, toasted in a dry frying pan over low heat until light brown**

1. Bring a large pot of water to a boil. Cook the pasta *al dente*, according to manufacturer's instructions. Drain thoroughly and refrigerate. Trim the scallions, discarding all but 3 inches of the green tops. Chop the white part and set aside. Cut the green portion into thin rings and set aside.

2. Heat the oil in a heavy wok or skillet over high heat. Add the beef and stir-fry for 30 seconds. Remove the beef from the pan with a slotted spoon and place in a mixing bowl. Add the *shiitake* mushrooms to the pan, reduce the heat to medium, and sauté the mushrooms for 5 minutes, stirring constantly. Combine the beef, mushrooms, and pasta in a large mixing bowl along with the scallion white and cucumber; refrigerate, covered with plastic wrap.

3. Combine the dressing ingredients in a jar with a tight-fitting lid. Shake well and toss the dressing with the salad. Chill for at least an hour, tossing occasionally to coat all parts of the salad with the dressing. To serve, arrange the salad on a platter or individual plates and sprinkle with the green scallion rings.

NOTE: The salad can be prepared up to a day in advance and kept refrigerated, tightly covered with a plastic wrap. The salad can be served either chilled or at room temperature. Boneless, skinless chicken breast or pork tenderloin can be substituted for the beef.

WINE NOTE
The spicy flavors of this dish call for a California Zinfandel or an Hermitage or Côte Rotie from the Rhône Valley in France.

Sesame Pork, Pasta, and Vegetable Salad

Pork tenderloin is an extremely lean cut of meat. When combined with the colorful, crunchy vegetables and delicate angel hair pasta, this Asian-inspired salad is deceivingly filling for its low calorie count.   *Serves 6*

FOR THE SALAD

½ pound fresh angel hair pasta
1 tablespoon dark sesame oil
1 tablespoon vegetable oil
1 teaspoon finely minced garlic
½ pound pork tenderloin, trimmed and cut into fine shreds
3 carrots, peeled and cut into fine julienne
3 celery stalks, washed and cut into fine julienne
⅓ pound snow peas, stringed and cut into fine julienne

FOR THE DRESSING

⅓ cup chicken stock, preferably unsalted (page 266)
1 tablespoon dry Sherry
2 tablespoons rice wine vinegar
2 tablespoons reduced-sodium soy sauce
¼ teaspoon ground Szechwan pepper
¼ cup sesame seeds, toasted in a dry frying pan over low heat until light brown

1. Bring a large pot of water to a boil over high heat. Add the angel hair pasta, and when the water returns to a boil, drain the pasta in a colander, then place in a mixing bowl and toss with the sesame oil. Place the mixing bowl, covered with plastic wrap, in the refrigerator.

2. Heat the vegetable oil in a large skillet or wok over high heat. Add the garlic and stir-fry for 30 seconds or until fragrant, making sure the garlic does not burn, or it will become bitter. Add the pork, carrot, celery, and snow peas and stir-fry for 2 to 3 minutes, until the pork has been cooked through and the vegetables are cooked but remain crunchy. Combine the pork and vegetable mixture with the pasta.

TOTAL TIME
1½ hours (room temperature) or 3 hours (chilled)
WORK TIME
25 minutes

PER SERVING
285 calories
24 mg cholesterol
4 g fat
335 mg sodium

3. Combine the dressing ingredients, and add this mixture to the pork and pasta bowl. Allow the salad to mellow in flavor for at least 30 minutes before serving.

NOTE: The salad can be prepared up to a day in advance and kept refrigerated, tightly covered with plastic wrap. The dish can be served either at room temperature or chilled as a salad and can also be served hot, tossing the pasta with the pork and vegetable mixture to heat it through just before serving. If you're using dried pasta rather than fresh angel hair, follow the cooking directions provided by the manufacturer.

WINE NOTE
The light Asian flavors here will marry well with a Riesling from Alsace or a Sancerre or Pouilly-Fumé from the Loire Valley.

Main Dishes

Grilled Chicken Kabobs
Chicken Loaf with Watercress
Cold Poached Chicken Breasts with Spicy Melon Relish
Lemon Chicken
Chicken Breasts with Balsamic Vinegar
Grilled Chicken and Red Pepper Tacos
Coq au Vin
Herbed Chicken Legs
Chicken and Eggplant Cannelloni
Tandoori Chicken
Jambalaya
Turkey Stew with Marsala and Sage
Turkey Chili
Turkey with Lemon Sauce
Turkey Tonnato
Roasted Monkfish in Plum Wine Sauce
Fish Steamed in Napa Cabbage with Red Pepper Sauce
Salmon with Basil Cream Sauce
Caribbean Grouper
Seafood Sausages
Tuna Brochettes with Smoked Tomato Sauce
Southwestern Halibut
Creole Swordfish
Asian Grouper
Pasta with Seafood Baked in Foil
Pasta with Fresh Tomato Sauce and Crab
Alfred's Meat Loaf
Beef Braised in Stout Beer
Peppers Stuffed with Beef and Orzo
Veal Scaloppine with Fresh Shiitake Mushroom Sauce
Braised Veal Shanks
Veal Stew in Mustard Sauce
Stuffed Flank Steak

While eating a number of little dishes might be in vogue for restaurant dining, cooking at home rarely involves elaborate preparation of every dish and course. We tend to invest our energies in one show-stopper dish, usually the main dish.

The majority of these main dishes are based on either poultry or fish, and all are deceptively easy to prepare. The tantalizing flavor comes from the combination of ingredients, not from any great culinary skills needed for their successful completion.

I believe in cooking seasonally, and this is especially important in selecting a main dish. Not only do the vegetables that augment the protein change in seasonal availability, and therefore price, but also the cooking methods and nature of the dishes we want to eat vary with the temperature. The same chicken breast will appeal to us more in the winter as a hearty Coq au Vin (page 128) than during the summer when it might be Lemon Chicken (page 124). And a grilled Caribbean Grouper (page 145) might not seem as satisfying in cold weather as Southwestern Halibut (page 149).

For warm weather, try the Grilled Chicken Kabobs (page 120) in a light, tangy lemon marinade or the Tuna Brochettes with Smoked Tomato Sauce (page 148) for a hearty grilled fish dish. The Turkey Tonnato (page 139), a variation on the Italian cold veal roll with tuna sauce, can be served as an elegant party entree. The vibrant flavor of grilled Tandoori Chicken (page 132), so succulent you won't miss the skin, transforms the casual summer barbecue to a dramatic gastronomic event.

For cold weather, the slowly braised meat dishes, such as Beef Braised in Stout Beer (page 160) and Braised Veal Shanks (page 164), will be as comforting as a roaring fire. For a fiercely cold night, you can't beat a steaming bowl of Turkey Chili (page 136), dotted with black turtle beans.

Menu selection usually starts with the main dish and builds in both directions after the choice is made. Take into account how much total time you wish to spend preparing the dinner and what flavors, colors, and textures are represented in the entree selection. If you're selecting, for example, the elegant Seafood Sausages (page 146), the meal becomes rather formal, and other dishes should conform to that mode. On the other hand, Alfred's Meat Loaf (page 158) is casual and hearty, so stay with the theme of Mom-and-Apple-Pie.

Grilled Chicken Kabobs

TOTAL TIME
2 hours, including
marinating
WORK TIME
15 minutes

PER SERVING
140 calories
66 mg cholesterol
1 g fat
79 mg sodium

The fresh citrusy, herbed flavor from the marinade and the colorful peppers punctuating the skewers have made these kabobs a treat for the eyes and palate. They are incredibly easy to prepare and are wonderful for buffets since they do not require a knife.   *Serves 6*

1½ pounds boneless, skinless chicken breasts, trimmed (page 272)
¼ cup freshly squeezed lemon juice
¼ cup dry white wine
2 tablespoons grated lemon zest
3 shallots, peeled and chopped
3 garlic cloves, peeled and minced
2 tablespoons chopped fresh basil *or* ½ teaspoon dried
3 tablespoons chopped fresh parsley
2 tablespoons chopped fresh marjoram *or* ½ teaspoon dried
¼ teaspoon freshly ground white pepper
½ red bell pepper, seeds and ribs removed (page 269), cut into 2-inch squares
½ green bell pepper, seeds and ribs removed (page 269), cut into 2-inch squares
½ yellow bell pepper, seeds and ribs removed (page 269), cut into 2-inch squares

1. Pound the chicken to a uniform thickness of ¼ inch and cut it into 2-inch cubes. Combine remaining ingredients except the bell peppers in a glass or stainless-steel bowl. Add the chicken cubes and marinate, either at room temperature for 1 hour or refrigerated, covered with plastic wrap, for 2 to 4 hours.

2. Soak 6 bamboo skewers in water to cover for at least 20 minutes. Preheat a grill or broiler.

3. Thread the chicken onto the skewers, alternating with squares of the peppers. Grill or broil them for 10 to 12 minutes, turning them a quarter turn every few minutes.

NOTE: The kabobs can be served hot, at room temperature, or chilled. If you're serving them hot, cook them just before serving, since they have a tendency to dry out when reheated.

WINE NOTE
Try a Fumé Blanc or Sauvignon Blanc from California to match the assertive flavors here.

Chicken Loaf with Watercress

Meat loaf is a warming comfort food, and this version made with chicken fulfills the same needs. In this case, however, it is particularly good cold since there is virtually no fat. It goes well with Herbed Tomato Sauce (page 202).   *Serves 6*

TOTAL TIME
1½ hours; or 4 hours if served chilled
WORK TIME
15 minutes

PER SERVING
139 calories
77 mg cholesterol
3 g fat
390 mg sodium

1 pound boneless, skinless chicken breast, trimmed (page 272) and well chilled
½ pound onions (2 to 3 medium), peeled and coarsely chopped
¼ cup grated carrot
3 tablespoons bread crumbs
1 egg
3 egg whites
¼ teaspoon salt
¼ teaspoon cayenne pepper
2 quarts water
2 bunches (about ½ pound) of watercress, washed, tough stems removed
3 tablespoons low-fat (part skim milk) mozzarella cheese
Oil for loaf pan

1. Preheat the oven to 350 degrees. Place the chicken, onions, carrot, bread crumbs, egg, egg whites, salt, and pepper in the work bowl of a food processor fitted with the steel blade. Puree until smooth, scraping down the sides of the bowl as necessary. (This step can also be accomplished by grinding the chicken meat through a meat grinder and then pureeing the mixture in a blender.)

2. Bring the water to a boil over high heat. Place the watercress in a strainer and blanch it in boiling water for 15 seconds. Drain it over the sink, pressing with the back of a spoon to extract as much water as possible. Puree the watercress with the cheese in a blender or food processor fitted with the steel blade.

3. Place half the chicken mixture in a lightly oiled loaf pan and make a tunnel with the watercress in the center. Top with the remaining chicken and smooth the top with a spatula.

4. Bake in the center of the oven for 1 hour or until a meat thermometer registers 180 degrees. Serve immediately, at room temperature, or chilled (refrigerate for at least 3 hours).

NOTE: The loaf can be assembled a day in advance and baked just prior to serving, or it can be baked and reheated, covered with tin foil, in a 300-degree oven for 25 minutes.

WINE NOTE
A Pinot Blanc from Alsace or a white Burgundy from the Macon region will pair well with this mild dish.

Cold Poached Chicken Breasts with Spicy Melon Relish

While this dish is an elegant summer entree, you can also serve it as a salad by cutting the chicken into strips. The cool cantaloupe absorbs the spicing and enhances the delicacy of the poached chicken.   *Serves 6*

TOTAL TIME
2 hours, including chilling
WORK TIME
20 minutes

PER SERVING
221 calories
66 mg cholesterol
3 g fat
84 mg sodium

1½ pounds boneless, skinless chicken breasts, trimmed (page 272)
1 cup chicken stock, preferably unsalted (page 266)
2 teaspoons finely minced garlic
2 teaspoons grated fresh ginger
1½ tablespoons mustard seed
¼ cup dark brown sugar
¼ cup Sherry vinegar
1 (about 1 pound) ripe cantaloupe, halved, seeds discarded, cut into balls with the large end of a melon baller (or cut into ¾-inch dice)

1. Pound the chicken to a uniform thickness of ¼ inch (or have the butcher do it). Place the chicken stock in a skillet and bring to a boil over high heat. Add the chicken, reduce the heat to medium, and poach the breasts for 3 to 4 minutes. This will have to be done in batches. Reserve the enriched stock for another use. Cover the chicken breasts with plastic wrap and refrigerate until chilled.

2. Combine the remaining ingredients except cantaloupe in a heavy saucepan. Bring to a boil over medium heat and cook until reduced by half. Add the melon balls and poach them for 1 minute. Remove the melon with a slotted spoon and reduce the juices slightly. Pour over the melon and refrigerate until chilled, at least 2 hours.

3. To serve, top each chicken breast with some of the melon relish and sauce.

NOTE: The dish can be prepared up to two days in advance and kept refrigerated, tightly covered with plastic wrap.

WINE NOTE
While the fruit is spiced, this remains a delicate dish. Try serving a light white, such as a Sauvignon Blanc from California or a Sancerre from the Loire Valley.

Lemon Chicken

TOTAL TIME
2 to 8 hours, including marinating
WORK TIME
15 minutes

PER SERVING
180 calories
66 mg cholesterol
6 g fat
99 mg sodium

The chicken breast itself is imbued with a tangy, lemony taste. Reducing the marinade to a sauce makes this a quick and easy dish to prepare.   *Serves 6*

6 boneless, skinless chicken breast halves, trimmed (page 272)
3 lemons
1 cup dry white wine
2 garlic cloves, peeled and minced
4 shallots, peeled and chopped
1 tablespoon chopped fresh rosemary *or* ½ teaspoon dried
2 tablespoons chopped fresh oregano *or* 1 teaspoon dried
Pinch of salt
Pinch of freshly ground white pepper
2 tablespoons olive oil
1 teaspoon arrowroot mixed with 2 tablespoons cold water

1. Pound the chicken breasts to an even thickness of ⅓ inch (or have the butcher do it); do not pound the tenderloins. Grate the yellow zest from the lemons using a fine grater and then squeeze the lemon juice.

2. Combine the lemon juice with the remaining ingredients except oil and arrowroot in a glass or stainless-steel bowl. Add the chicken breasts and marinate for 2 hours at room temperature or up to 8 hours refrigerated, tightly covered with plastic wrap.

3. Drain the chicken, reserving the marinade, and pat dry with paper towels. Heat the oil in a skillet over high heat. Add the chicken breasts, being careful not to crowd the pan, and sauté over high heat for 3 minutes on each side. Remove the chicken and keep warm.

4. Pour the marinade into the pan and cook over high heat until reduced by half. Stir the arrowroot mixture into the sauce to thicken it slightly. To serve, spoon the sauce over the chicken breasts.

NOTE: The dish should not be marinated for more than the time specified. You can cook the chicken up to two days in advance and reheat it slowly in the sauce.

Chicken Breasts with Balsamic Vinegar

Pungent, aged balsamic vinegar is sweet enough to be used straight from the bottle as a condiment. It forms the basis for this robust sweet-and-sour wine sauce, with citrus zest and tarragon lending their piquant nuances.   *Serves 6*

TOTAL TIME
1½ hours, including marinating
WORK TIME
20 minutes

PER SERVING
249 calories
66 mg cholesterol
6 g fat
169 mg sodium

1½ **pounds boneless, skinless chicken breasts, trimmed (page 272)**
1 **cup white wine**
½ **cup freshly squeezed orange juice**
½ **cup balsamic vinegar**
½ **cup golden raisins**
½ **cup dried currants**
2 **tablespoons extra-virgin olive oil**
1 **tablespoon grated lemon zest**
2 **tablespoons grated orange zest**
2 **teaspoons chopped fresh tarragon** *or* ¼ **teaspoon dried**
¼ **teaspoon salt**
¼ **teaspoon freshly ground white pepper**

1. Pound the chicken fillets to a uniform thickness of ⅓ inch (or have the butcher do it); do not pound the tenderloins.

2. Pour the wine into a skillet and bring to a boil over medium-high heat. Add the chicken breasts, reduce the heat to a simmer, and poach the chicken for 5 to 7 minutes. Remove with a slotted spoon and set aside.

3. While the wine is heating, bring the orange juice and vinegar to a boil in a small saucepan. Remove from the heat and add the raisins and currants; let them soak for 15 minutes.

4. Add the reserved wine and the remaining ingredients to the orange juice pan; bring to a boil over high heat. Simmer, uncovered, until the mixture is reduced by half.

5. Cut the chicken fillets into slices. Pour the sauce over the chicken and allow it to sit at room temperature for at least 1 hour before serving. The dish can then be reheated, served at room temperature, or chilled.

NOTE: The dish can be prepared up to two days in advance and reheated slowly or served cold or at room temperature.

WINE NOTE
The strong vinegar flavor makes this a tough dish for wine, but a strongly flavored Gewürztraminer from Alsace is a good bet.

Grilled Chicken and Red Pepper Tacos

TOTAL TIME
1½ hours
WORK TIME
20 minutes

PER SERVING
353 calories
68 mg cholesterol
13 g fat
184 mg sodium

Hearty, with all the flavors now popular as part of new south-western cooking, these soft tacos are a perfect casual lunch or dinner. Serve them with Mixed Grilled Vegetable Salad with Rosemary Vinaigrette (page 74) if you're lighting a grill for the chicken.   *Serves 6*

1½ pounds boneless, skinless chicken breasts, trimmed (page 272)
2 red bell peppers, roasted and peeled (page 269), sliced
2 celery stalks, washed and sliced
1 medium red onion, peeled and chopped
½ cup cooked black beans (about 2 ounces dried)
¼ cup chopped fresh cilantro leaves
¼ cup balsamic vinegar
¼ cup vegetable oil
¼ cup freshly squeezed orange juice
¼ cup freshly squeezed lime juice
2 garlic cloves, peeled and minced
1 teaspoon ground coriander
½ teaspoon freshly ground pepper
¼ teaspoon salt
¼ cup plain nonfat yogurt
6 8-inch flour tortillas

1. Preheat a grill or broiler. Pound the chicken breasts to an even thickness of ½ inch (or have the butcher do it) and grill or broil on both sides until cooked through but not dried out—about 4 minutes on a side. (It makes sense to grill the peppers at the same time.) Slice and set aside.

2. Combine the bell peppers, celery, onion, black beans, and cilantro in a mixing bowl. Combine the remaining ingredients except the tortillas in a jar with a tight-fitting lid. Shake well and pour the dressing over the vegetables. Marinate the vegetables for 1 hour at room temperature.

3. Place a large skillet over medium heat and heat the tortillas for 30 seconds on each side to soften.

4. To serve, divide the chicken among the tortillas, placing it at the center of the tortilla. Divide the vegetables and their dressing on top of the chicken and roll the tortilla into a cylinder. Serve immediately; the dish should be at room temperature.

NOTE: The chicken breasts, vegetable mixture, and dressing can all be prepared a day in advance. Do not marinate the vegetables for more than 1 hour. Reheat the chicken, covered with aluminum foil, in a 300-degree oven for 15 minutes.

WINE NOTE
The best choice here is a *grand cru* Beaujolais or red Burgundy from France, a California Merlot, or a glass of chilled beer.

Coq au Vin

TOTAL TIME
40 minutes
WORK TIME
20 minutes

PER SERVING
186 calories
68 mg cholesterol
4 g fat
117 mg sodium

Using meat stock, red wine, herbs, and smoky bacon gives this chicken stew all the heartiness and robust flavor of a traditional *coq au vin*. Serve it with either steamed tiny potatoes or rice. *Serves 6*

2 slices bacon
2 teaspoons olive oil
1½ pounds boneless, skinless chicken breasts, trimmed (page 272) and cut into 1-inch cubes
2 cups veal or beef stock, preferably unsalted (page 267)
1 cup hearty red wine, such as Burgundy or Cabernet Sauvignon
1 teaspoon chopped fresh thyme *or* ¼ teaspoon dried
2 tablespoons chopped fresh parsley
1 bay leaf
1 tablespoon chopped fresh marjoram *or* ½ teaspoon dried
1 garlic clove, peeled and minced
¼ teaspoon freshly ground pepper
½ pound pearl onions
½ pound small fresh mushrooms, washed and trimmed
1 teaspoon arrowroot mixed with 2 tablespoons cold water

1. Cook the bacon in a deep skillet until crisp. Drain on paper towels, crumble, and discard the fat. Add the oil to the pan and heat over medium-high heat. Add the chicken breast cubes, in batches if necessary, and brown lightly. Remove with a slotted spoon and set aside.

2. Add the stock, wine, thyme, parsley, bay leaf, marjoram, garlic, pepper, and bacon to the pan. Bring to a boil over high heat and simmer for 15 minutes. While the sauce is simmering, blanch the onions in boiling water for 1 minute. Place in ice water; when cool enough to handle, trim the root ends and slip off the skins.

3. Add the onions and mushrooms to the pan and simmer for 10 minutes. Add the chicken and simmer for 5 minutes. Remove the onions, mushrooms, and chicken from the pan with a slotted spoon. Raise the heat to high and reduce until only 1 cup of sauce remains. Stir the arrowroot mixture into the sauce, cook-

ing until slightly thickened. Return the chicken mixture to the pan, reheat slightly, and serve immediately.

NOTE: The dish can be made up to three days in advance. Reheat, covered, over low heat, stirring occasionally, for about 10 minutes.

WINE NOTE
A rich French red Burgundy is the classic companion to coq *au vin*, and it will suit nicely. You could also serve a red Rhône, such as Hermitage or Côte Rotie, or a California Merlot.

Herbed Chicken Legs

While slightly higher in calories and fat, the dark meat of chicken is also more succulent and flavorful than the white meat. This easy dish keeps in all the moisture, and the juices released during baking form a light herbed sauce.   *Serves 6*

TOTAL TIME
40 minutes
WORK TIME
10 minutes

PER SERVING
206 calories
88 mg cholesterol
10 g fat
181 mg sodium

6 chicken leg quarters (thigh and drumstick), skinned
1 tablespoon oil
½ cup chicken stock, preferably unsalted (page 266)
3 garlic cloves, peeled and minced
2 shallots, peeled and chopped
¼ cup chopped fresh herbs (any combination of parsley, basil, oregano, rosemary, and marjoram)
¼ teaspoon freshly ground white pepper
¼ teaspoon salt, *or* ⅛ teaspoon if using salted canned stock

1. Preheat the oven to 400 degrees. Wash the chicken and pat it dry. Heat the oil in a large skillet or sauté pan over high heat. Brown the chicken on both sides, then place each piece in a square of parchment paper or heavy-duty foil large enough to enclose it.

2. Combine the remaining ingredients. Divide the mixture on top of each chicken leg quarter and seal the parchment or foil by crimping the edges tightly, starting at one corner and working clockwise.

3. Place the packages on a baking sheet and bake for 40 minutes in the center of the oven. Remove and cut a slit in the package to release the steam. Unwrap carefully and place each piece on a plate, using the juices as a sauce.

NOTE: The packages can be prepared up to six hours in advance and kept refrigerated. Add five minutes to the baking time.

WINE NOTE
A California Sauvignon Blanc or Chardonnay or a richer French white Burgundy will complement the flavors nicely, although the dish is hearty enough to support a red such as a Côtes du Rhône or *grand cru* Beaujolais from France.

Chicken and Eggplant Cannelloni

TOTAL TIME
3 hours
WORK TIME
30 minutes

PER SERVING
319 calories
69 mg cholesterol
8 g fat
447 mg sodium

Rather than using commercial *cannelloni* shells, which I find contain too much dough relative to the amount of filling, I started using egg roll skins to create tubular forms. They cook in the sauce, and the resulting dish is light yet filling.   *Serves 6*

3 pounds (3 medium) eggplant
1 pound boneless, skinless chicken breasts, trimmed (page 272)
1 tablespoon olive oil
1½ cups chopped onion
1½ teaspoons minced garlic
2 tablespoons freshly grated Parmesan cheese
¼ teaspoon salt
¼ teaspoon freshly ground black pepper
6 egg roll wrappers
2 cups Herbed Tomato Sauce (page 202)
½ cup grated low-fat (part skim milk) mozzarella cheese

1. Preheat the oven to 400 degrees. Prick the eggplant with a sharp meat fork and place on a baking sheet in the center of the oven.

2. Place the chicken breasts in a small baking pan and cover the pan with foil. Bake for 15 to 18 minutes, depending on thickness, or until the chicken breasts are cooked through. When cool enough to handle, shred the meat into large shreds.

3. Bake the eggplant for 40 to 50 minutes, turning after 20 minutes, or until they are uniformly soft. Remove the eggplant from the oven. They will look brown and will have deflated. When cool enough to handle easily, cut off the top and peel away the skin with your fingers. Drain any liquid that develops by shaking the pulp in a sieve. Chop the flesh either by hand or in a food processor fitted with the steel blade, pulsing it on and off. Set aside.

4. Heat the oil in a small skillet or sauté pan over medium heat. Add the onions and garlic and sauté, stirring frequently, for 10 minutes or until the onions are soft.

5. Preheat the oven to 350 degrees. Combine the eggplant, chicken, onions, garlic, Parmesan cheese, salt, and pepper. Divide the mixture evenly and place a portion along the top edge of each egg roll wrapper. Gently roll them into tube shapes and lay them seam side down in an 8- by 11-inch baking pan.

6. Pour the tomato sauce over the top of the rolls, cover the pan with foil, and bake in the center of the preheated oven for 20 minutes. Remove the foil, sprinkle the mozzarella cheese evenly over the top, and return the pan to the oven for 10 minutes. Serve immediately.

NOTE: The eggplant/chicken mixture and the tomato sauce can be prepared up to two days in advance, and the *cannelloni* can be assembled up to six hours in advance. Do not bake it, however, until just before serving.

WINE NOTE
For this Italian-inspired dish with a hearty tomato sauce, try an Italian red Chianti or a white Gavi di Gavi or one of the bigger California Chardonnays.

Tandoori Chicken

TOTAL TIME
6 to 24 hours, includ-
ing marinating
WORK TIME
20 minutes

PER SERVING
273 calories
109 mg cholesterol
9 g fat
150 mg sodium

While most chicken dishes grilled without the skin tend to become dry, the marinating leaves this Indian dish moist and spicy, with an appealing bright red color.   *Serves 8*

2 (3- to 3½-pound) frying chickens, cut into serving pieces, wings
   reserved for another use (or whatever parts of the chicken you like,
   counting on either a breast or thigh/leg quarter per person)
4 garlic cloves, peeled
1 large onion, peeled and sliced
2 cups plain nonfat yogurt
3 tablespoons freshly squeezed lemon juice
1 tablespoon paprika
½ teaspoon freshly ground black pepper
1 teaspoon ground cumin
1 teaspoon ground coriander
½ teaspoon ground cinnamon
Pinch of ground cloves
1 slice (about the size of a quarter) peeled fresh ginger
¼ teaspoon salt
Lemon wedges for garnish

1. Remove all the skin from the chicken pieces, reserving it for stock. Use a sharp paring knife to make random cuts in the flesh all the way to the bone. Make about 6 slashes per breast and about 4 per thigh and leg. Wash the chicken pieces and place them in a stainless-steel or glass baking dish.

2. Place the remaining ingredients except lemon wedges in a blender or food processor fitted with the steel blade. Puree the mixture and pour it over the chicken.

3. Refrigerate the chicken, covered with plastic wrap, for at least 6 hours or preferably overnight, turning the pieces occasionally.

4. Preheat a grill or broiler. Drain the pieces from the marinade and shake them over the sink to remove any excess. Grill or broil, turning as necessary, for about 12 to 15 minutes.

5. The chicken can be served hot, at room temperature, or cold, with lemon wedges for garnish.

NOTE: The chicken can marinate for up to 24 hours and can be reheated, covered, in a 300-degree oven.

WINE NOTE
A good choice with this full-flavored dish would be a Gewürztraminer or Riesling from Alsace or a red wine such as Côtes du Rhône or Beaujolais.

Jambalaya

Cajun jambalaya, with a combination of chicken, pork, and seafood, is one of my favorites from the bayou country. This healthier version contains all the traditional spiciness and heartiness. This is a wonderful dish for a buffet dinner, since you can multiply the recipe almost endlessly with little extra work, and your guests will need only a fork.   *Serves 8*

2 tablespoons vegetable oil
½ cup chopped reduced-sodium ham
2 large onions, peeled and coarsely chopped
2 celery stalks, washed and coarsely chopped
1 green bell pepper, seeds and ribs removed (page 269), coarsely chopped
6 scallions, including 3 inches of the green, trimmed and chopped
3 garlic cloves, peeled and minced
1 cup brown rice
1 pound boneless, skinless chicken breasts, trimmed (page 272) and cut into 2-inch cubes
2 bay leaves
½ to 1 teaspoon cayenne pepper (to taste)
1 tablespoon chopped fresh oregano *or* 1 teaspoon dried
2 teaspoons chopped fresh thyme *or* ½ teaspoon dried
½ teaspoon salt
1 cup salt-free tomato sauce
1 14-ounce can tomatoes, drained and chopped
1 cup fish stock (page 268) or clam juice
½ pound medium shrimp, peeled and deveined

TOTAL TIME
1 hour
WORK TIME
25 minutes

PER SERVING
257 calories
73 mg cholesterol
6 g fat
550 mg sodium

1. Preheat the oven to 350 degrees. Heat the vegetable oil over medium-high heat in a 4-quart ovenproof casserole. Add the ham and sauté for 1 minute. Add the fresh vegetables and garlic. Sauté for 5 minutes, stirring often, until the onion is translucent. Add the brown rice and sauté for 3 more minutes, stirring constantly.

2. Add the chicken, bay leaves, cayenne pepper, oregano, thyme, and salt. Cook for 2 minutes.

3. Add the tomato sauce, tomatoes, and fish stock. Bring to a boil, cover the casserole, and place in the center of the oven. Cook for 20 minutes. Stir the casserole, add the shrimp, and return to the oven for 10 to 15 minutes or until the liquid has been absorbed and the rice is tender. Serve immediately.

NOTE: You can make the dish up to two days in advance; however, remove it from the oven after the initial 20 minutes. It will still be slightly liquid. Before serving, place it in a 350-degree oven for 30 minutes, then add the shrimp and continue to bake for 10 minutes.

WINE NOTE
Try a red Côtes du Rhône from France, a Barbera or Chianti from Italy, or a Cabernet Sauvignon or Zinfandel from California with this hearty dish.

Turkey Stew with Marsala and Sage

While cooking with heady Marsala is part of Italian cuisine, adding fresh sage to this hearty, comforting stew is also reminiscent of the flavors of traditional American poultry stuffing. Serves 6

TOTAL TIME
45 minutes
WORK TIME
20 minutes

PER SERVING
185 calories
76 mg cholesterol
4 g fat
115 mg sodium

1 tablespoon unsalted butter
1½ pounds turkey breast meat, cut into 1-inch cubes
½ pound fresh mushrooms, washed, trimmed, and halved if large
½ pound (2 to 3 medium) onions, peeled and diced
1 garlic clove, peeled and minced
1½ cups turkey or chicken stock, preferably unsalted (page 266)
⅓ cup Marsala wine
1 tablespoon chopped fresh sage *or* ½ teaspoon dried
Pinch of salt
Pinch of freshly ground white pepper
1 teaspoon arrowroot mixed with 2 tablespoons cold water

1. Melt the butter in a large deep skillet over medium-high heat. Add the turkey, not overcrowding the pan, and brown on all sides. This should be done in batches. Remove the turkey with a slotted spoon and set aside. Reduce the heat to medium and add the mushrooms, onions, and garlic. Sauté, stirring frequently, for 5 to 7 minutes or until the onions are translucent.

2. Add the stock, wine, sage, salt, and pepper to the pan and bring to a boil over high heat. Simmer the mixture, stirring frequently, until reduced by half. Return the turkey to the pan and cook over low heat, uncovered, for 20 minutes, stirring occasionally.

3. Stir the arrowroot mixture into the stew, cooking for a minute to slightly thicken the juices. Serve immediately.

NOTE: The stew can be made up to three days in advance. Reheat, covered, over low heat, stirring occasionally.

WINE NOTE
If you're serving a white, choose a full, rich California Chardonnay. If a red is preferred, choose a *grand cru* Beaujolais or Côtes du Rhône from France or a California Merlot.

Turkey Chili

TOTAL TIME
1 hour
WORK TIME
15 minutes

PER SERVING
302 calories
70 mg cholesterol
6 g fat
456 mg sodium

Kit Carson's last words were reported as "If only I had time for one more bowl of chili," and this version, made with lean ground turkey breast in lieu of beef, is as satisfying and filling on a cold winter night as any you have tasted.   Serves 6

1 tablespoon vegetable oil
1 onion, peeled and chopped
3 garlic cloves, peeled and minced
1 red bell pepper, seeds and ribs removed (page 269), finely diced
1 green bell pepper, seeds and ribs removed (page 269), finely diced
1½ pounds turkey breast meat, coarsely ground
2 tablespoons flour
3 tablespoons chili powder
2 tablespoons ground cumin
2 teaspoons powdered cocoa
1 to 2 teaspoons cayenne pepper
¼ cup tarragon vinegar
2 tablespoons strong brewed coffee
2 14-ounce cans plum tomatoes, crushed
¼ teaspoon salt
2 cups cooked black beans

1. Heat the oil over medium-high heat in a Dutch oven or deep skillet. Add the onion, garlic, red bell pepper, and green bell pepper; sauté, stirring frequently, for 5 minutes. Add the ground turkey and sauté for 5 minutes, stirring constantly and breaking up any lumps with the spoon.

2. Stir in the flour, chili powder, cumin, and cocoa. Stir over low heat, stirring frequently, for 3 minutes to cook the spices. Add the remaining ingredients except the black beans and bring to a boil over medium heat. Simmer the chili, stirring occasionally, for 40 to 45 minutes, until thick and the turkey is tender. Add the black beans and cook for 5 additional minutes.

NOTE: The chili can be made up to three days in advance and refrigerated, tightly covered with plastic wrap. It can also be frozen for up to a month.

WINE NOTE
A good cold beer is best, or choose a spicy California Zinfandel.

Turkey with Lemon Sauce

Even "skinny" sauces can create the illusion of richness if their flavors are concentrated through reduction. This sauce for turkey, garnished with colorful fresh spinach, adds the tangy taste of lemon juice to the reduced stock and wine.   Serves 6

2 pounds boneless turkey breast meat
⅔ cup dry white wine
2 tablespoons freshly squeezed lemon juice
2 cups turkey or chicken stock, preferably unsalted (page 266)
1 garlic clove, peeled and minced
3 tablespoons chopped fresh marjoram *or* 1 teaspoon dried
Pinch of freshly ground white pepper
¼ teaspoon salt (omit if using salted canned stock)
1 teaspoon arrowroot mixed with 2 tablespoons cold water
2 teaspoons unsalted butter
3 pounds fresh spinach, washed and stemmed, *or* 1 10-ounce package
    frozen leaf spinach, defrosted

TOTAL TIME
25 minutes
WORK TIME
15 minutes

PER SERVING
219 calories
96 mg cholesterol
4 g fat
238 mg sodium

1. Preheat a grill or broiler. Cut the turkey meat into 6 cutlets and pound to an even thickness of ½ inch (or have the butcher do it); set aside.

2. In a small saucepan, combine the wine, lemon juice, stock, garlic, marjoram, pepper, and salt. Bring to a boil over high heat, reduce the heat to medium, and reduce by half. Stir the arrowroot mixture into the sauce and stir until lightly thickened. Whisk in the butter and keep the sauce warm.

3. Grill or broil the turkey cutlets for 3 minutes on each side or until the juices run clear. Heat a large skillet over high heat and add the spinach, turning it with a spatula. It will wilt and decrease in volume almost instantly. If you're using frozen spinach, squeeze it well to remove excess moisture and slowly heat it in a skillet. Do not cook it for more than 2 minutes. Drain the spinach if necessary.

4. To serve, place a portion of spinach on a plate and top with a turkey cutlet. Spoon the sauce on top.

NOTE: If you're boning a whole turkey breast, use the bones to make the stock. The sauce can be made up to two days in advance and kept refrigerated. Do not grill the turkey or cook the spinach until just before serving.

WINE NOTE
A white Burgundy from France or a California Chardonnay will provide a nice balance to the flavors of the dish.

Turkey Tonnato

Turkey breast can usually substitute for veal to reduce the cost—as well as the calories and cholesterol—of a dish. This Italian summer classic is a personal favorite, with a tangy tuna sauce enlivening the delicate roasted turkey.   *Serves 6*

TOTAL TIME
4 hours, including chilling
WORK TIME
10 minutes

1 (3-pound) turkey breast (to yield 1½ pounds of meat)
1 9¼-ounce can white tuna packed in water, drained
½ cup freshly squeezed lemon juice
¼ cup extra-virgin olive oil
½ teaspoon freshly ground pepper
Pinch of salt
¼ cup plain nonfat yogurt
2 tablespoons small capers, rinsed
12 thin lemon slices for garnish

PER SERVING
316 calories
94 mg cholesterol
14 g fat
332 mg sodium

1. Preheat the oven to 375 degrees. Place the turkey breast on a rack in a roasting pan and roast it for 1½ hours or until a meat thermometer registers 170 degrees when placed in the thickest part of the meat. Remove from the oven, remove the meat from the carcass, reserving the bones and skin for stock, and carve the meat into 6 servings. Refrigerate, covered with plastic wrap, until chilled—about 2 hours.

2. In a blender or food processor fitted with the steel blade, puree the remaining ingredients except capers and lemon slices. Scrape into a bowl and stir in the capers.

3. To serve, coat each portion of turkey with the sauce and garnish with thin slices of lemon.

NOTE: The turkey and tuna sauce can both be prepared up to two days in advance. Keep them tightly covered with plastic wrap in the refrigerator and do not coat the slices until ready to serve.

WINE NOTE
The Italian flavors here will shine against Italian Pinot Grigio, Vernaccia, or Orvieto or a more strongly flavored Alsace Riesling or a Chablis from France.

Roasted Monkfish in Plum Wine Sauce

TOTAL TIME
2½ hours, including marinating

WORK TIME
25 minutes

PER SERVING
250 calories
57 mg cholesterol
4 g fat
271 mg sodium

Known as "poor man's lobster" and once considered a trash fish in America, monkfish (or *lotte*) has become popular due to its similarity in texture and delicate flavor to the prized crustacean. The sweetness of Chinese plum wine is the perfect foil for the fish, its sweetness balanced by the vinegar and chilies.　*Serves 6*

3 pounds thick monkfish fillets

FOR THE MARINADE

8 thin slices (about the size of a dime) fresh ginger
3 garlic cloves, peeled and minced
1 cup plum wine
¾ cup dry Sherry
Juice of 1 lemon
½ cup rice wine vinegar
½ cup white wine vinegar
2 teaspoons finely grated lemon zest
2 tablespoons reduced-sodium soy sauce
3 dried Chinese chilies
1 tablespoon coriander seed
2 tablespoons chopped fresh cilantro or parsley
1 teaspoon cayenne pepper

2 ounces dried *shiitake* mushrooms
1 cup sliced celery
¼ pound *enoki* mushrooms, washed and trimmed
8 scallions, including 2 inches of the green, trimmed and chopped

1. If the monkfish fillets are not trimmed, use a sharp paring knife and remove the shiny membrane covering the fillets. Trim to an even thickness, saving the scraps for fish stock.

2. In a glass or stainless-steel bowl, combine the marinade ingredients. Add the monkfish and marinate for 2 hours at room temperature or for 6 hours refrigerated, covered with plastic wrap.

3. Soak the dried *shiitake* mushrooms in boiling water to cover for 15 minutes, pushing them down with the back of a spoon to absorb the water. Drain, stem, and slice.

4. Preheat the oven to 450 degrees. Remove the monkfish from the marinade, reserving the marinade. Place in a baking dish and bake for 10 to 12 minutes or until the flesh springs back to the touch. Remove and keep warm.

5. While the monkfish is roasting, boil down the marinade in a small saucepan until reduced by half. Strain the sauce and return it to the pan. Add the celery and *shiitake* and simmer for 5 minutes. To serve, place a monkfish fillet on the plate and top with some of the sauce. Scatter *enoki* mushrooms and chopped scallions over the fillets.

NOTE: The same treatment works well for thick halibut or swordfish steaks, which can be grilled as well as roasted. The fish can be cooked a day in advance; roast it for only seven minutes and then reheat in a 300-degree oven for 12 to 15 minutes.

WINE NOTE
The Asian flavors in this dish are assertive. Try a Gewürztraminer from Alsace to balance them.

Fish Steamed in Napa Cabbage with Red Pepper Sauce

TOTAL TIME
30 minutes
WORK TIME
20 minutes

PER SERVING
234 calories
81 mg cholesterol
9 g fat
231 mg sodium

This Asian-inspired dish is as dramatic as it is delicious. The filling combines pale sole with brightly toned salmon scented with sesame and soy, and the brilliant red sauce is sparked with pungent ginger.   *Serves 6*

12 leaves Napa or savoy cabbage
1 pound salmon fillets, preferably a bright orange species, skinned (page 272)
1 pound sole fillets
1 tablespoon vegetable oil
1 teaspoon dark sesame oil
¼ cup finely minced scallion, white part only
1 tablespoon freshly squeezed lemon juice
2 teaspoons reduced-sodium soy sauce

FOR THE SAUCE

1½ cups fish stock (page 268)
2 red bell peppers, roasted and peeled (page 269)
1½ additional teaspoons freshly squeezed lemon juice
1 tablespoon grated fresh ginger
Pinch of salt
Pinch of freshly ground white pepper

1. Bring a pot of water to a boil and blanch the cabbage leaves until pliable, about 2 minutes. Drain and set aside.

2. Cut the salmon and sole into ½-inch cubes and set aside. Heat the vegetable and sesame oils in a small skillet over medium heat. Add the scallions and sauté, stirring frequently, for 5 minutes. Add to the fish along with 1 tablespoon lemon juice and the soy sauce. Lay out 2 cabbage leaves so they are overlapping slightly and divide the mixture in the center of the leaves. Roll the cabbage, tucking in the sides to enclose the filling, and secure the rolls with toothpicks. Place them in a bamboo steamer and steam over boiling water for 7 to 10 minutes.

3. While the rolls are steaming, puree the stock, peppers, 1½ teaspoons lemon juice, ginger, salt, and pepper in a blender or food processor fitted with the steel blade. Pour into a small saucepan and bring to a boil over medium heat. Reduce by half, stirring frequently.

4. To serve, place a pool of sauce on the plate and top with a cabbage roll.

NOTE: The cabbage rolls can be refrigerated for one day before cooking, tightly covered with plastic wrap. Do not steam until just before serving. The sauce can also be prepared a day in advance and refrigerated. Reheat over low heat, stirring occasionally.

WINE NOTE
The strong Asian flavors need a wine with a spicy, pungent aroma and flavor. Try a Gewürztraminer from Alsace.

Salmon with Basil Cream Sauce

The fresh taste of basil is highlighted by the white wine and cream in this brilliant green sauce that tops delicate orange salmon. This is an elegant entree and easy to prepare.
Serves 6

2 pounds salmon fillets, skinned (page 272)
1½ tablespoons unsalted butter
3 shallots, peeled and minced
1 garlic clove, peeled and minced
1½ cups chopped fresh basil
¼ cup chopped fresh parsley
¾ cup dry white wine
⅓ cup light cream
1 tablespoon freshly squeezed lemon juice
¼ teaspoon freshly ground white pepper
¼ teaspoon salt

WORK TIME
10 minutes
TOTAL TIME
20 minutes

PER SERVING
284 calories
100 mg cholesterol
15 g fat
167 mg sodium

1. Cut the salmon into 6 equal serving pieces, wash, and pat dry on paper towels. Melt the butter in a large skillet over medium-high heat. Sear the salmon on both sides for about 2 to 3 minutes, keeping the center slightly rare since the fish will continue to cook after it is taken from the pan. Remove the fish from the pan with a slotted spatula and keep warm. Reduce the heat to low and add the shallots and garlic to the pan. Sauté, stirring frequently, for 5 minutes.

2. Add the remaining ingredients to the pan and cook over medium heat, stirring frequently, until the mixture is reduced by half. To serve, reheat the fish slightly in the sauce, if necessary, and serve the sauce around the salmon fillets.

NOTE: The fish can be prepared up to three hours in advance. Reheat the fish in the sauce over low heat, uncovered, for 10 minutes.

WINE NOTE
A French white Burgundy or a Vouvray from the Loire Valley will complement this dish nicely.

Caribbean Grouper

This is a subtle and delicious marinade suitable for any delicate fish. Since grouper reminds me of trips to the islands, the marinade was inspired by other tropical ingredients.   *Serves 6*

3 pounds grouper (about ½ inch thick) or any other white-fleshed fillet, such as halibut, whitefish, or snapper
4 shallots, peeled and chopped
4 garlic cloves, peeled and minced
Juice of 2 limes
1 cup freshly squeezed orange juice
¼ cup dark rum
1 cup white wine
¼ cup reduced-sodium soy sauce
2 tablespoons chopped fresh rosemary *or* 2 teaspoons dried
¼ cup chopped fresh parsley
¼ teaspoon freshly ground white pepper
¼ teaspoon salt

TOTAL TIME
2½ to 8½ hours,
including marinating
WORK TIME
15 minutes

PER SERVING
248 calories
84 mg cholesterol
2 g fat
615 mg sodium

1. Remove the skin from the fillet, if necessary, and go over the fillet carefully with your fingers to remove any hidden small bones. Wash and pat dry with paper towels.

2. Combine the remaining ingredients, add the fish, and marinate in a glass or stainless-steel pan, covered with plastic wrap, in the refrigerator for at least 2 hours or up to 8 hours.

3. Preheat a grill or broiler. Remove the fish from the marinade, reserving the marinade. Grill the fish for 3 to 4 minutes on each side, depending on thickness, turning gently. The fish should still be slightly translucent in the center since it will continue to cook after being taken off the grill.

4. While the fish is grilling, boil down the marinade until it is reduced by half. Spoon a few tablespoons over each portion of fish. Serve immediately or at room temperature.

WINE NOTE
A spicy white, such as a California Sauvignon Blanc or an Alsatian Gewürztraminer, or a Sancerre would balance the spices of the dish.

Seafood Sausages

TOTAL TIME
45 minutes
WORK TIME
15 minutes

PER SERVING
242 calories
163 mg cholesterol
5 g fat
422 mg sodium

This is an elegant dish, which belies how incredibly easy it is to make. The sausages are formed versions of a delicately herbed fish mousse, given textural and visual diversity by the scallops and shrimp in the puree.   *Serves 6*

1 pound fillet of sole or any other firm-fleshed white fish, such as
    snapper, halibut, or grouper, washed and cut into 1-inch pieces
1 pound bay scallops, or sea scallops cut into eighths
2 egg whites
⅓ cup light cream
¼ teaspoon salt
¼ teaspoon freshly ground white pepper
4 drops Tabasco sauce
2 tablespoons chopped fresh parsley
1 teaspoon chopped fresh oregano *or* ¼ teaspoon dried
2 teaspoons chopped fresh basil *or* ¼ teaspoon dried
1 pound medium shrimp, peeled, deveined, and roughly chopped
Vegetable oil
3 bunches fresh watercress, washed, tough stems removed

1. Make sure all the fish is well chilled. Place the sole in the work bowl of a food processor fitted with the steel blade. Add one quarter of the scallops. Add the egg whites, cream, salt, pepper, and Tabasco; puree the mixture until smooth, scraping down the sides of the bowl as necessary. Add the herbs and mix briefly to combine.

2. Scrape the mixture into a mixing bowl and stir in the remaining scallops and the shrimp. Lightly oil 12 pieces of heavy-duty aluminum foil, about 8 inches square. Place a spoonful of the sausage mixture on one side and form with your fingers into a cylinder. Roll the foil, twisting the ends to seal the packages tightly. Repeat until all sausages are formed.

3. Bring water to a boil in a stockpot over high heat. Add the sausage packages and regulate the heat so that they are just simmering. Cover the pot and simmer the sausages for 15 minutes.

4. Remove them from the water with tongs and let them sit for 10 minutes. Gently unwrap them over the sink, allowing any water that has seeped in to drain.

5. While the sausages are resting, heat a skillet over medium-high heat. Sauté the watercress for 1 minute or until wilted. Drain if necessary.

6. To serve, arrange a bed of watercress on a plate and top with 2 sausages.

NOTE: There are two ways to do this dish in advance: either the sausages can be made to step 3 and refrigerated for a day, or they can be completely cooked up to two days in advance and reheated, covered with aluminum foil, in a 300-degree oven for 15 minutes. Do not sauté the watercress in advance.

WINE NOTE
Since this is derived from the classic French repertoire, a French white Burgundy will do well. Try a good Macon-Villages or, to splurge, a Chassagne- or Puligny-Montrachet.

Tuna Brochettes with Smoked Tomato Sauce

TOTAL TIME
Minimum of 3½ hours,
including marinating
WORK TIME
15 minutes

PER SERVING
363 calories
72 mg cholesterol
15 g fat
274 mg sodium

Grilled tuna has all the tenderness and richness of a beef *filet mignon*, which is why a red wine marinade enhances these qualities perfectly. The Smoked Tomato Sauce (page 203) is a complementary topping, and a bit of spinach adds more color to the elegant presentation. *Serves 6*

2½ pounds fresh tuna, preferably in one piece
1 cup dry red wine
2 tablespoons olive oil
1 tablespoon freshly squeezed lemon juice
1 tablespoon chopped fresh rosemary *or* ½ teaspoon dried
1 tablespoon chopped fresh basil *or* ½ teaspoon dried
2 tablespoons chopped fresh parsley
2 teaspoons chopped fresh thyme *or* ¼ teaspoon dried
¼ teaspoon freshly ground black pepper
¼ teaspoon salt
1 pound fresh spinach, washed and stemmed
2 cups Smoked Tomato Sauce (page 203)

1. Cut the tuna into 2-inch chunks and thread onto bamboo skewers. Place the skewers in a flat glass or stainless-steel pan just large enough to hold them.

2. In a jar with a tight-fitting lid, combine the red wine, olive oil, lemon juice, rosemary, basil, parsley, thyme, pepper, and salt. Shake well to emulsify and pour the marinade over the tuna brochettes.

3. Marinate in the refrigerator, covered with plastic wrap, for a minimum of 3 hours, turning occasionally. The brochettes can marinate for up to 8 hours.

4. Just before serving, wilt the spinach by heating a 12-inch skillet over high heat. Add the spinach, turning with a spatula, and within 1 minute it will wilt and become bright green. Drain if necessary.

5. Preheat a grill or broiler. Cook the tuna for 2 to 3 minutes on each side or until the flesh in the center is hot but still translucent (or to desired doneness).

6. To serve, place a line of spinach at the top of a plate and place a brochette below. Spoon a portion of the Smoked Tomato Sauce over the top of the brochette. The brochettes can be served either hot or at room temperature.

WINE NOTE
Here is an opportunity to violate the classic, and usually safe, rule of white wine with fish and red wine with meat. Try a light red, such as one from the Loire Valley in France, or a lesser Beaujolais.

Southwestern Halibut

This spicy preparation is frequently used in the Southwest for sautéed meats. The sauce's vivid red color is matched by the gutsy flavor. *Serves 6*

2 pounds halibut steaks, ¾ to 1 inch thick, cut into 6 equal serving
   pieces
1½ tablespoons vegetable oil
10 garlic cloves, peeled and thinly sliced
1 *jalapeño* pepper, seeds and ribs removed (page 269), very finely
   chopped
3 red bell peppers, seeds and ribs removed (page 269), finely chopped
1½ teaspoons paprika
1½ teaspoons chili powder
2 cups dry white wine
½ cup finely chopped fresh cilantro
Pinch of cayenne pepper
¼ teaspoon salt

TOTAL TIME
30 minutes
WORK TIME
15 minutes

PER SERVING
221 calories
48 mg cholesterol
7 g fat
185 mg sodium

1. Wash the steaks and set aside. Heat the oil in a large skillet over medium heat and add the garlic, *jalapeño*, and red pepper. Sauté for 5 minutes, stirring frequently. Place the steaks on top and sprinkle with the paprika and chili powder. Add the white wine, bring to a boil over high heat, cover the pan, reduce the heat, and simmer the fish for 6 to 8 minutes, depending on thickness.

2. Remove the fish from the pan with a slotted spatula and keep warm. Raise the heat to high and reduce the sauce until only ¾ cup remains, stirring frequently. Stir the remaining ingredients into the sauce and spoon the sauce over the fish. Serve hot, at room temperature, or chilled.

NOTE: Swordfish, tuna, or any thick fish steak can be substituted for the halibut. The fish can be prepared up to a day in advance and refrigerated, tightly covered with plastic wrap. Either serve chilled or bring to room temperature; do not reheat.

WINE NOTE
You should serve a very big white wine to stand up to the heat of the chilies, such as a California Chardonnay or a Gewürztraminer from Alsace.

Creole Swordfish

TOTAL TIME
25 minutes
WORK TIME
15 minutes

PER SERVING
240 calories
59 mg cholesterol
8 g fat
356 mg sodium

The "Holy Trinity" of Creole cooking is onions, celery, and green bell peppers. These vegetables in a thick, rich tomato sauce, enlivened by hot pepper and the Tabasco sauce native to Louisiana, make this a spicy, savory entree.   *Serves 6*

2 pounds swordfish steaks, approximately 1 inch thick, cut into 6 equal serving pieces
1 tablespoon olive oil
1 cup finely chopped onion
1 cup finely chopped celery
3 garlic cloves, peeled and minced
1 green bell pepper, seeds and ribs removed (page 269), finely chopped
½ cup dry white wine
1 14-ounce can crushed tomatoes packed in tomato puree
½ to 1 teaspoon Tabasco sauce (to taste)
Pinch of cayenne pepper
¼ cup chopped fresh parsley
2 teaspoons chopped fresh thyme *or* ½ teaspoon dried
¼ teaspoon salt

1. Wash the swordfish steaks and pat dry on paper towels. Set aside. Heat the oil in a large skillet over medium-high heat. Add the onions, celery, garlic, and green pepper. Sauté, stirring frequently, for 5 minutes or until the onions are translucent. Add the swordfish steaks along with the remaining ingredients and bring to a boil over medium heat. Poach the swordfish, partially covered, for 6 to 8 minutes, depending on thickness.

2. Remove the swordfish from the pan with a slotted spatula and keep warm. Raise the heat to high and reduce the sauce by one third, stirring frequently. To serve, spoon the sauce over the swordfish steaks. The swordfish can be served either hot or at room temperature.

NOTE: This dish is better not reheated.

WINE NOTE
The spices should lead to serving a full-flavored California Chardonnay with this main dish.

Asian Grouper

TOTAL TIME
20 minutes
WORK TIME
10 minutes

PER SERVING
214 calories
42 mg cholesterol
6 g fat
377 mg sodium

With some steamed rice, this dish becomes your entire meal. A bright panoply of crunchy vegetables cooked in a savory, yet delicate sauce accompanies the quickly sautéed cubes of fish. *Serves 6*

1½ pounds grouper fillets, cut into 1-inch pieces
12 dried *shiitake* mushrooms
1 cup boiling water

FOR THE SAUCE

½ cup dry Sherry
3 tablespoons reduced-sodium soy sauce
3 tablespoons freshly squeezed lime juice
2 teaspoons sugar
¼ teaspoon ground Szechwan pepper

1 tablespoon dark sesame oil
1 tablespoon vegetable oil
1 tablespoon finely chopped fresh ginger
4 garlic cloves, peeled and minced
4 scallions, trimmed and cut into 1-inch lengths
2 celery stalks, washed and sliced
¼ pound snow peas, stringed
1 red bell pepper, seeds and ribs removed (page 269), cut into julienne
¼ pound fresh *shiitake* mushrooms, washed, stemmed, and sliced

1½ teaspoons cornstarch dissolved in 2 tablespoons cold water

1. Wash the fish cubes and pat dry on paper towels. Soak the dried mushrooms in the boiling water, pushing them down with the back of a spoon, for 15 minutes; set aside. When soft, stem the mushrooms and chop them coarsely. Set aside.

2. Have the sauce ingredients mixed together in a small bowl and handy. Heat the sesame and vegetable oils in a heavy wok or skillet over high heat. Add the ginger and garlic and stir-fry for 30 seconds, stirring constantly, until the ingredients are fragrant. Add the fish cubes and sear on both sides, turning gently with a wok spatula. Remove from the pan and add the scallions, celery, snow peas, red pepper, and fresh and dried *shiitake* mushrooms. Stir-fry the vegetables for 2 minutes, then return the fish to the pan and add the sauce. Bring to a boil and simmer for 2 minutes, then stir in the cornstarch mixture. Simmer briefly until lightly thickened. Serve immediately.

NOTE: Any firm-fleshed white fish or boneless, skinless chicken breast can be substituted. As with most Asian food, most of the preparation of this dish is in the slicing and dicing. This can be done a day in advance, with the component parts kept tightly covered with plastic wrap in the refrigerator. Do not complete the dish until just before serving.

WINE NOTE
The Asian flavors will pair with a Sancerre or Pouilly-Fumé from the Loire Valley or a Gewürztraminer from Alsace.

Pasta with Seafood Baked in Foil

TOTAL TIME
2½ hours, including
soaking
WORK TIME
20 minutes

PER SERVING
335 calories
115 mg cholesterol
9 g fat
345 mg sodium

In Italy, the best pasta dishes are frequently the simplest, depending on the freshness of the ingredients and the blending of flavors. In this case, the presentation is dramatic; a large silver trophy arrives at the table, and when it is cut open, the heady aroma fills the dining room.   *Serves 6*

18 mussels
18 medium-sized hard-shelled clams
2 tablespoons cornmeal
¼ pound small squid
½ cup water
½ pound large shrimp, peeled and deveined, shells reserved
½ pound dried thin spaghetti
3 tablespoons fruity olive oil
3 garlic cloves, peeled and minced
½ teaspoon crushed red pepper
½ cup dry white wine
1 14-ounce can Italian plum tomatoes, drained and chopped
¼ teaspoon salt
¼ cup finely chopped fresh parsley

1. Scrub the mussels and clams with a stiff brush under cold running water, discarding any that are not firmly closed. Scrape off the mussel beards with a sharp paring knife. Place the mollusks in cold water to cover and sprinkle the cornmeal on top of the water. Place the bowl in the refrigerator for 2 hours, then scrub them again and set aside.

2. If the squid is small, serve whole. If large, cut the sack into rings and remove and discard the head and the hard section joining the tentacles (or have the fishmonger do it). Set aside.

3. Place the mussels and clams in a deep pot with the water and the reserved shrimp shells and bring to a boil over high heat. Steam for 3 to 5 minutes, shaking the pot a few times to redistribute the shellfish. Remove from the pot with a slotted spoon, discarding any that did not open. Set aside and boil the liquid down to ½ cup. Strain through a coffee filter or cheesecloth-lined sieve and set aside.

4. Bring a large pot of water to a boil and add the spaghetti. Cook for only half the time given in the instructions, drain, and toss with 1 tablespoon of the oil. Set aside.

5. Preheat the oven to 450 degrees. Have a large sheet of heavy-duty foil available. Heat the remaining oil in a large skillet over medium-high heat. Add the garlic and red pepper and sauté, stirring constantly, for 3 minutes. Add the squid and shrimp and sauté for 2 minutes. Add the wine, tomatoes, reserved seafood stock, and salt; simmer for 3 minutes.

6. Place the pasta on the foil and pour the sauce on top. Stir to blend and then arrange the mussels and clams on top. Seal the foil by crimping the edges and place on a baking sheet. Bake in the center of the oven for 10 minutes. Remove and bring to the table on a platter. Open with scissors, toss with parsley, and serve.

NOTE: The dish can be prepared up to two hours in advance prior to the final baking. Add five minutes to the baking time.

WINE NOTE
Try one of the bigger California Chardonnays or an Italian Gavi di Gavi. Or you could serve a light red, such as a Beaujolais, with this rich dish.

Pasta with Fresh Tomato Sauce and Crab

TOTAL TIME
45 minutes
WORK TIME
20 minutes

PER SERVING
294 calories
38 mg cholesterol
5 g fat
224 mg sodium

Summer is not only the best time for succulent vine-ripened tomatoes; it is also the season when delicate, sweet crab meat is in the greatest abundance in the market. This lightly herbed sauce is the perfect foil for this prized crustacean.   *Serves 6*

1 head of garlic
1½ tablespoons olive oil
6 scallions, including 2 inches of the green, chopped
6 shallots, peeled and minced
12 large ripe tomatoes, peeled, seeded, and chopped (page 271)
1½ tablespoons chopped fresh basil *or* ¾ teaspoon dried
2 teaspoons chopped fresh rosemary *or* ¼ teaspoon dried
2 teaspoons chopped fresh oregano *or* ¼ teaspoon dried
Pinch of freshly ground black pepper
¼ teaspoon salt
½ pound fresh lump crab meat, picked over to remove any fragments
   of shell and cartilage
½ pound fresh angel hair pasta
6 fresh basil or oregano sprigs for garnish (optional)

1. Preheat the oven to 350 degrees. Place the garlic on a baking sheet in the center of the oven for 15 minutes or until the cloves are soft. When cool enough to handle, pop 4 cloves out of their skins, reserving the rest for another use, and set aside.

2. While the garlic is roasting, heat the olive oil in a large skillet over medium heat. Add the scallions and shallots and sauté for 5 minutes, stirring frequently, or until the shallots are translucent. Add 8 of the tomatoes and the roasted garlic, basil, rosemary, oregano, pepper, and salt. Simmer for 20 minutes or until the sauce is very thick, pushing down frequently to mash the tomatoes. Add the remaining tomatoes and all but 6 tablespoons of the crab. Simmer for 5 minutes. Remove from heat and set aside but keep warm.

3. Bring a large pot of water to a boil and add the pasta. When the water returns to a boil, drain the pasta and toss with the hot sauce. To serve, divide the pasta among plates and top with a sprinkling of reserved crab meat and a sprig of basil or oregano if desired.

NOTE: The sauce can be made up to a day in advance, and kept refrigerated, tightly covered with plastic wrap. The sauce should be reheated over a low flame, uncovered, for 10 minutes, stirring frequently. Do not cook the pasta until just before serving.

WINE NOTE
While the tomatoes and scallions might call for red wine, the crab meat needs white. So compromise with a rich, full-flavored California Chardonnay.

Alfred's Meat Loaf

TOTAL TIME
1½ hours
WORK TIME
20 minutes

PER SERVING
254 calories
103 mg cholesterol
11 g fat
388 mg sodium

By "stretching" the veal with vegetables, you get all the heartiness of a meat loaf with a fraction of the calories and fat. The tunnel of spinach in the center creates a more attractive presentation for the down-to-earth dish, which is lightly spiced. This dish is named for real estate magnate Alfred Taubman, who suggested the dish.   *Serves 6*

2 teaspoons vegetable oil
2 cups finely chopped onion
2 garlic cloves, peeled and minced
1 carrot, peeled and finely grated
1 pound lean ground veal
¼ cup plain bread crumbs
1 egg
2 egg whites
2 tablespoons freshly grated Parmesan cheese
1 teaspoon paprika
¼ teaspoon cayenne pepper
¼ teaspoon salt
1½ teaspoons chopped fresh rosemary *or* ¼ teaspoon dried
3 pounds fresh spinach, washed and steamed, *or* 1 10-ounce package frozen chopped spinach, defrosted
1 ounce low-fat (part skim milk) mozzarella cheese, grated (about 2½ tablespoons)
2 cups Herbed Tomato Sauce; optional (page 202)

1. Heat the oil in a skillet over medium heat. Add the onions and garlic and sauté, stirring frequently, for 10 to 12 minutes or until the onions are soft.

2. Scrape the mixture into a mixing bowl and add the carrot, veal, bread crumbs, egg, egg whites, Parmesan cheese, paprika, cayenne, salt, and rosemary. Mix well with a wooden spoon or your hands until light in texture. Set aside.

THE GOURMET GAZELLE COOKBOOK

3. Preheat the oven to 350 degrees. If you're using fresh spinach, heat a skillet over high heat. Add the spinach, turning it with a spatula, until the spinach wilts, adding spinach as room permits. Drain spinach if necessary. Chop the spinach and mix with the cheese. If you're using frozen spinach, place it in a colander and press with the back of a spoon to extract as much moisture as possible and then mix with the cheese.

4. Form half the meat into a rectangle about 9 inches long and 4 inches wide on a baking sheet. Make a tunnel of spinach in the center and then top with the remaining meat, smoothing the top and sides to form a loaf. Bake for 1 hour in the center of the oven or until a meat thermometer registers 160 degrees. Slice and serve with Herbed Tomato Sauce if desired. The meat loaf can also be served cold or at room temperature.

NOTE: The meat loaf can be made up to two days in advance. Reheat, covered with foil, in a 300-degree oven for 20 minutes and do not slice until ready to serve. Or, it can be assembled a day in advance, kept covered with plastic wrap in the refrigerator, and baked just before serving.

WINE NOTE
If you choose a red, try a Beaujolais from France. For a white, a Vouvray or white Burgundy from the Macon region of France will go well.

Beef Braised in Stout Beer

TOTAL TIME
2 hours
WORK TIME
15 minutes

PER SERVING
276 calories
66 mg cholesterol
11 g fat
166 mg sodium

Beef braised in beer, *Carbonnades à la Flamande*, is a classic Belgian dish. In this case, the beer used is a dark stout, rather than light lager, so the stew is a rich brown color and has a robust, piquant flavor.   *Serves 6*

1½ pounds boneless lean beef, such as round, trimmed of all visible fat and cut into 2-inch cubes
2 tablespoons vegetable oil
2 cups diced onion
2 garlic cloves, peeled and minced
1 pound fresh mushrooms, washed, trimmed, and halved if large
2 cups Guinness stout beer
1½ cups veal or beef stock, preferably unsalted (page 267)
2 tablespoons dark brown sugar
1 teaspoon chopped fresh thyme *or* ¼ teaspoon dried
3 tablespoons chopped fresh parsley
1 bay leaf
¼ teaspoon freshly ground black pepper
¼ teaspoon salt (omit if using salted canned stock)
2 teaspoons cornstarch mixed with 2 tablespoons cold water
1 tablespoon balsamic vinegar

1. Wash the meat and pat dry with paper towels. Heat the oil in a Dutch oven over medium-high heat. Brown the beef cubes on all sides and remove them with a slotted spoon. This will have to be done in a few batches.

2. Reduce the heat to medium and add the onions, garlic, and mushrooms. Sauté for 5 minutes, stirring often. Return the meat to the pan and add the remaining ingredients except cornstarch and vinegar. Bring to a boil over high heat, reduce the heat to a simmer, and braise the stew, covered, for 1½ to 2 hours or until the meat is tender.

3. Remove the meat and vegetables from the pan, discarding the bay leaf, and reduce the gravy by one third, stirring frequently. Stir in the cornstarch mixture, simmering for 2 minutes until thickened. Return the meat and vegetables to the pan and stir in the vinegar. Reheat the stew, if necessary.

NOTE: If you can't make the stew the day before, make it early in the day and chill it so that any fat will harden and can be removed. Reheat slowly, stirring occasionally.

WINE NOTE
Try a California Cabernet Sauvignon, French red Bordeaux, or red Burgundy with this hearty beef dish.

Peppers Stuffed with Beef and Orzo

Orzo is a pasta resembling grains of rice and is used frequently in Greek cookery. Its toothsome texture complements the herbed beef and vegetables for these hearty stuffed peppers.   Serves 6

TOTAL TIME
1 hour
WORK TIME
20 minutes

PER SERVING
255 calories
44 mg cholesterol
7 g fat
149 mg sodium

6 red, yellow, or green bell peppers
1 tablespoon olive oil
1 pound lean round of beef, trimmed of all visible fat and ground
½ cup chopped red onion
3 garlic cloves, peeled and minced
2 celery stalks, washed and chopped
¼ pound fresh mushrooms, washed and chopped
¾ cup orzo
1½ cups beef or veal stock, preferably unsalted (page 267)
1 tablespoon chopped fresh oregano *or* ½ teaspoon dried
2 tablespoons balsamic vinegar
¼ teaspoon freshly ground black pepper
¼ teaspoon salt (omit if using salted canned stock)

1. Cut the top inch off the peppers, discard the stems, and pull out the ribs and seeds. Chop the caps and set aside.

2. Heat the oil in a skillet over medium-high heat. Add the beef and cook, breaking up any lumps, for 5 minutes. Add the onion, garlic, celery, mushrooms, and reserved pepper caps to the pan; cook for 10 minutes over medium heat, stirring frequently, or until the vegetables are soft.

3. While the vegetables are sautéing, wash the orzo in a sieve and combine with the stock in a small saucepan. Bring to a boil and simmer the orzo for 5 minutes, uncovered, or until just tender. Drain, reserving ½ cup of the cooking liquid.

4. Preheat the oven to 400 degrees. Add the reserved cooking liquid to the beef and vegetables, along with the remaining ingredients. Simmer for 5 minutes, stir in the *orzo*, and stuff the peppers. Place the peppers in a baking dish and cook, lightly covered with foil, for 25 minutes. Serve immediately.

NOTE: The peppers can be stuffed up to a day in advance and refrigerated, tightly covered with plastic wrap. Allow them to reach room temperature before baking. Lean ground lamb can be substituted for the beef.

WINE NOTE
A Barolo, Barbera, or bigger Chianti from Italy will complement the dish, as will a red Bordeaux from France or a California Cabernet Sauvignon.

Veal Scaloppine with Fresh Shiitake Mushroom Sauce

TOTAL TIME
30 minutes
WORK TIME
20 minutes

PER SERVING
250 calories
80 mg cholesterol
15 g fat
188 mg sodium

Based on a combination of subtle flavors—wild mushrooms, a hint of nut oil, and delicate veal—this is a wonderful recipe for that special dinner when your preparation time is limited. You can have it on the table within minutes.   *Serves 6 to 8*

2 tablespoons walnut oil
2 pounds veal scallops, pounded to ⅛-inch thickness
2 tablespoons unsalted butter
¼ pound fresh *shiitake* mushrooms, cleaned, stemmed, and sliced
¼ pound fresh mushrooms, cleaned and sliced
4 shallots, peeled and chopped
2 garlic cloves, peeled and minced
2 cups veal or chicken stock, preferably unsalted (page 267)
1 teaspoon chopped fresh thyme *or* ¼ teaspoon dried
¼ teaspoon freshly ground black pepper
¼ teaspoon salt (omit if using salted canned stock)
½ teaspoon arrowroot mixed with 1 tablespoon cold water

1. Heat the walnut oil in a 12-inch skillet over medium-high heat. When hot, sear the veal on both sides, turning quickly. Remove with a slotted spatula to a platter and repeat until all veal is seared.

2. Add the butter to the pan, then add the *shiitake,* mushrooms, shallots, and garlic. Sauté, stirring frequently, for 5 minutes or until the shallots are translucent and the mushrooms have softened.

3. Add the stock, thyme, pepper, and salt. Bring to a boil over medium heat and simmer until the stock is reduced by half. Add the arrowroot mixture to the pan and stir in evenly. Allow the mixture to simmer for an additional minute or until slightly thickened.

4. Return the veal to the pan and bring back to a boil to heat the veal through. Do not let the veal cook further, or it will toughen. Serve immediately.

NOTE: This dish can be made up to a day in advance through step 3. Reheat the sauce over low heat to a simmer and then add the veal to reheat it briefly. In place of the fresh *shiitake,* any wild mushroom can be used, such as Italian *porcini,* morels, *chanterelles,* or oyster mushrooms.

WINE NOTE
A classic French white Burgundy or a rich California Chardonnay will pick up the wild mushroom taste.

Braised Veal Shanks

TOTAL TIME
2 hours
WORK TIME
15 minutes

PER SERVING
346 calories
120 mg cholesterol
16 g fat
232 mg sodium

Slowly braised meats are my favorite winter comfort food. These veal shanks, buttery tender and savory, are healthier than equivalent dishes since the bone marrow is removed before cooking.   *Serves 6*

6 meaty veal shanks (about ½ to ¾ pound each, depending on the
    size of the center bone; each one should yield about 6 ounces meat)
2 tablespoons flour
1 tablespoon olive oil
1 cup chopped onion
1 teaspoon minced garlic
¾ pound fresh mushrooms, washed and halved if large
2 cups chicken stock, preferably unsalted (page 266)
¾ cup Madeira wine
½ cup dry white wine
¼ cup chopped fresh parsley
1 tablespoon chopped fresh rosemary *or* 1 teaspoon dried
1 tablespoon chopped fresh oregano *or* ½ teaspoon dried
¼ teaspoon freshly ground black pepper
¼ teaspoon salt (omit if using salted canned stock)

1. With a small sharp paring knife, remove all marrow from the center of the bone in the veal shank and discard.

2. Wash the shanks and pat dry with paper towels. Rub the meat with flour. Heat the olive oil in a 14-inch skillet over medium-high heat. Brown the shanks on both sides and remove with a slotted spatula. Set aside.

3. Reduce the heat to low and add the onions and garlic. Sauté, stirring frequently, for 5 minutes or until the onions are translucent.

4. Return the veal to the pan and add the remaining ingredients. Bring to a boil over high heat, cover, and reduce the heat so that the veal is just simmering.

5. Braise for 1½ hours or until the veal is fork-tender. Strain the juices into a saucepan and bring to a boil, reducing the juices by half. Pour over the veal and reheat if necessary. Serve immediately.

THE GOURMET GAZELLE COOKBOOK

NOTE: As with all braised dishes, it's better to make this a day in advance both for superior flavor and so that any fat that has been released by the meat forms a layer that can be removed before the shanks are reheated. Reheat, covered, in a 350-degree oven for 20 minutes or until hot.

WINE NOTE
Try a rich French white Burgundy or a dry California Chardonnay to complement the herbaceous sauce.

Veal Stew in Mustard Sauce

There is a sweet-and-sour undertone to this comforting stew, with dried currants and mustard enlivening the sauce. The delicate, tender cubes of veal absorb the flavors.   *Serves 6*

1½ pounds boneless lean veal, such as round, trimmed of all visible
   fat and cut into 2-inch cubes
1 tablespoon vegetable oil
1 cup chopped onion
2 garlic cloves, peeled and minced
3 carrots, peeled and sliced
½ cup dried currants
2 cups veal stock, chicken stock, or a combination of chicken and beef
   stock, preferably unsalted (page 267)
2 tablespoons grainy mustard
¼ teaspoon freshly ground black pepper
2 teaspoons cornstarch mixed with 2 tablespoons cold water
1 tablespoon white wine vinegar

1. Wash the veal cubes and pat dry. Heat the oil in a heavy-bottomed Dutch oven over medium-high heat. Brown the veal on all sides, removing the cubes with a slotted spoon when browned. This will have to be done in a few batches.

TOTAL TIME
2 hours
WORK TIME
20 minutes

PER SERVING
287 calories
80 mg cholesterol
13 g fat
162 mg sodium

2. Reduce the heat to medium-low, add the onion and garlic, and sauté, stirring frequently, for 5 minutes. Return the veal to the pan and add the carrots, currants, stock, mustard, and pepper. Bring to a boil, reduce the heat so the stew is just simmering, and braise the stew, covered, for 1½ hours or until the meat is fork-tender.

3. Stir the cornstarch mixture into the stew. Allow it to simmer for 2 minutes to thicken. Stir in the vinegar.

NOTE: As with all stews and braised dishes, it is suggested that this stew be made a day in advance and refrigerated so that all fat can be removed. The recipe also works well with skinless chicken pieces.

WINE NOTE
The full flavors here require an Italian Barolo, California Zinfandel, or French red Rhône, such as a Côte Rotie or Hermitage.

Stuffed Flank Steak

Flank steak is a wonderfully tender and lean cut of beef, and the herbed vegetable stuffing becomes a complementary starch. While the dish is excellent hot, it can also be served at room temperature at a buffet.   *Serves 6*

TOTAL TIME
40 minutes
WORK TIME
25 minutes

PER SERVING
271 calories
52 mg cholesterol
16 g fat
286 mg sodium

1¼ pounds flank steak, cut from the thick end
2 tablespoons unsalted butter
1 green bell pepper, seeds and ribs removed (page 269), chopped
1 red bell pepper, seeds and ribs removed (page 269), chopped
1 large onion, peeled and chopped
2 garlic cloves, peeled and minced
2 tablespoons beef or veal stock, preferably unsalted (page 267)
2 tablespoons freshly grated Parmesan cheese
½ cup plain bread crumbs
1 tablespoon chopped fresh parsley
½ teaspoon chopped fresh oregano *or* pinch of dried
½ teaspoon chopped fresh basil *or* pinch of dried
½ teaspoon chopped fresh thyme *or* pinch of dried
Pinch of fennel seed
Pinch of celery seed
¼ teaspoon freshly ground black pepper
¼ teaspoon salt

1. Cut a deep pocket in the center of the flank steak that extends to within ½ inch of the sides of the meat (or have the butcher do it). Set aside.

2. Melt the butter in a 12-inch skillet over medium heat. Add the green pepper, red pepper, onion, and garlic; sauté about 12 minutes, stirring frequently, until the vegetables are soft. Remove the pan from the heat and stir in the remaining ingredients. Stir well to combine.

3. Preheat a grill or broiler. Gently stuff the vegetable mixture into the pocket of the steak and skewer the opening closed with turkey-trussing skewers or toothpicks. Sprinkle the meat with freshly ground pepper.

4. Grill the steak on both sides to your taste, about 4 minutes per side for medium-rare. Allow the meat to rest for 5 minutes, then carve it into slices. Serve immediately.

NOTE: The stuffing can be prepared up to two days in advance and kept refrigerated. Heat it in a 300-degree oven for 15 minutes before stuffing the meat and do not stuff the meat until just before broiling.

WINE NOTE
This herbaceous dish pairs well with a California Cabernet Sauvignon or Zinfandel or a French red wine from the Rhône.

Vegetables
and
Side Dishes

Cranberry-Glazed Acorn Squash
Artichoke Hearts with Basil and Garlic
Asian Asparagus
Brussels Sprouts with Lemon and Parsley
Red Cabbage Cooked with Wine
Sautéed Cucumbers with Dill
Braised Endive
Deviled Leeks
Baked Vidalia Onions
Spaghetti Squash au Gratin
Spaghetti Squash Primavera
Creamed Spinach
Spinach Soufflé
Green Beans with Prosciutto
Stuffed Zucchini
Potato Onion Pudding
Stuffed Baked Potatoes
New Potatoes with Rosemary
Garlic Roasted Potatoes
Grilled Polenta
Mushroom Barley Casserole
Parsley Rice Pilaf
Braised Wild Rice with Pine Nuts
Sweet Potatoes and Apples

What makes a meal memorable is the integration of the total plan and the care taken to select each dish so that a variety of contrasting yet complementary textures, colors, and flavors is presented. This selection process, which is almost unconscious for experienced cooks, extends to the vegetables and starches.

Usually the main dish is the first dish selected; it didn't get to be called the main course by accident. The selection of accompaniments, as well as the dishes to precede and follow the main course, involves a series of decisions determined by personal style.

If the main dish is simple—a piece of marinated and grilled fish, for instance—I tend to select an appetizer served with a sauce. I also have certain other predilections. Since fish is usually pale, I tend to select a green vegetable, and since fish is delicate, I believe some form of rice is more in keeping with the texture and flavor than potatoes.

While these decisions are personal, I think there are certain generalities that apply: The more complex and elaborate the main dish, the simpler the vegetable and starch, and vice versa. Not only is this scheme aesthetically pleasing, it's also realistic. If you're spending hours preparing a main dish, you want to complete the side dishes with lightning speed.

The dishes in this chapter are conceived for those evenings when you are leaning toward the simple main dish and can, therefore, make the side dishes your stars.

Adding assertive seasonings to vegetables makes them hearty and satisfying but still low in calories, cholesterol, and sodium. The addition of *prosciutto* as a flavoring with tomatoes turns simple green beans into an earthy Italian mélange. Mushrooms and carrots are really the primary ingredients in a barley side dish, yet the sense of starchy satisfaction is derived from the barley.

While stir-frying and steaming are both in vogue today, I adore both braised vegetables and the heartier vegetables that take well to this cooking method. Since the salad served with a meal is usually crunchy, I like having textural diversity, so the vegetable chosen is toothsome or satiny.

You will find hearty Red Cabbage Cooked with Wine (page 176), piquant Deviled Leeks (page 179) flavored with mustard, and sweet Baked Vidalia Onions (page 180) gratinéed with Parmesan cheese.

And since potatoes are my favorite starch, for both their inherent texture and their versatility, you'll find in this chapter a range of recipes, from Stuffed Baked Potatoes (page 190), which taste rich and creamy, to Garlic Roasted Potatoes (page 193)—my version of French fries.

Cranberry-Glazed Acorn Squash

TOTAL TIME
1½ hours
WORK TIME
10 minutes

PER SERVING
113 calories
5 mg cholesterol
2 g fat
6 mg sodium

Acorn squash is sweet enough to be served in lieu of sweet potatoes. This dish is an ideal holiday vegetable, with the tart, tangy cranberry sauce contrasting its flavor and red color with the vibrant orange squash.   *Serves 6*

2 (¾ pound) acorn squash
½ cup Cranberry Sauce (page 217)
¼ cup freshly squeezed orange juice
1 tablespoon unsalted butter
1 tablespoon finely grated orange zest

1. Preheat the oven to 350 degrees. Place the acorn squash in a baking dish and bake for 1 hour, turning occasionally. When cool enough to handle, cut in half and discard the seeds. Peel and cut the flesh into 1½-inch cubes. Place back in the baking dish.

2. Combine the remaining ingredients in a small saucepan. Place over medium heat and bring to a boil, stirring occasionally. Drizzle the glaze evenly over the squash and place back in the oven for 10 minutes. Serve immediately.

NOTE: The acorn squash can be baked up to two days in advance and kept refrigerated, tightly covered with plastic wrap. Do not glaze it until just before serving, adding five minutes to the baking time.

Artichoke Hearts with Basil and Garlic

Buttery, tender artichoke hearts take well to this Italian method of preparation. This is a vibrant and aromatic dish that goes nicely with fish, meat, or poultry.   *Serves 6*

TOTAL TIME
45 minutes
WORK TIME
10 minutes

PER SERVING
63 calories
0 cholesterol
5 g fat
49 mg sodium

3 cups water
6 large artichokes
2 tablespoons fruity olive oil
1 teaspoon finely minced garlic
2 tablespoons chopped fresh basil *or* ½ teaspoon dried
Pinch of salt
Pinch of freshly ground white pepper

1. Bring the water to a boil over high heat. Holding the artichoke in your free hand, cut off the leaves 1 inch above the heart and discard. Trim the stem. Steam the artichoke hearts for 25 to 30 minutes or until the tip of a knife inserted in the stem meets with no resistance.

2. Remove from the steamer and, when cool enough to handle, take off the remaining leaves, leaving as much pulp attached to the heart as possible. Scrape out the hairy choke from the center with a small spoon and dice the artichoke hearts into 1-inch chunks.

3. Heat the olive oil in a small skillet over medium heat. Add the garlic and basil and sauté, stirring constantly, for 2 minutes. Add the artichoke hearts and sprinkle with salt and pepper. Sauté for 3 more minutes, stirring gently, or until the hearts are heated through. Serve immediately.

NOTE: The artichokes can be steamed up to two days in advance and kept, tightly covered with plastic wrap, in the refrigerator. Do not sauté them until just before serving.

Asian Asparagus

TOTAL TIME
20 minutes
WORK TIME
15 minutes

PER SERVING
41 calories
0 cholesterol
2 g fat
221 mg sodium

Asparagus, one of the harbingers of spring, remains crunchy when prepared in this Asian manner, and the seasoning mixture complements its flavor. The same treatment can be applied to stalks of broccoli, cut into flowerets, with the stalks peeled and sliced.   *Serves 6*

1½ **pounds fresh asparagus**
2 **teaspoons vegetable oil**
¼ **cup water**
Pinch of sugar
1 **garlic clove, peeled and minced**
1 **teaspoon dark sesame oil**
1 **tablespoon reduced-sodium soy sauce**
1 **tablespoon oyster sauce**
1 **tablespoon dry Sherry**
2 **teaspoons rice wine vinegar**
Pinch of crushed red pepper
2 **tablespoons finely chopped scallion, including white and green**

1. Break the hard stems off the asparagus and peel the base of the stem if necessary. Roll-cut the asparagus by slicing the tip off on the diagonal and then, while holding the knife at the same angle, rolling the stalk of asparagus one-quarter turn between cuts. Wash the asparagus pieces and drain well in a colander.

2. Heat the vegetable oil in a wok or large skillet over high heat. When hot, add the asparagus and stir-fry for 1 minute. Add the water and sugar, then cover the pan. Steam the asparagus for 3 minutes, shaking the pan a few times.

3. While the asparagus is steaming, combine the remaining ingredients. Uncover the asparagus pan and cook for an additional minute over high heat to evaporate some of the remaining moisture. Add the seasoning mixture and cook for 1 minute, stirring constantly to coat the pieces. Serve immediately.

NOTE: The timing of this recipe is for thick asparagus spears. If you're using thin stalks, cut back on the steaming time. The asparagus can be cut up to a day in advance and kept refrigerated in a plastic bag.

Brussels Sprouts with Lemon and Parsley

Sometimes the simplest vegetable preparations are the best. Lemon, butter, and parsley—a classic combination—greatly elevate this miniature member of the cabbage family. True to their winter season, these sprouts go well with slowly braised hearty stews. *Serves 6*

2 10-ounce containers fresh Brussels sprouts
1½ tablespoons unsalted butter
¼ cup freshly squeezed lemon juice
¼ cup chopped fresh parsley
¼ teaspoon salt
Pinch of freshly ground pepper

TOTAL TIME
25 minutes
WORK TIME
15 minutes

PER SERVING
65 calories
8 mg cholesterol
3 g fat
113 mg sodium

1. Bring a large pot of water to a boil. Trim the root end of the sprouts, pull off any discolored outer leaves, and cut in half if large. Have a bowl of ice water handy. Cook the sprouts in the boiling water for 8 minutes. Drain briefly in a colander, then plunge into the ice water to stop the cooking action. Drain again, shaking the colander to remove as much excess water as possible.

2. Melt the butter in a skillet over medium heat. Add the sprouts, stirring to coat them, and cook over low heat for 5 minutes, stirring occasionally. Raise the heat to high and toss with the remaining ingredients. Serve immediately.

NOTE: The sprouts can be blanched up to a day in advance and kept refrigerated, covered with plastic wrap. Sauté them just before serving.

Red Cabbage Cooked with Wine

TOTAL TIME
8 hours, including
marinating
WORK TIME
20 minutes

PER SERVING
134 calories
0 cholesterol
3 g fat
115 mg sodium

Sweet-and-sour braised red cabbage is part of the German heritage of robust foods. In addition to the traditional game main dishes it frequently accompanies, this dish is wonderful with roasted poultry or pork.   *Serves 6*

1 2-pound head of red cabbage
⅓ cup red wine vinegar
2 tablespoons sugar
¼ teaspoon salt (omit if using salted canned stock)
¼ teaspoon freshly ground pepper
1 tablespoon vegetable oil
1 cup finely chopped onion
1 apple, peeled and grated
1 cup dry red wine
1 cup chicken stock, preferably unsalted (page 266)
1 cinnamon stick
2 bay leaves
⅓ cup fruit-only red currant or raspberry jam

1. Remove the outer leaves from the cabbage and cut it into quarters. Cut out the core and thinly slice the cabbage. This can be done quickly with a food processor fitted with the slicing disk. Place in a large glass or stainless-steel mixing bowl.

2. Toss the cabbage with the vinegar, sugar, salt, and pepper. Place a plate on top and let the cabbage sit for 6 hours at room temperature or refrigerate overnight.

3. Preheat the oven to 350 degrees. Heat the oil in a large ovenproof casserole over medium heat. Add the onions and sauté, stirring frequently, for 5 minutes. Add the apple and continue to sauté for 3 minutes. Add the cabbage, with any juices that have accumulated, along with the wine, stock, cinnamon, and bay leaves; bring to a boil over high heat. Cover the pan and place in the center of the oven for 1½ hours, stirring occasionally.

4. Remove the pan from the oven and discard the cinnamon stick and bay leaves. Stir in the jam and bring to a boil over medium heat. Cook, stirring frequently, for 15 minutes or until the cabbage is very soft and the juices are syrupy. Serve immediately.

NOTE: The cabbage can be prepared up to three days in advance. Reheat over low heat, stirring often, for 10 minutes.

Sautéed Cucumbers with Dill

This recipe was the result of a felicitous accident. One evening I decided, at the last minute, not to make cream of cucumber soup. The base of sautéed cucumbers, enlivened by the fresh taste of dill, became a delicious vegetable, excellent with grilled fish or roasted poultry. *Serves 6*

TOTAL TIME
20 minutes
WORK TIME
10 minutes

PER SERVING
24 calories
3 mg cholesterol
1 g fat
44 mg sodium

1½ tablespoons unsalted butter
3 large cucumbers, peeled, seeded, and cut into ¼-inch slices
¼ teaspoon salt
Pinch of freshly ground white pepper
3 tablespoons chopped fresh dill *or* 1½ teaspoons dried
2 teaspoons freshly squeezed lemon juice

1. Melt the butter in a covered skillet over medium heat. Add the cucumbers, salt, and pepper and cover the pan. Cook over medium heat, stirring occasionally, for 7 to 10 minutes or until the cucumbers are soft.

2. Raise the heat to high and add the dill. Cook for 5 minutes, stirring frequently. Sprinkle with lemon juice and serve immediately.

NOTE: The cucumbers can be prepared up to six hours in advance. Reheat over low heat, uncovered, for 5 to 7 minutes.

Braised Endive

TOTAL TIME
25 minutes
WORK TIME
10 minutes

PER SERVING
48 calories
8 mg cholesterol
3 g fat
34 mg sodium

The natural pungency of creamy, elegant Belgian endive is tempered by a quick stove-top braising. This is a dramatic vegetable dish that goes well with both hearty meats and delicate seafood and poultry.   *Serves 6*

6 (about 1¼ pounds) Belgian endive
1½ tablespoons unsalted butter
1 teaspoon sugar
2 tablespoons freshly squeezed lemon juice
½ cup chicken stock, preferably unsalted (page 266)
3 tablespoons chopped fresh herbs (any combination of oregano,
   basil, rosemary, marjoram) *or* 2 teaspoons dried
1 tablespoon chopped fresh parsley
Pinch of salt (omit if using salted canned stock)
Pinch of freshly ground white pepper

1. Rinse the endive, pat dry, and trim the root end. Melt the butter in a skillet over medium heat. Add the endive along with the sugar, lemon juice, and chicken stock. Bring to a boil, cover the pan, and braise the endive over low heat for 5 minutes. Turn in quarter turns and braise for total of 20 minutes.

2. Uncover the pan, raise the heat to medium-high, and add the herbs, parsley, salt, and pepper. Cook for an additional few minutes or until the pan juices have reduced by two thirds. Serve immediately.

NOTE: The endive can be prepared up to six hours in advance and kept at room temperature. Reheat over low heat.

Deviled Leeks

Leeks are the most subtle and mildly flavored member of the onion family. These characteristics are amplified not only by a slow braising, but also by contrast with the mustard and Parmesan coating.   Serves 6

TOTAL TIME
35 minutes
WORK TIME
10 minutes

PER SERVING
104 calories
7 mg cholesterol
3 g fat
246 mg sodium

1 tablespoon unsalted butter
12 small leeks, including 2 inches of the green, washed and trimmed (page 271)
3 tablespoons chicken stock, preferably unsalted (page 266)
¼ cup white wine
1 tablespoon chopped fresh marjoram *or* ½ teaspoon dried
Pinch of freshly ground white pepper
2 tablespoons Dijon mustard
⅓ cup plain bread crumbs
2 tablespoons freshly grated Parmesan cheese

1. Preheat the oven to 375 degrees. Melt the butter in a large skillet over medium heat. Add the leeks and sauté for 5 minutes. Add the stock, wine, marjoram, and pepper and bring to a boil. Cover the pan, reduce the heat to low, and cook the leeks for 10 minutes, rolling them over occasionally.
2. Arrange the leeks in a baking dish and pour the braising liquid over them. Spread them evenly with the mustard and sprinkle with bread crumbs and Parmesan. Place in the center of the oven and bake, uncovered, for 10 minutes. Serve immediately.

NOTE: The leeks can be braised up to two days in advance. Do not brown them until just before serving.

Baked Vidalia Onions

TOTAL TIME
1 hour
WORK TIME
10 minutes

PER SERVING
48 calories
1 mg cholesterol
1 g fat
36 mg sodium

While most people associate Georgia with peaches, my favorite crop from the state are the incredibly sweet Vidalia onions that come to market in May and June. This wine-and-stock braising highlights their flavor beautifully. Alternatives, although they're not quite as sweet, are Walla Walla onions from Washington state or Maui onions from Hawaii.   *Serves 6*

6 Vidalia, Walla Walla, or Maui onions
1 cup chicken stock, preferably unsalted (page 266)
½ cup dry white wine
Pinch of freshly ground white pepper
1 teaspoon chopped fresh rosemary *or* ¼ teaspoon dried
½ teaspoon chopped fresh thyme *or* pinch of dried
2 tablespoons freshly grated Parmesan cheese

1. Preheat the oven to 375 degrees. Peel the onions, trimming the root and cutting a slice off the top so they will sit flat. Place the onions in a baking dish just large enough to hold them, such as a 9- by 13-inch dish, with the root ends up.

2. Combine the chicken stock, wine, pepper, rosemary, and thyme. Pour over the onions, cover the baking pan with foil, and bake in the center of the oven for 30 minutes. Turn the onions so that the root ends are down and bake an additional 20 minutes.

3. Pour off all but a few tablespoons of the braising liquid. (Reserve it for the next time you make stock, since it adds a depth of flavor.) Sprinkle the onions with Parmesan cheese and return to the oven for 5 minutes. Serve immediately.

NOTE: The onions can be baked up to two days in advance to the point of sprinkling with the cheese. Reheat them in a 300-degree oven, then drain the braising liquid and sprinkle with cheese.

Spaghetti Squash au Gratin

Spaghetti squash is a recent addition to the produce department, and it can be sauced as one would spaghetti or treated as one would any squash. It's very high in fiber and as low in calories as any of its better-known relatives. This dish can be served as a vegetable or in place of a starch.   *Serves 6*

1 2-pound spaghetti squash
2 tablespoons chopped fresh marjoram *or* ½ teaspoon dried
¼ teaspoon freshly ground white pepper
Pinch of salt
1 tablespoon freshly grated Parmesan cheese

1. Place a couple of inches of water in a deep pot, insert a vegetable steamer, and bring to a boil over high heat. Cut the squash into quarters and scrape out the seeds. Place the quarters in the steamer flesh side down and steam for 20 to 30 minutes or until your finger leaves an impression on the shell.

2. Remove from the steamer and, when cool enough to handle, take a table fork and gently "comb" the squash lengthwise into a mixing bowl. The strands will fall into your bowl like pieces of spaghetti.

3. Preheat the broiler. Combine the squash with the marjoram, pepper, and salt. Place in a 1-quart baking dish and sprinkle with Parmesan cheese. Place under the broiler for 2 minutes and serve immediately.

NOTE: The squash can be prepared through step 2 up to two days in advance. Keep it refrigerated, covered with plastic wrap, and reheat it covered in a 350-degree oven for 15 minutes.

TOTAL TIME
45 minutes
WORK TIME
10 minutes

PER SERVING
60 calories
0 cholesterol
1 g fat
122 mg sodium

Spaghetti Squash Primavera

TOTAL TIME
1 hour
WORK TIME
20 minutes

PER SERVING
93 calories
7 mg cholesterol
3 g fat
201 mg sodium

Colorful *pasta primavera* seems like an Italian classic, but it's the invention of Sirio Maccioni of New York's Le Cirque. Here the concept is transformed by using spaghetti squash in lieu of pasta. For the small quantities of vegetables used with the spaghetti squash, it's easier to buy them already prepped at the salad bar of the supermarket. *Serves 6*

1 2-pound spaghetti squash
1 cup broccoli flowerets
1 cup cauliflower flowerets
1 carrot, peeled and sliced
1 green bell pepper, seeds and ribs removed (page 269), cut into thin strips
1 red bell pepper, seeds and ribs removed (page 269), cut into thin strips
½ cup grated low-fat (part skim milk) mozzarella cheese
½ cup chicken stock, preferably unsalted (page 266)
2 tablespoons freshly grated Parmesan cheese
2 tablespoons chopped fresh basil *or* 1½ teaspoons dried
¼ teaspoon salt (omit if using salted canned stock)
Pinch of freshly ground white pepper

1. Place a couple of inches of water in a deep pot, insert a vegetable steamer, and bring to a boil over high heat. Cut the squash into quarters and scrape out the seeds. Place the quarters in the steamer flesh side down and steam for 20 to 30 minutes or until your finger leaves an impression on the shell. Five minutes before the squash will be finished, add the broccoli, cauliflower, carrot, green pepper, and red pepper to the steamer. Have ready a bowl of ice water.

2. Remove from the steamer and plunge all the vegetables except the squash into ice water to stop the cooking action. Then drain and set aside. When the squash is cool enough to handle, take a table fork and gently "comb" it lengthwise into a mixing bowl. The strands will fall into your bowl like pieces of spaghetti.

3. Combine the remaining ingredients in a large saucepan. Bring to a boil over medium heat, stirring frequently, until the cheese has melted.

4. Add the spaghetti squash and other vegetables to the pan and heat over medium heat until the mixture is hot, stirring gently. Serve immediately.

NOTE: The vegetables and sauce can be prepared up to a day in advance and kept refrigerated, tightly covered with plastic wrap. Heat the sauce, then add the vegetables.

Creamed Spinach

TOTAL TIME
20 minutes
WORK TIME
20 minutes

PER SERVING
87 calories
7 mg cholesterol
3 g fat
311 mg sodium

Creamed spinach is a traditional favorite to accompany baked or grilled meat or poultry. This version enhances the creamy texture with the robust flavors of cheese.   *Serves 6*

4 pounds fresh spinach, washed and stemmed, *or* **2 10-ounce packages frozen leaf spinach, defrosted**
2 teaspoons unsalted butter
¼ cup finely chopped onion
2 teaspoons flour
½ cup skim milk
¼ cup low-fat (part skim milk) mozzarella cheese
1 tablespoon freshly grated Parmesan cheese
Pinch of freshly ground white pepper
¼ teaspoon salt

1. Place a large skillet over high heat. Add handfuls of the spinach, turning it with a spatula as it wilts. It will take about 5 minutes to wilt all the spinach. Transfer to a colander to drain, pressing with the back of a spoon to extract some of the liquid. If you're using defrosted frozen spinach, drain it in a colander.

2. In a 2-quart saucepan, melt the butter over medium-low heat. Add the onion and sauté, stirring frequently, for 7 minutes or until the onions are soft. Stir in the flour and sauté, stirring constantly, for 2 minutes. Raise the heat to medium and whisk in the remaining ingredients. Bring to a boil, whisking until smooth.

3. Add the spinach and stir until it returns to a boil. Serve immediately.

NOTE: You can cook the spinach and sauce up to a day in advance and keep them refrigerated, covered with plastic wrap. The flavor of the dish remains fresher, however, if they are combined and heated just before serving.

Spinach Soufflé

Light in texture and bright green in color, this soufflé is a showstopper to accompany a simple entree, or it can be a lunch all by itself.   Serves 6

TOTAL TIME
50 minutes
WORK TIME
15 minutes

PER SERVING
76 calories
8 mg cholesterol
3 g fat
55 mg sodium

Softened butter for the *soufflé* dish
⅓ cup plain bread crumbs
1 10-ounce package frozen chopped spinach, defrosted
1 tablespoon unsalted butter
2 tablespoons flour
½ cup skim milk
Pinch of freshly ground white pepper
3 tablespoons freshly grated Parmesan cheese
6 egg whites

1. Preheat the oven to 400 degrees. Grease the inside of a 6-cup *soufflé* dish and coat the interior with bread crumbs, shaking over the sink to remove any excess. Place the spinach in a strainer and push with the back of a spoon to extract as much liquid as possible. Set aside.

2. Melt the butter in a small saucepan over low heat. Add the flour and cook, stirring constantly, over low heat for 3 minutes to cook the flour. Whisk in the milk, pepper, and cheese and bring to a boil, whisking constantly, until thick. Stir in the spinach and set aside.

3. Place the egg whites in a totally grease-free bowl and beat at medium speed until frothy. Increase the speed to high and beat until stiff peaks form. Gently fold the spinach mixture into the egg whites and scrape into the prepared *soufflé* dish. Place in the center of the oven and immediately reduce the temperature to 375 degrees. Bake for 35 to 45 minutes, until the *soufflé* has puffed and the top is brown; the baking time depends on whether you like *soufflés* wet or dry in the center. Serve immediately.

NOTE: The spinach base can be prepared up to six hours in advance. Do not beat the egg whites or bake the *soufflé* until immediately before serving.

Green Beans with Prosciutto

TOTAL TIME
25 minutes
WORK TIME
15 minutes

PER SERVING
71 calories
3 mg cholesterol
3 g fat
85 mg sodium

The savory, smoky flavor of the ham melds with the vegetables to form a robust sauce for green beans. Serve this with grilled poultry or meats for a hearty addition to a meal.   *Serves 6*

1½ pounds green beans, washed, stemmed, and cut into 2-inch pieces
1 tablespoon vegetable oil
2 garlic cloves, peeled and minced
½ cup finely chopped red onion
4 tablespoons finely chopped (about 1 ounce) *prosciutto* or Smithfield ham
½ cup peeled, seeded, and finely diced tomato (page 271)
1 tablespoon chopped fresh oregano *or* ½ teaspoon dried
Pinch of freshly ground black pepper
2 teaspoons freshly squeezed lemon juice

1. Have a bowl of ice water handy. Place the beans in a vegetable steamer and place in a deep pot with a couple of inches of water. Bring to a boil over high heat and steam the beans for 4 minutes. Remove the steamer from the pot and plunge the beans into the ice water to stop the cooking action and set the color. When cool, drain and set aside.

2. Heat the oil in a skillet over medium heat. Add the garlic and onions and sauté, stirring often, for 5 to 7 minutes or until the onions are soft.

3. Add the *prosciutto*, tomatoes, and oregano; sauté 2 minutes. Return the beans to the pan and heat through. Sprinkle with pepper and lemon juice and serve immediately.

NOTE: This recipe also tastes delicious made with cauliflower or broccoli flowerets or Italian broccoli rabe. The beans can be blanched and the sauce can be prepared up to a day in advance, kept separately in the refrigerator. Reheat the sauce over low heat, then add the beans to reheat.

Stuffed Zucchini

A few of these sections standing vertically on a plate are far more dramatic than the traditional presentation of a horizontally halved zucchini. The filling is creamy and a vivid green tone. The vegetable works well with any simple entree.   Serves 6

TOTAL TIME
45 minutes

WORK TIME
20 minutes

PER SERVING
80 calories
7 mg cholesterol
4 g fat
211 mg sodium

3 medium (1½ pounds) zucchini
1 tablespoon olive oil
½ cup finely chopped onion
1 pound fresh spinach, washed and stemmed
½ cup grated low-fat (part skim milk) mozzarella cheese
Pinch of freshly ground white pepper
Pinch of freshly grated nutmeg
¼ teaspoon salt
2 tablespoons freshly grated Parmesan cheese

1. Have a bowl of ice water handy. Bring a pot of water to a boil and parboil the zucchini for 5 minutes or until the flesh yields slightly but is not mushy. Plunge the zucchini into the ice water to stop the cooking action and set the color.

2. When cool, trim the ends from the zucchini and cut each into 4 equal lengths. Using a melon baller, scrape out the pulp, leaving a ¼-inch shell on the sides and ½ inch on one end. Chop the pulp and set aside.

3. Heat the olive oil in a 12-inch skillet over medium heat. Add the onions and sauté, stirring frequently, for 5 minutes or until the onions are translucent. Add the zucchini pulp and sauté for 5 minutes more. Raise the heat to high and add the spinach. Sauté, stirring often, for 2 minutes; it will wilt almost instantly and radically decrease in volume.

4. Preheat the oven to 350 degrees. Using a slotted spoon, transfer the mixture to a blender or food processor fitted with the steel blade. Add the mozzarella, pepper, nutmeg, and salt. Puree until smooth, then fill the zucchini sections with the mixture.

5. Stand the zucchini sections on a baking sheet and sprinkle with Parmesan cheese. Place in the center of the oven for 15 minutes. Serve immediately.

NOTE: You can make the stuffed zucchini up to two days in advance and keep them refrigerated, tightly covered with plastic wrap. Allow them to sit at room temperature for two hours before baking.

Potato Onion Pudding

I've never met a potato I didn't like, and this creamy, rich-tasting pudding is one of my favorite ways of eating potatoes. It's almost like the filling of a potato *knish*, with the taste of the browned onions throughout and the contrast of the crunchy crust with the creamy pudding.   Serves 6

TOTAL TIME
2 hours
WORK TIME
20 minutes

PER SERVING
203 calories
54 mg cholesterol
5 g fat
213 mg sodium

4 large Idaho baking potatoes
1 tablespoon unsalted butter
2 cups coarsely chopped onion
¾ cup low-fat (part skim milk) mozzarella cheese
½ cup skim milk
2 tablespoons chicken stock, preferably unsalted (page 266)
1 egg
¼ teaspoon freshly ground black pepper
¼ teaspoon salt

1. Preheat the oven to 400 degrees. Wash the potatoes and prick several times with a sharp meat fork. Bake in the center of the oven for 50 to 60 minutes or until soft. Remove from the oven, split in half, and scrape the potato pulp into a bowl.

2. While the potatoes are baking, melt the butter in a 12-inch skillet or sauté pan over medium-high heat. Add the onions and sauté, stirring frequently, for 20 minutes or until the onions are well browned and caramelized. Set aside.

3. Lower the oven temperature to 375 degrees. Combine the potato pulp and browned onions with the remaining ingredients. Beat until smooth with a hand mixer or in a food processor fitted with the steel blade. If you're using a food processor, do not add the onions until the other ingredients are smooth, then add them and pulse on and off to incorporate without pureeing them. Scrape the mixture into a lightly oiled 8- by 8-inch baking dish or a 6-cup *soufflé* dish.

4. Bake in the center of the oven for 30 minutes or until the pudding is slightly puffed and browned. Serve immediately.

NOTE: The pudding can be prepared through step 3 up to two days in advance and kept refrigerated, tightly covered with plastic wrap. Either allow it to reach room temperature or add five minutes to the baking time.

Stuffed Baked Potatoes

TOTAL TIME
1½ hours
WORK TIME
15 minutes

PER SERVING
130 calories
3 mg cholesterol
1 g fat
273 mg sodium

These creamy potatoes fool people. The orange tone leads you to think they're filled with Cheddar cheese, then the flavor conveys all the richness of a potato stuffed with sour cream and chives. They are the perfect side dish for any grilled or broiled meat or poultry.   *Serves 6*

3 large Idaho baking potatoes
¾ cup chicken stock, preferably unsalted (page 266)
½ cup finely chopped onion
3 garlic cloves, peeled and finely minced
1½ teaspoons paprika
¼ teaspoon cayenne pepper
½ teaspoon salt (use only ¼ teaspoon if using salted canned stock)
1 cup plain nonfat yogurt
½ cup minced chives
3 tablespoons freshly grated Parmesan cheese

1. Preheat the oven to 400 degrees. Scrub the potatoes with a stiff brush and prick them in several places with a meat fork. Bake in the center of the oven for 1 hour or until tender when pierced with a knife.

2. While the potatoes are baking, place the chicken stock, onion, and garlic in a small saucepan. Bring to a boil over medium heat and simmer, uncovered, for 10 minutes, stirring occasionally.

THE GOURMET GAZELLE COOKBOOK

3. Remove the potatoes from the oven and cut in half. Scrape the pulp into a bowl, reserving the shells. Add the onion mixture along with the remaining ingredients except Parmesan. Beat with an electric mixer until light and fluffy.

4. Stuff the potato mixture back into the shells, with either a spoon or a pastry bag fitted with a large tip. Sprinkle with Parmesan cheese and place back in the oven for 10 minutes. Serve immediately.

NOTE: The potatoes can be stuffed up to two days in advance. To cook straight from the refrigerator, preheat the oven to 375 degrees and bake for 20 to 25 minutes.

New Potatoes with Rosemary

TOTAL TIME
50 minutes
WORK TIME
5 minutes

PER SERVING
132 calories
0 cholesterol
5 g fat
44 mg sodium

Tender, buttery new potatoes are enhanced by the bright flavor of fresh rosemary. Serve this dish with poached or roasted poultry or fish; it is also delicious with grilled lamb.   *Serves 6*

1½ pounds small red potatoes
2 tablespoons olive oil
¼ teaspoon salt
Pinch of freshly ground white pepper
2 tablespoons chopped fresh rosemary *or* **1 teaspoon dried**

1. Preheat the oven to 350 degrees. Scrub the potatoes and spread the olive oil in an ovenproof casserole. Thinly slice the potatoes and toss with the oil to coat them. Sprinkle with the seasonings, cover the casserole, and bake in the center of the oven for 45 minutes, turning gently after 20 minutes. Serve immediately.

NOTE: The potatoes can also be cooked with a combination of herbs, such as oregano, basil, marjoram, and parsley. They can be prepared up to six hours in advance and reheated in the oven for 15 minutes.

Garlic Roasted Potatoes

These potatoes attain the same golden, crunchy crust as ones that are deep-fried, and the garlic is a delicious addition. They are a wonderful side dish for any baked or grilled meat or poultry item.   Serves 6

TOTAL TIME
40 minutes
WORK TIME
10 minutes

PER SERVING
177 calories
0 cholesterol
4 g fat
193 mg sodium

6 medium baking potatoes
2 tablespoons olive oil
1 tablespoon minced garlic
½ teaspoon salt
½ teaspoon freshly ground black pepper

1. Preheat the oven to 450 degrees. Place a nonstick or lightly greased baking sheet in the oven to preheat.

2. Peel the potatoes and cut each lengthwise down the center and then into 2-inch cubes. Toss the potato cubes with the remaining ingredients. Lay the cubes on the baking sheet and bake for 30 minutes, turning them with a strong spatula a few times so that all sides brown. Serve immediately.

NOTE: For a different look, you can used 18 quartered small new potatoes, scrubbing them and leaving the skins attached.

Grilled Polenta

TOTAL TIME
3 hours, including chilling
WORK TIME
30 minutes

PER SERVING
103 calories
1 mg cholesterol
3 g fat
53 mg sodium

I've often thought that the person actually cooking the polenta loses weight in the process, due to the energy involved in beating the thick dough. Most of the work for this recipe can be done in advance. The chicken stock and grilled taste enhance the polenta, a classic Italian dish, served alone or topped with sauce.   *Serves 6*

2½ cups chicken stock, preferably unsalted (page 266)
¾ cup polenta or very finely ground yellow cornmeal
2 tablespoons freshly grated Parmesan cheese
1 tablespoon vegetable oil

1. Bring the stock to a boil in a heavy-bottomed 4-quart sauce-pan over high heat. Slowly stir in the polenta, whisking constantly to prevent lumps from forming. It will become thick almost instantly.

2. Reduce the heat so that the mixture is barely simmering and beat with a heavy whisk or wooden spoon for 20 to 30 minutes or until it forms a mass in the middle of the pot and the spoon can stand straight up.

3. Remove from the heat and beat in the Parmesan cheese. Oil a 9- by 13-inch baking dish and spoon the mixture into it. Smooth with a spatula or oil your hands and smooth when cool enough to touch.

4. Brush the top with oil and place, uncovered, in the refrigerator to chill for at least 2 hours.

5. Preheat a charcoal or gas grill. Cut the polenta into square or diamond shapes and place on the hot grill. Turn carefully after 2 minutes and grill on the other side for 2 minutes. Serve immediately.

NOTE: The recipe can be made up to two days in advance through step 4. Grill the polenta just before serving.

Mushroom Barley Casserole

This hearty casserole, flavored with wild mushrooms, complements any grilled or broiled main dish. It's also good for buffet parties since the recipe can be multiplied with no adjustments needed.   *Serves 6*

TOTAL TIME
1 hour
WORK TIME
15 minutes

PER SERVING
113 calories
0 cholesterol
4 g fat
151 mg sodium

6 dried mushrooms (such as morels, *shiitake,* or *porcini*)
1 cup boiling water
½ cup pearl barley
1½ tablespoons unsalted butter
2 ounces fresh *shiitake* mushrooms, washed, stemmed, and sliced
¼ pound fresh mushrooms, washed and sliced
1 carrot, peeled and diced
6 shallots, peeled and chopped
1 tablespoon chopped fresh parsley
2 cups beef or veal stock, preferably unsalted (page 267)
¼ teaspoon freshly ground pepper
¼ teaspoon salt (omit if using salted canned stock)

1. Soak the dried mushrooms in the boiling water for 15 minutes. Drain, reserving the soaking liquid, and rub the mushrooms with your fingers under cold running water to remove any grit that might be clinging to them. Chop the mushrooms and strain the soaking liquid through a sieve lined with a paper coffee filter or cheesecloth. Set aside. Rinse the barley in a strainer and set aside.

2. Preheat the oven to 375 degrees. Melt the butter over medium heat in a heavy 2-quart ovenproof casserole. Add the *shiitake,* mushrooms, carrot, and shallots. Sauté, stirring frequently, for 5 minutes. Add the barley and stir for 1 minute to coat the grains. Add the reserved mushroom soaking liquid and remaining ingredients. Bring to a boil, cover the casserole, and place in the center of the oven for 20 minutes. Stir, adding more liquid if the mixture seems dry, and return to the oven for 10 minutes. Serve immediately.

NOTE: The recipe can be prepared up to two days in advance. Reheat in a 300-degree oven, sprinkling about ¼ cup of water over the mixture so that it doesn't dry out.

Parsley Rice Pilaf

TOTAL TIME
30 minutes
WORK TIME
10 minutes

PER SERVING
117 calories
4 mg cholesterol
2 g fat
94 mg sodium

Parsley gives this versatile dish its fresh flavor, and the vegetables add depth and nutrients as they subtract calories. It elevates all simple entrees.   *Serves 8*

1 tablespoon unsalted butter
1 cup finely chopped onion
½ cup finely chopped celery
½ cup finely chopped green pepper
1 cup long-grain white rice
2½ cups chicken stock, preferably unsalted (page 266)
½ cup chopped fresh parsley
½ teaspoon chopped fresh tarragon *or* pinch of dried
Pinch of freshly ground white pepper
¼ teaspoon salt (omit if using salted canned stock)

1. Melt the butter over medium heat in a 2-quart saucepan. Add the onion, celery, and green pepper; sauté, stirring frequently, for 5 minutes or until the onions are translucent. Add the rice and sauté for 2 minutes to coat the grains, stirring constantly.

2. Stir in the remaining ingredients. Bring to a boil, then cover the pan, reduce the heat, and simmer for 20 minutes or until the rice is soft and the liquid has been absorbed. Serve immediately.

NOTE: The rice can be made up to two days in advance and reheated over low heat or in a 300-degree oven, stirring often.

Braised Wild Rice with Pine Nuts

The naturally nutty flavor of wild rice is brought out by the crunchy pine nuts. In addition to being a wonderful side dish with any hearty roasted meat or poultry, this is also a useful stuffing for whole chickens or turkeys.   *Serves 6*

TOTAL TIME
2 hours
WORK TIME
10 minutes

PER SERVING
135 calories
5 mg cholesterol
5 g fat
121 mg sodium

¾ cup wild rice
1 tablespoon unsalted butter
½ cup diced onion
½ cup diced carrot
2½ to 3 cups chicken stock, preferably unsalted (page 266)
1 sprig fresh thyme *or* pinch of dried
1 bay leaf
¼ teaspoon freshly ground black pepper
¼ teaspoon salt (omit if using salted canned stock)
3 tablespoons pine nuts, toasted in a 325-degree oven for 7 to 10
   minutes or until lightly browned

1. Preheat the oven to 325 degrees. Place the wild rice in a strainer and rinse under cold running water about 2 minutes, until the water runs clear. Shake the strainer to remove as much excess water as possible. Melt the butter over medium heat in a 2-quart ovenproof casserole and add the onion, carrot, and wild rice. Sauté over medium heat, stirring constantly, for 3 minutes. Add the remaining ingredients except the pine nuts and bring to a boil.

2. Cover the casserole and place in the center of the oven for 1 to 1½ hours or until the rice is very fluffy and tender and has absorbed the liquid. Stir occasionally, adding more stock if the rice becomes dry before it is fluffy. Serve immediately, garnishing each serving with some of the pine nuts.

NOTE: The rice can be made up to two days in advance and reheated in a 300-degree oven for 15 to 20 minutes, stirring occasionally. Do not add pine nuts until just before serving, or they will become soggy.

Sweet Potatoes and Apples

TOTAL TIME
1½ hours
WORK TIME
15 minutes

PER SERVING
195 calories
0 cholesterol
.5 g fat
18 mg sodium

This candied sweet potato recipe is just as delicious as its fattening cousins, made the traditional way with a lot of butter. The spicing is complemented by the rum, and the apples add their flavor and also cut back on the total calories.   *Serves 6*

2 pounds sweet potatoes
2 large cooking apples
¼ cup dark rum
¼ cup dark brown sugar
2 tablespoons molasses
¼ teaspoon ground cinnamon
¼ teaspoon freshly grated nutmeg

1. Preheat the oven to 400 degrees. Scrub the sweet potatoes, prick them with a fork, and bake them on the upper rack until tender—30 to 45 minutes, depending on size. Remove from the oven and, when cool enough to handle, peel away the skin with a paring knife. Cut into halves lengthwise and place in a lightly greased ovenproof casserole just large enough to hold them in one layer.

2. Peel the apples and cut into sixths. Slice each section into thin slices. Combine the apples in a saucepan with the remaining ingredients. Bring to a boil over medium heat and cook the mixture, stirring frequently, for 5 minutes.

3. Reduce the oven temperature down to 375 degrees. Pour the apple mixture over the sweet potatoes and bake for 15 minutes, spooning the juices over the potatoes a few times. Serve immediately.

NOTE: The potatoes can also be made a day in advance and reheated, covered with aluminum foil, in a 350-degree oven, or the dish can be assembled up to six hours in advance and then baked just before serving.

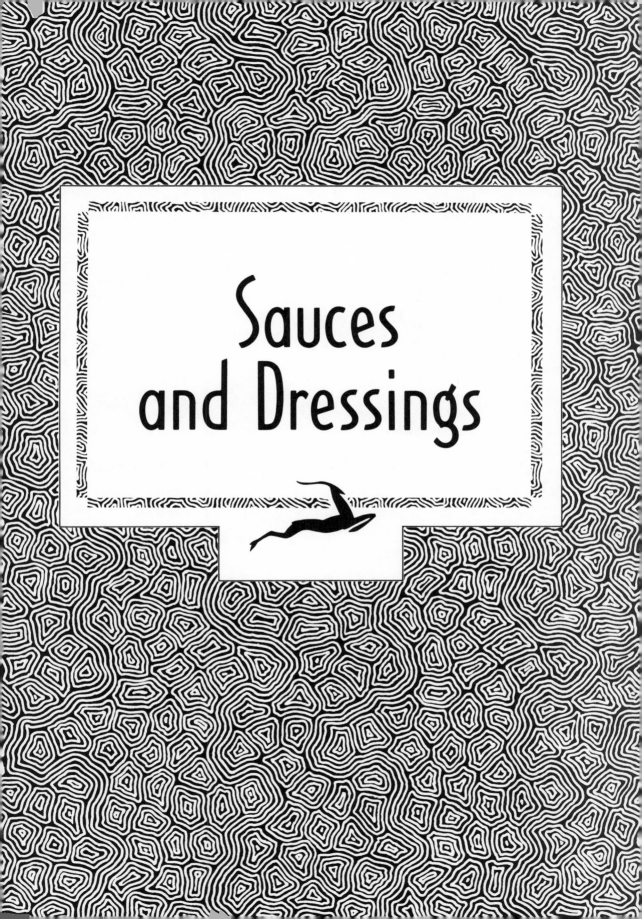

Sauces
and Dressings

Herbed Tomato Sauce
Smoked Tomato Sauce
Veal Sauce
Onion Sauce
Basil Sauce
Fresh Tomato Salsa
Cucumber Sauce
Spinach Sauce
Pear Dressing
Yogurt Dill Dressing
Blue Cheese Dressing
Rosemary Vinaigrette
Balsamic Vinaigrette
Ginger Dressing
Celery Seed Dressing
Applesauce
Cranberry Sauce
Red Onion Marmalade

What can make the difference between an ordinary meal and one that's truly special are the small touches—the salad dressing that excites the palate rather than merely coating the greens, the sauce topping a simple piece of grilled fish that enhances its flavor, or the pasta sauce that thickly coats the strands with aromatic richness.

Dressings are no more difficult than shaking a jar, and the difference between using fresh ingredients—be it garlic, rosemary, or ginger—rather than processed is noticeable.

The dressings included in this chapter derive their flavor from a dominant ingredient, so they make a strong statement and turn even a wedge of iceberg lettuce into something satisfying and interesting. The Yogurt Dill Dressing (page 210) and Blue Cheese Dressing (page 211) can also be used as a dip for vegetable *crudités*, and the Pear Dressing (page 210) can be used to enliven fruit salads as well as tossed greens.

Since salad dressings can be kept for up to a week, make a few to begin your week and then alternate to suit your fancy.

While the Veal Sauce (page 204), thick and rich with a combination of fresh and woodsy dried mushrooms, is intended primarily to be served atop pasta, many of the other sauces serve multiple uses. The Onion Sauce (page 205), containing the same hearty flavor as a bowl of steaming onion soup, is at home on steak as well as spaghetti, and the Herbed Tomato Sauce (page 202), blending wine and thyme with the tomatoes, can be used on meat, fish, or poultry.

Sauces serving as a relish are also included in this chapter. It would not be Thanksgiving without Cranberry Sauce (page 217), and Applesauce (page 216) accompanies a number of traditional meals, as well as doing double duty for dessert on occasion. In these versions of the American standards, the flavor of the fruits is allowed to be the star, subtly enhanced with liquors and wines.

Developing recipes always reflects personal taste preferences and usually produces a few special favorites of which the cook never tires. The Red Onion Marmalade (page 218) is such a dish. While it is intended as a special garnish, I have literally eaten it for lunch. And Smoked Tomato Sauce (page 203) creates such wonderful anticipatory aromas as it simmers, you'll be prepared for the luscious taste it imparts to any grilled entree.

Herbed Tomato Sauce

TOTAL TIME
40 minutes
WORK TIME
15 minutes

PER SERVING
99 calories
0 cholesterol
4 g fat
502 mg sodium

The combination of wine and thyme with the tomatoes is subtle yet stunning. You can use this thick sauce to top pasta and include anything from leftover diced chicken to crab meat as a protein; it can also be used on grilled or poached fish, chicken, or even hamburgers.   *Makes 6 cups or 8¾ cup servings*

3 28-ounce cans Italian plum tomatoes
2 tablespoons olive oil
1 large onion, peeled and chopped
2 garlic cloves, peeled and minced
⅓ cup dry red wine
1 tablespoon chopped fresh thyme *or* 1 teaspoon dried
Pinch of freshly ground black pepper
Pinch of salt

1. Drain the tomatoes, reserving the liquid to add to a stock. Seed and chop them finely.

2. Heat the oil in a 4-quart saucepan over medium heat. Add the onion and garlic and sauté, stirring frequently, for 5 minutes or until the onions are translucent.

3. Add the tomatoes and remaining ingredients. Bring to a boil, reduce the heat to a simmer, and cook the sauce until it is thick and reduced by one third, about 20 to 25 minutes. Stir frequently as the sauce thickens to make sure it does not stick to the pot.

NOTE: The sauce can be prepared up to five days in advance or frozen for up to three months.

Smoked Tomato Sauce

The tantalizing smoked flavor—use mesquite chips if possible—comes through in every bite of this sauce, which is essentially a cooked *salsa*. It can be used for topping baked, grilled, or broiled meat, fish, or poultry.   *Makes 6 cups or 8 ¾-cup servings*

TOTAL TIME
1 hour
WORK TIME
25 minutes

PER SERVING
76 calories
0 cholesterol
2 g fat
143 mg sodium

8 large ripe tomatoes
1 head of garlic
1 red bell pepper
3 medium onions, halved
2 canned green chilies, drained
2 tablespoons freshly squeezed lime juice
1 tablespoon olive oil
2 tablespoons chopped fresh oregano *or* 1 teaspoon dried
2 tablespoons chopped fresh parsley
¼ teaspoon cayenne pepper
Pinch of salt

1. Light a covered charcoal grill. Soak wood chips, preferably mesquite, in water for 20 minutes. When the coals are prepared, push them to one side of the grill and place the wood chips on top. Place the tomatoes and whole head of garlic on the side of the grill not over the coals and place the red pepper and onions directly over the heat. Cover the grill. Turn the pepper to char all sides and turn the onions after 15 minutes. Smoke the vegetables for a total of 30 minutes.

2. Remove the vegetables from the grill. Peel the onions; peel, core, and seed the tomatoes. Peel the pepper (see page 269) and pop 2 cloves of garlic from the head; they will pop out of the skin.

3. Place all the vegetables, along with the remaining ingredients, in a blender or food processor fitted with the steel blade. Puree until smooth.

4. Pour the puree into a 2-quart saucepan and bring to a boil over medium heat. Lower the heat and simmer the sauce, uncovered, for 15 minutes, stirring frequently. Remove from heat and refrigerate until ready to use.

NOTE: This sauce will keep in a tightly covered jar for up to a week or can be frozen for up to three months.

Veal Sauce

TOTAL TIME
1 hour
WORK TIME
25 minutes

PER SERVING
140 calories
44 mg cholesterol
8 g fat
100 mg sodium

The woodsy flavor of wild mushrooms gives this hearty sauce a complex taste. Its deep color and thick consistency belie its low calorie count.   *Serves 6*

1 cup water
½ ounce dried *porcini*
1 pound lean veal, trimmed of all fat and ground
1 pound fresh mushrooms, cleaned and quartered
2 medium carrots, peeled and sliced
2 medium onions, peeled and sliced
1 cup sliced celery
3 garlic cloves, peeled and minced
5 cups chicken or veal stock, preferably unsalted (page 267)
2 tablespoons salt-free tomato paste
1 tablespoon chopped fresh rosemary *or* ½ teaspoon dried
2 tablespoons chopped fresh oregano *or* 1 teaspoon dried
2 teaspoons cornstarch mixed with ¼ cup cold water

1. Bring the water to a boil in a small saucepan and add the dried mushrooms, pushing them down into the water. Allow them to soften for 15 minutes, then drain, reserving the soaking liquid. Wash the mushrooms under cold running water, rubbing with your fingers to remove any grit that is clinging, and strain the soaking liquid through a sieve lined with a coffee filter or cheesecloth.

2. Place the veal in a heavy 3-quart saucepan over medium-high heat. Sauté the veal, stirring to break it up into small pieces, for 5 minutes. Add the mushrooms, carrots, onions, celery, and garlic. Sauté, stirring frequently, for 5 more minutes.

3. Add the chicken stock, tomato paste, half the rosemary, half the oregano, and the reserved soaking liquid; bring to a boil over high heat, stirring to distribute the tomato paste. Lower the heat and simmer the sauce, uncovered, for 25 to 30 minutes or until reduced by half.

4. Add the cornstarch mixture to the sauce along with the remaining herbs and simmer for 2 minutes more or until thickened. Serve immediately.

NOTE: The sauce can be made up to three days in advance and kept refrigerated, tightly covered with plastic wrap. It can also be frozen for up to six months.

Onion Sauce

While this robust, thick sauce is an alternative to tomato sauce for pasta, it is equally good topping for any grilled or broiled meat or poultry. The long cooking of the onions brings out their natural sweetness, and the fresh herbs added just before serving add pungency.   *Serves 6*

TOTAL TIME
1 hour
WORK TIME
15 minutes

PER SERVING
157 calories
3 mg cholesterol
8 g fat
125 mg sodium

2 tablespoons olive oil
3 pounds yellow onions, peeled and thinly sliced
2 teaspoons sugar
4 garlic cloves, peeled and minced
6 cups veal stock, preferably unsalted (page 267)
4 tablespoons freshly grated Parmesan cheese
1 tablespoon chopped fresh marjoram *or* ½ teaspoon dried
2 teaspoons chopped fresh thyme *or* ¼ teaspoon dried
3 tablespoons chopped fresh parsley
2 tablespoons sherry vinegar

1. Heat the oil in a heavy-bottomed 4-quart saucepan over medium heat. Add the onions, tossing to coat them well. Cover the pan and sweat the onions, stirring occasionally, for 20 minutes.

2. Stir in the sugar and garlic. Raise the heat to medium-high and caramelize the onions for 15 minutes or until brown, stirring frequently. Add the veal stock and reduce by half.

3. Stir in the remaining ingredients and serve immediately.

NOTE: The sauce will last for a week, tightly covered and refrigerated, or it can be frozen for up to three months.

Basil Sauce

TOTAL TIME
10 minutes
WORK TIME
10 minutes

PER SERVING
98 calories
2 mg cholesterol
1 g fat
73 mg sodium

Bright green and perfumed with fresh basil, this sauce has as its base the flavor characteristics of traditional *pesto* sauce. Use it on hot or cold pasta, to top poached chicken or fish, or create a cold pasta salad with other vegetables and poached chicken breast. *Serves 6*

3 garlic cloves, peeled
1½ cups fresh basil leaves, washed and stemmed
1 cucumber, peeled, seeded, and sliced
½ green bell pepper, seeds and ribs removed (page 269), sliced
½ yellow bell pepper, seeds and ribs removed (page 269), or sliced green pepper
6 scallions, trimmed, including 2 inches of the green
¼ cup red wine vinegar
3 tablespoons olive oil
3 tablespoons freshly grated Parmesan cheese
Pinch of salt
Pinch of freshly ground white pepper

1. Place all ingredients in a blender or food processor fitted with the steel blade. Puree, scraping down the sides of the bowl as necessary.

NOTE: The sauce can be made a day in advance and refrigerated, tightly covered. It begins to lose flavor after that time.

Fresh Tomato Salsa

The increasing popularity of *salsa*, the traditional Mexican relish, is part of the trend of new southwestern cooking. This version is piquant without being overly spicy, so it pairs well with even delicate dishes. *Makes 3 cups or 6 ½-cup servings*

TOTAL TIME
4½ hours, including chilling
WORK TIME
20 minutes

PER SERVING
53 calories
0 cholesterol
3 g fat
36 mg sodium

6 large ripe tomatoes, peeled, seeded, and diced (page 271)
½ cup chopped red onion
¼ cup chopped red bell pepper
2 garlic cloves, peeled and minced
3 tablespoons drained chopped canned green chilies
3 tablespoons chopped fresh cilantro or parsley
1 tablespoon chopped fresh oregano *or* ½ teaspoon dried
½ teaspoon cayenne pepper
2 tablespoons red wine vinegar
1 tablespoon olive oil

1. Combine all ingredients in a large glass or stainless-steel bowl. Toss well and refrigerate for at least 4 hours before serving, tossing occasionally.

NOTE: The *salsa* can be made up to three days in advance and kept refrigerated, covered with plastic wrap.

Cucumber Sauce

TOTAL TIME
40 minutes
WORK TIME
10 minutes

PER SERVING
49 calories
1 mg cholesterol
.2 g fat
141 mg sodium

This sauce is an excellent topping for cold poached or broiled fish or cold steamed potatoes. For a party, poach a whole salmon and use this sauce as a glaze, decorating it with overlapping cucumber slices for fish scales.   *Serves 6*

3 cucumbers, peeled, seeded, and very thinly sliced
¼ teaspoon salt
1½ cups plain nonfat yogurt
2 teaspoons prepared horseradish
1 tablespoon chopped scallion, white part only
2 teaspoons tarragon vinegar
2 teaspoons freshly squeezed lemon juice
¼ teaspoon freshly ground white pepper

1. Place the cucumber slices in a colander and toss with the salt. Allow to sit for 30 minutes over a mixing bowl or in the sink; then rinse well and pat dry on paper towels.

2. Place the cucumbers in a blender or food processor fitted with the steel blade. Add the remaining ingredients and puree until smooth. Serve well chilled.

NOTE: The sauce can be made up to two days in advance and kept refrigerated in a tightly covered jar.

Spinach Sauce

This quick and easy pasta sauce is a variation on the classic *pesto*, since it derives some of its flavors from garlic, basil, and cheese, but most of its substance from spinach. It is also excellent on grilled chicken breasts or poached fish.   *Serves 6*

TOTAL TIME
25 minutes
WORK TIME
20 minutes (10 if using frozen spinach)

PER SERVING
106 calories
12 mg cholesterol
5 g fat
371 mg sodium

4 pounds fresh spinach, washed and stemmed *or* 1 pound frozen leaf spinach, defrosted and squeezed dry
1½ tablespoons unsalted butter
2 garlic cloves, peeled and minced
1 cup chicken stock, preferably unsalted (page 266)
¼ cup chopped fresh basil *or* 2 teaspoons dried
⅓ cup freshly grated Parmesan cheese
¼ teaspoon salt
¼ teaspoon freshly ground white pepper

1. If you're using fresh spinach, heat a large skillet over high heat. Add the spinach, turning it with a spatula as it wilts and adding spinach as room permits. When wilted, drain in a colander, pressing with the back of a spoon to extract excess liquid.

2. Melt the butter in the bottom of a saucepan over medium heat. Add the garlic and sauté, stirring frequently, for 5 minutes. Add the spinach, chicken stock, and basil and bring to a boil over high heat. Cook, stirring frequently, until reduced by half. Stir in the cheese, salt, and pepper and puree in a blender or food processor fitted with the steel blade. Scrape into a bowl and serve immediately.

NOTE: The sauce can be prepared up to two days in advance and refrigerated, tightly covered. Reheat over low heat, stirring frequently, for about 10 minutes.

Pear Dressing

TOTAL TIME
5 minutes
WORK TIME
5 minutes

PER TABLESPOON
19 calories
0 cholesterol
1 g fat
15 mg sodium

The combination of pears and nuts in this vinaigrette produces a vibrant and unusual sweet-and-sour flavor. It can be served on fruit salads and simple cold poultry as well as in a green salad.   *Makes 2 cups*

2 ripe pears, peeled, cored, and diced
5 tablespoons raspberry vinegar
1 tablespoon Dijon mustard
¼ cup unsalted cashews
2 tablespoons walnut oil
¼ cup vegetable oil
¼ teaspoon freshly ground white pepper
1 teaspoon chopped fresh thyme *or* **¼ teaspoon dried**
1 tablespoon chopped fresh marjoram *or* **½ teaspoon dried**
1 tablespoon chopped fresh oregano *or* **½ teaspoon dried**

1. Place all ingredients in a blender or food processor fitted with the steel blade. Puree until smooth.

NOTE: The dressing can be kept refrigerated for a week in a jar with a tight-fitting lid.

Yogurt Dill Dressing

TOTAL TIME
5 minutes
WORK TIME
5 minutes

PER TABLESPOON
6 calories
.5 mg cholesterol
.1 g fat
7 mg sodium

Tangy yogurt is a natural pairing with the fresh taste of dill. This dressing is thick enough to be used as a dip with *crudités* and is also a good substitute for mayonnaise on coleslaw or potato salad.   *Makes 1½ cups*

1 cup plain nonfat yogurt
1 tablespoon finely chopped onion
¼ cup finely chopped cucumber
Pinch of freshly ground black pepper
¼ cup minced fresh dill *or* **1 tablespoon dried**

1. Combine the yogurt, onion, cucumber, and pepper in a blender or food processor fitted with the steel blade. Puree until smooth. Scrape into a bowl and stir in the dill.

NOTE: The dressing can be kept up to a week in a tightly covered jar in the refrigerator.

Blue Cheese Dressing

Blue cheese dressing is a popular favorite and clearly caloric when made the traditional way with sour cream and mayonnaise. This version imparts the same sharp taste, with a fraction of the calories. *Makes 3 cups*

TOTAL TIME
3 minutes
WORK TIME
3 minutes

2 cups plain nonfat yogurt
½ cup low-fat buttermilk
½ cup crumbled blue cheese, packed
¼ teaspoon freshly ground white pepper

PER TABLESPOON
11 calories
1 mg cholesterol
.5 g fat
29 mg sodium

1. Place all ingredients in a blender or food processor fitted with the steel blade. Puree until smooth and scrape into a container with a tight-fitting lid.

NOTE: While delicious as soon as it is made, I think this dressing improves if made a day in advance so that the flavors can intensify and blend. It keeps refrigerated for five days.

Rosemary Vinaigrette

TOTAL TIME
5 minutes
WORK TIME
5 minutes

PER TABLESPOON
27 calories
0 cholesterol
3 g fat
24 mg sodium

The combination of vinegar and lemon juice makes this a light dressing that allows the flavors of today's exotic salad ingredients—such as arugula and *radicchio*—to come through.
Makes 1 ¼ cups

¼ cup vegetable oil
¼ cup chicken stock, preferably unsalted (page 266)
¼ cup white wine vinegar
¼ cup freshly squeezed lemon juice
2 tablespoons chopped fresh rosemary *or* 1 teaspoon dried
1 tablespoon Dijon mustard
½ teaspoon freshly ground pepper

1. Combine all ingredients in a jar with a tight-fitting lid. Shake well to emulsify. Chill before serving.

NOTE: The dressing keeps up to a week.

Balsamic Vinaigrette

The heady aged balsamic vinegar gives this dressing pungency without the sharp acidity imparted by lighter vinegars. It has an underlying sweet-and-sour taste and goes well with most wines.   *Makes 1½ cups*

TOTAL TIME
5 minutes
WORK TIME
5 minutes

PER TABLESPOON
23 calories
0 cholesterol
2 g fat
23 mg sodium

6 tablespoons balsamic vinegar
½ cup freshly squeezed orange juice
4 tablespoons freshly squeezed lemon juice
¼ cup olive oil
1 tablespoon chopped fresh marjoram or oregano *or* ½ teaspoon dried
Pinch of freshly ground black pepper
Pinch of cayenne pepper
¼ teaspoon salt

1. Combine all ingredients in a jar with a tight-fitting lid. Shake well to emulsify and refrigerate until used.

NOTE: The dressing will keep for a week in the refrigerator.

Ginger Dressing

TOTAL TIME
5 minutes
WORK TIME
5 minutes

PER TABLESPOON
6 calories
0 cholesterol
2 g fat
77 mg sodium

In addition to enlivening greens, this vibrant salad dressing, based on a traditional Chinese combination of ingredients, can also be used as a quick and easy marinade for boneless chicken breasts or fish. *Makes 1 cup*

2 tablespoons sesame seed, toasted in a dry skillet over low heat until
 light brown
1 tablespoon grated fresh ginger
2 garlic cloves, peeled and minced
Pinch of crushed red pepper
½ cup rice wine vinegar
1 tablespoon dry Sherry
2 tablespoons reduced-sodium soy sauce
2 tablespoons dark sesame oil

1. Combine all ingredients in a jar with a tight-fitting lid. Shake well.

NOTE: The dressing will keep, tightly covered, up to a week in the refrigerator.

Celery Seed Dressing

This slightly sweet, delicate dressing works well on fruit salads as well as vegetable salads. The celery seed adds a spicy note to the mixture without transforming it into a savory sauce. *Makes 1 cup*

TOTAL TIME
5 minutes
WORK TIME
5 minutes

PER TABLESPOON
26 calories
0 cholesterol
2 g fat
10 mg sodium

2 tablespoons honey
⅓ cup raspberry vinegar
1 tablespoon freshly squeezed orange juice
¼ cup chicken stock, preferably unsalted (page 266)
2 tablespoons vegetable oil
1 tablespoon finely minced shallot
1 teaspoon celery seed
Pinch of freshly ground white pepper
Pinch of salt

1. Combine all ingredients in a jar with a tight-fitting lid. Shake until well blended and chill until ready to serve.

NOTE: The dressing can be kept refrigerated for up to a week, tightly covered. Shake well before serving.

Applesauce

TOTAL TIME
3 hours, including chilling
WORK TIME
10 minutes

PER SERVING
75 calories
0 cholesterol
.3 g fat
2 mg sodium

Cooking the apples with their peels not only makes preparing the applesauce quicker; the skins also add a rosy glow to the finished sauce. The wine enhances the fruit's flavor.   *Serves 6*

4 red delicious or McIntosh apples, washed, cored, and quartered
⅓ cup dry white wine
2 tablespoons dark brown sugar
¼ teaspoon ground cinnamon

1. Place the apples in a heavy-bottomed 4-quart saucepan and add remaining ingredients. Cover the pot and bring to a boil over medium-high heat.

2. Reduce the heat to low. Cook the apples, stirring occasionally, for 20 to 30 minutes or until the apples are soft.

3. Transfer the mixture to a blender or food processor fitted with the steel blade and puree. Chill well, at least 2 hours, before serving.

NOTE: The applesauce will keep well for up to a week, tightly covered, in the refrigerator.

Cranberry Sauce

What would a roasted turkey be without cranberry sauce? The *crème de cassis* intensifies the berry flavor, so much less sugar is required. *Makes 2 cups or 8 ¼-cup servings*

1 12-ounce bag fresh cranberries
⅓ cup sugar
⅓ cup freshly squeezed orange juice
2 teaspoons *crème de cassis*
2 teaspoons dark rum
1 teaspoon grated orange zest

TOTAL TIME
2½ hours, including chilling
WORK TIME
20 minutes

PER SERVING
66 calories
0 cholesterol
1 g fat
1 mg sodium

1. Place the cranberries in a colander and pick them over to remove any shriveled berries and twigs.

2. Combine the cranberries with the remaining ingredients in a heavy-bottomed 2-quart saucepan. Bring to a boil over medium heat, reduce the heat to a simmer, and cook the sauce, stirring frequently, for 12 to 15 minutes. The berries will pop, and the sauce will thicken.

3. Scrape into a pint container and chill until cold, at least 2 hours.

NOTE: The sauce lasts for a month, tightly covered, in the refrigerator.

Red Onion Marmalade

TOTAL TIME
2½ hours
WORK TIME
15 minutes

PER SERVING
67 calories
0 cholesterol
2 g fat
63 mg sodium

This robust sweet-and-sour condiment can accompany any grilled meat or poultry entree.   *Makes 3 cups or 9 ⅓-cup servings*

1 tablespoon olive oil
4 large red onions, peeled and sliced
½ cup red wine
½ cup white wine
2 tablespoons balsamic vinegar
⅓ cup sugar
¼ teaspoon salt
Pinch of freshly ground pepper

1. Heat the olive oil in a 2-quart ovenproof casserole over medium heat. Add the onions, separating them into rings, and toss with the oil. Reduce the heat to low, cover the pan, and sweat the onions, stirring occasionally, for 20 minutes.

2. Preheat the oven to 400 degrees. Add the remaining ingredients to the casserole; bring to a boil over high heat. Boil for 5 minutes, then place the uncovered casserole in the center of the oven.

3. Bake for 2 hours, stirring every 15 minutes, until the mixture is thick and the onions are tender. Serve hot, at room temperature, or cold.

NOTE: The marmalade will keep for a week, tightly covered in the refrigerator. With hot foods, either serve it at room temperature or heat it slowly in a saucepan.

Baked Goods

Apricot Ginger Muffins
Corn Muffins
Bran Muffins
Cherry Muffins
Pumpkin Muffins
Apple Muffins
Jalapeño Corn Muffins
Banana Bread
Carrot Bread
Red Pepper Popovers
Almond Meringue Cookies
Chocolate Hazelnut Meringue Cookies
Citrus Angel Food Cake
Chocolate Angel Food Cake

Waking up to the smell of muffins baking in the oven or ending dinner with a crispy cookie is a pleasure not inconsistent with eating healthfully. However, the typically high fat and sugar content of baked goods must be controlled.

In place of fat, these recipes rely on fruits and vegetables to deliver the sensation of moisture to muffins and quick breads. These ingredients also become an important flavor component and lend their frequently vivid colors.

All of the muffins and breads here are part of New American cookery and are flavorful baked goods based on traditional models that have been updated.

The muffins are intended both for breakfast and to serve as a starch at other meals. The Cherry Muffins (page 225) utilize the tart Michigan dried cherries now available at specialty food stores, and the Apricot Ginger Muffins (page 222) are dotted with tangy bits of dried fruit and crystallized ginger that explode with flavor at each bite. For a blander taste, the richness of the Corn Muffins (page 223) comes from canned cream-style corn.

Savory baked goods can be just as satisfying as those that are sweet, so try the Jalapeño Corn Muffins (page 228) or the Red Pepper Popovers (page 231) to enliven a simple entree.

Meringues and angel food cakes comprise the other section of this chapter, since they are two categories of baked goods requiring the use of egg whites only. Angel food cakes are Pennsylvania Dutch in origin and can be topped with fresh fruit or frozen yogurt to create a more elaborate dessert.

Meringues are a contribution of the French to world cookery, and they are a perfect treat for that simple meal ending with just a cup of coffee. Another benefit is that a batch of meringues, if kept in an airtight biscuit tin to reduce exposure to humidity, will keep for a few weeks. That means many crispy treats for minimal effort.

Apricot Ginger Muffins

TOTAL TIME
25 minutes
WORK TIME
10 minutes

PER MUFFIN
130 calories
46 mg cholesterol
2 g fat
140 mg sodium

The ginger adds an unexpected spiciness to these moist, delicious muffins. The ginger is complemented by the dried apricots, which add bits of color along with their tangy flavor.   *Makes 12*

Vegetable oil for muffin tins
1½ cups whole-wheat flour
½ cup unbleached white flour
1 tablespoon baking powder
⅓ cup sugar
1 cup low-fat buttermilk
1 tablespoon vegetable oil
½ cup grated peeled apple
2 eggs
1 teaspoon finely chopped crystallized ginger
2 tablespoons finely chopped dried apricots

1. Preheat oven to 400 degrees. If you're not using nonstick pans, lightly oil and flour 12 muffin tins.

2. In one mixing bowl, combine the whole-wheat flour, white flour, baking powder, and sugar. In another bowl, whisk together the buttermilk, oil, apple, and eggs.

3. Stir the liquids into the dry ingredients, beating the mixture with a wooden spoon to combine. Beat until combined but not overly smooth. Stir in the chopped ginger and apricots, mixing to distribute them evenly.

4. Divide the batter evenly among the muffin tins and bake in the center of the oven for 15 to 18 minutes or until browned. Place the pan on a rack to cool for 5 minutes, then remove the muffins from the tins.

NOTE: The muffins can be made a day in advance and should be kept refrigerated, covered with plastic wrap. Reheat, covered with foil, in a 300-degree oven for 10 minutes, if desired.

Corn Muffins

These muffins are as at home on the dinner table as on the breakfast table. Although they have very little oil, they are rich and moist from the pureed corn, which also intensifies their flavor. *Makes 12*

TOTAL TIME
30 minutes
WORK TIME
10 minutes

PER MUFFIN
157 calories
23 mg cholesterol
5 g fat
260 mg sodium

1 egg
¼ cup vegetable oil
¾ cup canned cream-style corn
1 cup skim milk
1 cup flour
¾ cup yellow cornmeal
1 tablespoon baking powder
½ teaspoon salt
⅓ cup sugar
Vegetable oil for muffin tins

1. Preheat the oven to 350 degrees. In a large mixing bowl, whisk together the egg, oil, corn, and skim milk. In another mixing bowl, combine the remaining ingredients.

2. If you're not using nonstick coated muffin tins, lightly oil and flour 12 muffin tins. Combine the dry and wet ingredients, beating lightly with a wooden spoon; do not overbeat. Divide the batter among the muffin tins and bake in the center of the oven for 15 to 20 minutes or until the tops are lightly browned and a toothpick inserted in the center comes out dry. Allow the muffins to sit for 5 minutes before removing them from the muffin tins.

NOTE: The muffins are best eaten right from the oven. They can be kept in the freezer, tightly wrapped in aluminum foil or a plastic bag, for up to a month. Reheat wrapped in aluminum foil in a 300-degree oven for 10 minutes.

Bran Muffins

TOTAL TIME
30 minutes
WORK TIME
10 minutes

PER MUFFIN
119 calories
23 mg cholesterol
2 g fat
101 mg sodium

Tangy dried currants and sweet grated apple blend with the spices in these muffins to produce moist, tender muffins that fill the kitchen with their aroma while baking. *Makes 12*

Vegetable oil for muffin tins
½ cup bran flake cereal
1½ cups whole-wheat flour
¾ teaspoon baking soda
¼ cup dark brown sugar
1 tablespoon grated orange zest
½ teaspoon ground cinnamon
¼ teaspoon freshly grated nutmeg
⅓ cup dried currants
⅓ cup freshly squeezed orange juice
½ cup grated fresh apple
1 cup low-fat buttermilk
1 egg
1 tablespoon vegetable oil

1. Preheat the oven to 350 degrees. If you're not using nonstick muffin tins, lightly oil and flour 12 muffin tins. In a large mixing bowl, combine the cereal, flour, baking soda, sugar, orange zest, cinnamon, and nutmeg. Combine the dried currants and orange juice in a small saucepan and bring to a boil over high heat. Remove the pan from the heat and allow the currants to soften for 5 minutes.

2. In another mixing bowl, combine the orange juice and currants with the remaining ingredients and beat until well mixed. Combine the wet with the dry ingredients, beating with a wooden spoon until well mixed but not overly smooth. Divide the mixture among the muffin tins and bake in the center of the oven for 25 minutes or until the muffins are brown on top and a toothpick inserted in the center comes out clean. Place on a rack to cool for 5 minutes, then remove the muffins from the pan.

NOTE: The muffins are best right from the oven, but they can be reheated by wrapping them in aluminum foil and placing them in a 300-degree oven for 10 minutes. They can be frozen for up to a few months, tightly wrapped in aluminum foil and placed in an airtight plastic bag.

Cherry Muffins

American Spoon Foods, one of the country's best sources of delicious sugarless fruit preserves, also packages wonderful dried Michigan cherries (page 279). They add a luscious red color as well as tangy tart flavor to the muffins. *Makes 12*

TOTAL TIME
40 minutes
WORK TIME
10 minutes

PER MUFFIN
106 calories
24 mg cholesterol
2 g fat
94 mg sodium

½ cup dried cherries
Vegetable oil for muffin tins
1½ cups whole-wheat flour
½ cup bran flake cereal
¾ teaspoon baking soda
¼ cup sugar
1 cup low-fat buttermilk
1 tablespoon vegetable oil
1 egg
1 cup grated peeled apple
2 teaspoons grated lemon zest

1. Soak the cherries in boiling water to cover for 15 minutes to plump. Preheat the oven to 400 degrees. If you're not using nonstick tins, lightly oil and flour 12 muffin tins.

2. In a large mixing bowl, combine the flour, cereal, baking soda, and sugar. In another bowl, whisk together the remaining ingredients.

3. Stir the liquids into the dry ingredients, using a wooden spoon. Stir to combine, but do not beat until totally smooth. Drain the cherries and stir into the mixture.

4. Divide the batter evenly among the prepared muffin tins and place in the center of the oven. Bake for 15 to 18 minutes or until browned. Place on a rack to cool for 5 minutes, then remove the muffins from the pan.

NOTE: The muffins can be made a day in advance and should be kept refrigerated, covered with plastic wrap. Reheat, covered with foil, in a 300-degree oven for 10 minutes if desired.

Pumpkin Muffins

TOTAL TIME
25 minutes
WORK TIME
5 minutes

PER MUFFIN
147 calories
45 mg cholesterol
2 g fat
244 mg sodium

These fragrant, dark muffins are not only for Thanksgiving. Serve them in lieu of a starch for any fall or winter meal. They contain all of the traditional spicing of pumpkin pie.   *Makes 12*

Vegetable oil for muffin tins
2½ cups unbleached white flour
2 teaspoons baking powder
2 teaspoons baking soda
⅛ teaspoon salt
2 eggs
1 tablespoon vegetable oil
1½ cups pureed fresh or canned pumpkin
⅓ cup dark brown sugar
¼ teaspoon ground cloves
½ teaspoon ground cinnamon
¼ teaspoon freshly grated nutmeg

1. Preheat the oven to 400 degrees. If you're not using nonstick muffin tins, lightly oil and flour 12 muffin tins.

2. In a large mixing bowl, combine the flour, baking powder, baking soda, and salt. In another bowl, combine the remaining ingredients, whisking until smooth.

3. Combine the dry and wet ingredients, beating lightly with a wooden spoon. Divide the batter among the prepared muffin tins and bake in the center of the oven for 15 to 18 minutes or until the tops are lightly browned and a toothpick inserted in the center comes out clean. Allow the muffins to sit in the muffin tins for 5 minutes, then remove and serve immediately.

NOTE: The muffins are best right from the oven. Reheat them, covered in foil, in a 300-degree oven for 10 minutes. They can also be frozen for up to a few months in an airtight plastic bag or heavily wrapped in foil.

Apple Muffins

Using both applesauce and apple butter turns these muffins into a fruity, lightly spiced treat. *Makes 12*

Vegetable oil for muffin tins
1½ cups whole-wheat flour
½ cup unbleached white flour
1 tablespoon baking powder
½ teaspoon ground cinnamon
¼ teaspoon freshly grated nutmeg
Pinch of ground allspice
Pinch of ground cloves
⅛ teaspoon salt
1 cup unsweetened applesauce
½ cup low-fat buttermilk
½ cup natural apple butter
1 tablespoon vegetable oil
1 egg

TOTAL TIME
25 minutes
WORK TIME
5 minutes

PER MUFFIN
127 calories
23 mg cholesterol
2 g fat
147 mg sodium

1. Preheat the oven to 400 degrees. If you're not using nonstick muffin tins, lightly oil and flour 12 muffin tins. In a large mixing bowl, combine the flours, baking powder, cinnamon, nutmeg, allspice, cloves, and salt. Whisk together the remaining ingredients in another mixing bowl until smooth.

2. Combine the wet and dry ingredients, stirring with a wooden spoon until well mixed but not totally smooth. Divide the batter among the prepared muffin tins and bake in the center of the oven for 15 to 18 minutes or until the tops are lightly browned and a toothpick inserted in the center comes out clean. Let the muffins sit in the tins for 5 minutes, then remove and serve immediately.

NOTE: The muffins are best right from the oven; however, they can be frozen, wrapped tightly in a plastic bag or aluminum foil, and then reheated at 300 degrees for 10 minutes.

Jalapeño Corn Muffins

TOTAL TIME
30 minutes
WORK TIME
10 minutes

PER MUFFIN
111 calories
30 mg cholesterol
3 g fat
228 mg sodium

The muffins are brightly flecked with red pepper and are brightly seasoned with a touch of fiery *jalapeño*. These are savory southwestern muffins that go well with any grilled meat or poultry. *Makes 12*

Vegetable oil for muffin tins
½ cup fresh or frozen corn kernels
1 teaspoon finely chopped *jalapeño* chili pepper (page 269)
1 cup yellow cornmeal
2 tablespoons unsalted butter, melted
½ cup milk
1 cup low-fat buttermilk
1 egg
2 egg whites
½ cup flour
1 tablespoon baking powder
½ teaspoon baking soda
¼ teaspoon salt
2 teaspoons sugar
¼ cup finely diced roasted red bell pepper (page 269) or pimiento

1. Preheat the oven to 400 degrees. If you're not using nonstick muffin tins, oil 12 muffin tins. Combine the corn, *jalapeño*, cornmeal, butter, milk, buttermilk, egg, and egg whites in a blender or food processor fitted with the steel blade. Puree until smooth.

2. Sift the dry ingredients into a mixing bowl and then combine with the corn mixture and red bell pepper, beating until smooth. Divide the batter among the muffin tins and bake in the center of the oven for 15 to 18 minutes or until a toothpick inserted in the center comes out clean. Allow the muffins to sit in the pan for 5 minutes, then remove them from the muffin tins.

NOTE: The muffins can be prepared up to two days in advance, cooled, kept at room temperature, tightly covered with plastic wrap, and reheated in a 300-degree oven for 10 minutes. They can also be frozen for up to a month, tightly sealed in a plastic bag.

Banana Bread

Rum enhances the delicacy of bananas, and this bread is densely textured and rich, so just a small slice is satisfying. *Makes 12 slices*

Vegetable oil for loaf pan
½ cup brown sugar
¼ cup granulated sugar
3 tablespoons unsalted butter
1 egg
3 large ripe bananas, peeled and mashed
2 tablespoons dark rum
½ teaspoon vanilla extract
2 cups flour
1 teaspoon baking soda
1 teaspoon baking powder
¼ teaspoon salt

TOTAL TIME
1½ hours
WORK TIME
15 minutes

PER SLICE
189 calories
30 mg cholesterol
4 g fat
159 mg sodium

1. Preheat the oven to 350 degrees. Oil and flour a loaf pan. Combine the brown sugar, sugar, and butter in a mixing bowl and beat until light and fluffy. Beat in the egg, bananas, rum, and vanilla and beat until smooth.

2. Sift the remaining ingredients together and lightly beat into the banana mixture. Scrape the batter into the pan and bake in the center of the oven for 50 minutes to 1 hour or until a toothpick inserted in the center comes out clean. Allow the bread to sit for 5 minutes, then remove it from the pan and cool it completely on a rack.

NOTE: The bread can be made up to two days in advance and kept, tightly covered with plastic wrap, once cooled. It can be frozen for up to two months in an airtight bag.

Carrot Bread

TOTAL TIME
2 hours
WORK TIME
15 minutes

PER SLICE
181 calories
30 mg cholesterol
4 g fat
161 mg sodium

The natural sweetness of carrots and their bright orange color make this aromatic spiced bread memorable.   *Makes 12 slices*

1½ cups finely grated carrot (about 4 or 5 carrots)
½ cup golden raisins
3 tablespoons unsalted butter
1½ cups water
¾ cup sugar
1 egg, lightly beaten
Vegetable oil for loaf pan
2 cups flour
1 teaspoon baking soda
1 teaspoon baking powder
1 teaspoon ground cinnamon
Pinch of ground cloves
Pinch of ground allspice
¼ teaspoon freshly grated nutmeg
¼ teaspoon salt

1. Combine the carrot, raisins, butter, water, and sugar in a saucepan and bring to a boil over medium heat. Simmer for 5 minutes, stirring frequently. Remove the pan from the heat, scrape the mixture into a mixing bowl, and refrigerate until cooled, at least 45 minutes. Beat in the egg and set aside.

2. Preheat the oven to 350 degrees. Oil and flour a loaf pan. Sift the remaining ingredients together and combine with the carrot mixture, beating with a wooden spoon. Scrape the batter into the prepared pan and bake in the center of the oven for 1 hour or until a toothpick inserted in the center comes out clean. Remove from the oven, allow it to rest 5 minutes in the pan, and then remove from the pan and cool on a rack.

NOTE: The bread can be made up to two days in advance and tightly covered with plastic wrap once cool; it can be frozen for up to two months, tightly sealed in a plastic bag.

Red Pepper Popovers

Popovers are actually more air than batter, and this old-fashioned American treat, when seasoned with fiery red pepper, needs no embellishment.   *Serves 6*

Vegetable oil for popover pans
1 cup flour
1 cup skim milk
1 egg
2 egg whites
1 tablespoon unsalted butter, melted
¼ teaspoon salt
¼ to ½ teaspoon crushed red pepper (to taste)

1. Preheat the oven to 425 degrees and oil 6 popover pans.

2. Combine all ingredients in a blender or food processor fitted with the steel blade and blend until smooth. Place the popover pans in the center of the oven to preheat for 3 minutes.

3. Divide the batter into the preheated popover pans and place in the center of the oven for 30 to 35 minutes or until puffy and golden brown. Serve immediately.

NOTE: While the batter can be prepared up to two days in advance and refrigerated, tightly covered, the popovers must be baked at the last minute, and they deflate rather quickly. Herbs or a few tablespoons of freshly grated Parmesan cheese can be substituted for the red pepper.

TOTAL TIME
40 minutes
WORK TIME
5 minutes

PER POPOVER
126 calories
52 mg cholesterol
3 g fat
140 mg sodium

Almond Meringue Cookies

TOTAL TIME
1½ hours
WORK TIME
15 minutes

PER COOKIE
11 calories
0 cholesterol
.7 g fat
5 mg sodium

These crispy almond-flavored meringues are very easy to make and an elegant treat for dessert or snacks. *Makes 30*

3 egg whites, at room temperature
½ teaspoon cream of tartar
1 teaspoon almond extract
¾ cup sugar
⅓ cup finely chopped almonds

1. Preheat the oven to 250 degrees. Line 2 cookie sheets with parchment paper or aluminum foil.

2. Place the egg whites in a totally grease-free bowl and beat at medium speed until frothy. Add the cream of tartar, raise the speed to high, and beat until soft peaks form. Beat in the almond extract and then the sugar, 1 tablespoon at a time. Continue to beat the meringue until shiny and stiff. Gently fold in the almonds and drop by tablespoons onto the baking sheets.

3. Bake in the center of the oven for 30 minutes, then turn the oven off and allow the meringues to sit in the oven, without opening the door, for another 30 minutes. Remove from the oven and allow the meringues to cool on the baking sheets before removing.

NOTE: The meringues will keep for more than a week in an airtight biscuit tin.

Chocolate Hazelnut Meringue Cookies

Meringues are simultaneously crispy and chewy. In this case their light texture is flavored with a combination of tempting cocoa and luscious ground hazelnuts.   *Makes 30*

TOTAL TIME
1½ hours
WORK TIME
15 minutes

PER COOKIE
35 calories
0 cholesterol
1 g fat
5 mg sodium

3 egg whites, at room temperature
½ teaspoon cream of tartar
¼ teaspoon vanilla extract
¾ cup sugar
4 tablespoons unsweetened cocoa powder
½ cup hazelnuts, toasted in a 350-degree oven for 7 minutes, then coarsely chopped

1. Preheat the oven to 250 degrees. Line 2 baking sheets with parchment paper or aluminum foil. Place the egg whites in a grease-free bowl and beat at medium speed until frothy. Add the cream of tartar, raise the speed to high, and beat the egg whites until soft peaks form. Beat in the vanilla extract and continue beating, adding the sugar 1 tablespoon at a time, until the meringue is shiny and stiff peaks form. Sift the cocoa over the top of the meringue and continue to beat for another moment. Fold in the chopped nuts.

2. Drop the batter by heaping teaspoons onto the sheets. Bake the meringues in the center of the oven for 30 minutes. Turn off the oven and leave the cookies in the oven for an additional 30 minutes. Remove the cookies from the oven and allow to cool on the baking sheets.

NOTE: The cookies will keep up to a week sealed in an airtight biscuit tin.

Citrus Angel Food Cake

TOTAL TIME
2½ hours
WORK TIME
25 minutes

PER SERVING
170 calories
0 cholesterol
.1 g fat
98 mg sodium

The tangy tastes of orange and lemon are consistent with the light, airy quality of angel food cake. This cake can serve as the base for many mixed fruit salads, as well as being delicious by itself.   Serves 8

¾ cup freshly squeezed orange juice
2 tablespoons finely grated orange zest
2 tablespoons finely grated lemon zest
¾ cup cake flour
⅛ teaspoon salt
1 cup sugar
10 egg whites, at room temperature
1 teaspoon cream of tartar

1. Preheat the oven to 350 degrees. Rinse a tube pan and shake it over the sink to remove excess moisture, but do not wipe it dry.

2. Place the orange juice, orange zest, and lemon zest in a small heavy saucepan and bring to a boil over medium heat. Reduce by three quarters, pour the mixture into a soup bowl, and refrigerate until cool. Sift the flour with the salt and ¼ cup of the sugar; set aside.

3. Place the egg whites in a grease-free mixing bowl and beat at medium speed until frothy. Add the cream of tartar, raise the speed to high, and beat until soft peaks form. Add the remaining sugar, 1 tablespoon at a time, and continue to beat until stiff peaks form and the meringue is glossy. Lower the speed to low and beat in the cooled orange juice mixture. Gently fold the flour mixture into the meringue and scrape the batter into the tube pan. Bake in the center of the oven for 45 minutes, then remove from the oven and invert the cake onto a cake rack or the neck of a wine bottle for at least 1½ hours or until cool. Run a knife or spatula around the outside of the pan to loosen the cake and invert onto a serving plate.

NOTE: The cake can be prepared up to a day in advance, tightly covered with plastic wrap after it has cooled and been inverted onto a serving plate.

Chocolate Angel Food Cake

Angel food cakes are light and cholesterol-free desserts. This one is flavored with cocoa powder for the chocoholic of your acquaintance.   *Serves 8*

TOTAL TIME
2½ hours
WORK TIME
20 minutes

PER SERVING
168 calories
0 cholesterol
.7 g fat
80 mg sodium

5 tablespoons unsweetened cocoa powder
¾ cup cake flour
Pinch of salt
1 cup sugar
10 egg whites, at room temperature
¾ teaspoon cream of tartar
1 teaspoon vanilla extract

1. Preheat the oven to 350 degrees. Rinse out a tube pan and shake it over the sink, but do not wipe it dry. Set aside.

2. Sift together the cocoa, flour, salt, and ¼ cup of the sugar. Set aside.

3. Place the egg whites in a grease-free bowl and beat at medium speed until frothy. Add the cream of tartar and continue beating, raising the speed to high, until soft peaks form. Continue beating, adding the remaining sugar, 1 tablespoon at a time, until the meringue forms stiff peaks and is shiny. With the mixer at the lowest speed, beat in the vanilla.

4. Gently fold the cocoa mixture into the egg whites, being careful to avoid streaks of white meringue. Scrape the batter into the tube pan and bake in the center of the oven for 40 to 45 minutes. Remove the cake from the oven and invert the pan onto a rack or onto the neck of a wine bottle. Allow the cake to cool for 90 minutes, undisturbed, then run a knife around the sides of the pan to loosen the cake and invert it onto a serving platter.

NOTE: The cake can be made up to a day in advance and left at room temperature, tightly covered with plastic wrap, once it has cooled. Serve topped with fresh sliced fruit, frozen yogurt, or Gazelle Cream (page 248) if desired.

Desserts

Cheesecake
Rice Pudding
Chocolate Pudding
Chardonnay Baked Apples
Zinfandel Poached Pears
Apple Pear Cobbler
Figs Poached in Grand Marnier
Gazelle Cream
Lemon Cheese Mousse
Peach Melba Mousse
Mocha Mousse
Bananas Baked with Rum
Strawberry Rhubarb Soufflé
Apricot Soufflé
Rhubarb Custard
Apple Strudel Pie
Strawberry Frozen Yogurt
Maple Bourbon Frozen Yogurt
Champagne Orange Sorbet
Kiwi Sorbet with Aquavit

To many people, it's not a meal unless it ends with dessert, and it certainly is not a party if there's nothing following the salad course. The good news is that it's possible to eat desserts every day without making caloric sacrifices.

Desserts, like every other course of a meal, run the gamut from light and ethereal to heavy and hearty. What unites most of the recipes in this chapter is a reliance on fruits as the main ingredient. The natural fructose of ripe fruit is sufficient in most cases to sweeten the dessert.

Rather than masking the succulent flavors of fruits with heavy treatments, most of the fruit recipes in this chapter merely augment those characteristics through restrained baking or poaching; enrichments are more frequently wine or liqueur than refined sugar. And of course the best fruit is fruit in season; the Chardonnay Baked Apples (page 244) and Figs Poached in Grand Marnier (page 247) are examples of seasonal recipes.

While I consider mixed fruit salad more appropriate for breakfast than dessert, topping the best seasonal fruit with Gazelle Cream (page 248) in lieu of whipped cream is an elegant way to end a dinner. Other light, formal desserts are Peach Melba Mousse (page 250) and the cholesterol-free soufflés, using a thick base of pureed fruit rather than an emulsified egg custard.

For more informal occasions, the Rice Pudding (page 242) and Cheesecake (page 240) are deceptively rich. These are comfort foods—thick, creamy, and subtly flavored.

Some of those who do not think it is a meal without dessert believe that dessert should be synonymous with ice cream. As alternatives, you will find in this chapter some sorbets and frozen yogurts that can be created year-round.

Frozen yogurts are more appealing than iced milks, since the consistency is more like ice cream, and the lightness of nonfat yogurt allows the flavors of such ingredients as maple syrup and strawberries to shine more vividly.

And for the formal dinner party, Champagne Orange Sorbet (page 259), served with a glass of Champagne, is the toast of the occasion.

Cheesecake

TOTAL TIME
4 hours, including chilling
WORK TIME
20 minutes

PER SERVING
209 calories
17 mg cholesterol
7 g fat
330 mg sodium

As with many high-calorie foods, only a little cream cheese is needed to give this cake its richness. The light texture of the cheesecake and its citrusy flavor make this a special dessert for any meal.   Serves 6

FOR THE CRUST

1 cup graham cracker crumbs
1½ tablespoons unsalted butter
½ teaspoon ground cinnamon

FOR THE CHEESECAKE

1 tablespoon unflavored gelatin
¼ cup skim milk
2 ounces cream cheese, softened to room temperature
⅓ cup sugar
1¼ cups low-fat cottage cheese
½ cup plain nonfat yogurt
½ teaspoon vanilla extract
2 tablespoons grated lemon zest
3 egg whites, at room temperature
Pinch of cream of tartar

1. For the crust, preheat the oven to 350 degrees. Combine the crust ingredients and press into the bottom and slightly up the sides of an 8-inch round cake pan. Bake in the center of the oven for 10 minutes. Remove and set aside to cool.

2. Sprinkle the gelatin on top of the skim milk to soften for 10 minutes. Place in a small saucepan and heat over medium heat, stirring constantly, until the gelatin is dissolved and no granules remain. Set aside to cool.

3. In a mixing bowl, beat the cream cheese with the sugar until light and fluffy. Add the cottage cheese, yogurt, vanilla, lemon zest, and gelatin mixture and beat until smooth. In a grease-free mixing bowl, beat the egg whites at medium speed until frothy. Add the cream of tartar, raise the speed to high, and beat until stiff peaks form. Gently fold the egg whites into the cheese mixture, then pour into the prepared crust and chill until set, at least 3½ hours.

NOTE: The cheesecake can be prepared up to two days in advance and refrigerated, tightly covered with plastic wrap.

Chocolate Pudding

Memories of childhood will be stirred by this creamy, thick pudding. You can top it with a tablespoon of Gazelle Cream (page 248) if desired.   *Serves 6*

1½ squares (1½ ounces) unsweetened chocolate
3 cups low-fat milk
½ cup sugar
2 tablespoons brandy
¼ cup cornstarch mixed with 2 tablespoons cold water

1. Break the chocolate into small pieces and combine with the milk, sugar, and brandy in a small heavy saucepan. Bring to a boil over medium heat and simmer, stirring occasionally, for 10 minutes or until the mixture is slightly reduced and the chocolate has melted into the milk.

2. Whisk the cornstarch mixture into the chocolate mixture. Bring to a boil and simmer, stirring constantly, for 5 minutes, beating until smooth. Pour into a bowl or individual glasses and refrigerate until well chilled, at least 1 hour.

NOTE: The pudding can be prepared up to two days in advance and kept refrigerated, tightly covered with plastic wrap.

TOTAL TIME
1½ hours, including chilling
WORK TIME
20 minutes

PER SERVING
180 calories
10 mg cholesterol
6 g fat
61 mg sodium

Rice Pudding

What could be a more soul-satisfying comfort food than creamy rice pudding? This version is flavored with tangy dried currants and a touch of orange from the marmalade and liqueur.
Serves 6

TOTAL TIME
3 hours, including chilling
WORK TIME
15 minutes

PER SERVING
158 calories
51 mg cholesterol
2 g fat
49 mg sodium

FOR THE RICE

½ cup long-grain white rice
1 cup water
1½ cups skim milk
2 tablespoons sugar
2 teaspoons unsalted butter
½ teaspoon vanilla extract
2 tablespoons dried currants
2 tablespoons fruit-only orange marmalade
1 tablespoon Grand Marnier or Cointreau

FOR THE PASTRY CREAM

3 tablespoons skim milk
2 teaspoons cornstarch
1 tablespoon sugar
1 egg

1. Bring the rice and water to a boil over medium heat. Blanch the rice for 5 minutes to remove some of the starch, drain, and return the rice to the pan along with the remaining rice ingredients. Bring to a boil over medium heat and reduce the heat to low. Cook the rice, covered, for 30 to 40 minutes, stirring occasionally, or until the rice is very tender and the mixture has thickened.

2. Scrape the rice into a mixing bowl and refrigerate with a sheet of plastic wrap directly on the surface so a skin will not form.

3. In a small saucepan, whisk together the milk, cornstarch, and sugar and bring to a boil over low heat, stirring constantly, beating until it is thick and smooth. Remove from the heat and whisk in the egg. Stir the pastry cream into the rice and chill until cold, at least 2 hours.

NOTE: The rice pudding can be prepared up to three days in advance and kept refrigerated, with plastic wrap directly on the surface.

Chardonnay Baked Apples

TOTAL TIME
40 minutes
WORK TIME
10 minutes

PER SERVING
115 calories
0 cholesterol
.4 g fat
4 mg sodium

The fruitiness of the wine is perfect to bring out the naturally sweet taste of apples. While this is a homey, comforting dessert, it can be enriched with some Gazelle Cream (page 248) or Maple Bourbon Frozen Yogurt (page 258).   Serves 6

6 large baking apples
⅓ cup golden raisins, plumped in ⅓ cup boiling water
⅔ cup cream Sherry
⅓ cup Chardonnay or other dry white wine
Pinch of freshly grated nutmeg

1. Preheat the oven to 350 degrees. Peel and core the apples. Place them in an ovenproof baking pan just large enough to hold them. Combine the remaining ingredients, place some of the raisins in the core of each apple, and pour the liquid in the bottom of the baking pan. Bake in the center of the oven, lightly covered with aluminum foil, for 20 minutes. Remove the foil and continue baking for 15 to 20 minutes or until the tip of a knife can be inserted with no resistance. Spoon the liquid over the apples a few times while baking. The apples can be served hot from the oven, at room temperature, or chilled.

NOTE: The apples will keep for up to a week, refrigerated and tightly covered with plastic wrap.

Zinfandel Poached Pears

The succulent, slightly spiced pears are not only elegant and delicious by themselves; sliced over *sorbet* or frozen yogurt they also serve as a colorful, delicious garnish. It's little more trouble to poach a large batch of them, and they will keep well for a week.   *Serves 6*

6 ripe pears, such as Bartlett or Bosc
1 lemon slice
2 cups Zinfandel or other spicy dry red wine
½ cup sugar
1 cinnamon stick
½ lemon, thinly sliced
½ orange, thinly sliced
3 cups water

1. Peel the pears, leaving the stem attached if possible. Using a melon baller or a small sharp paring knife, remove the cores. Immediately rub the pears with a slice of lemon to prevent discoloration.

2. Bring the remaining ingredients to a boil and simmer, uncovered, for 5 minutes. Add the pears and poach them gently, with the syrup barely simmering, for 15 to 20 minutes or until the tip of a paring knife pierces them with no resistance. Allow the pears to cool for 30 minutes in the syrup, then remove them with a slotted spoon. Pour the syrup around the pears, and refrigerate until well chilled, at least 3 hours. To serve, place a pear upright in a serving dish and spoon some of the poaching liquid around it.

NOTE: The pears can be refrigerated for up to a week. They will keep better if they are submerged in the poaching liquid.

TOTAL TIME
4 hours, including chilling
WORK TIME
15 minutes

PER SERVING
173 calories
0 cholesterol
.7 g fat
4 mg sodium

Apple Pear Cobbler

TOTAL TIME
1 hour
WORK TIME
15 minutes

PER SERVING
267 calories
15 mg cholesterol
7 g fat
5 mg sodium

This is a homey dessert that's delicious right from the oven, perhaps topped with a tablespoon of Gazelle Cream (page 248) to augment its crunchy streusel with some additional richness. *Serves 6*

3 cooking apples, such as Granny Smith
3 ripe pears, such as Bartlett or Bosc
3 tablespoons freshly squeezed lemon juice
¼ cup freshly squeezed orange juice
2 tablespoons grated orange zest
¼ teaspoon ground cinnamon
Pinch of freshly grated nutmeg
¼ cup sugar
½ cup uncooked rolled oats
¼ cup flour
⅓ cup dark brown sugar
3 tablespoons unsalted butter

1. Preheat the oven to 350 degrees. Peel and quarter the apples and pears and cut out their cores with a small paring knife. Thinly slice the fruit and immediately toss with the lemon juice to prevent discoloration. Combine the fruit with the orange juice, orange zest, cinnamon, and nutmeg. Arrange the fruit in an even layer in a 9- by 13-inch baking dish.

2. Combine the remaining ingredients in a small bowl and use your fingers to create a coarse meal. Pat the topping over the fruit and bake in the center of the oven for 45 minutes. Serve immediately, at room temperature, or chilled.

NOTE: The cobbler can be made up to two days in advance and refrigerated, covered with plastic wrap. If you'd like to serve it hot, reheat in a 300-degree oven for 15 minutes, covered for the first 10 minutes.

THE GOURMET GAZELLE COOKBOOK

Figs Poached in Grand Marnier

Fresh figs need but a brief poaching to enhance their natural sweetness and luxurious texture. The light liqueur sauce high-lights all of the flavor and textural characteristics.   *Serves 6*

12 ripe fresh figs
1 cup white dessert wine, such as a late-harvest Riesling
1 cup freshly squeezed orange juice
3 tablespoons grated orange zest
¼ cup Grand Marnier

1. Cut the figs in half and set aside. Combine the remaining ingredients in a stainless-steel or enamel saucepan and bring to a boil over high heat. Lower the heat and simmer until only 1 cup of liquid remains. Add the figs and gently poach them for 5 minutes. Remove with a slotted spoon, pour the syrup over the figs, and chill until cold, at least 2 hours.

NOTE: The figs can be poached up to three days in advance and refrigerated, tightly covered with plastic wrap.

TOTAL TIME
3 hours, including chilling
WORK TIME
15 minutes

PER SERVING
127 calories
0 cholesterol
.4 g fat
5 mg sodium

Gazelle Cream

PREPARATION TIME
5 minutes

PER SERVING
136 calories
31 mg cholesterol
9 g fat
67 mg sodium

This is a wonderfully flavorful, rich alternative to whipped cream with a fraction of the calories and cholesterol. The analysis given to the left is for the cream only. If you top fruit with it, the fruit you select will determine your actual calorie count. Count on ½ cup fruit—berries, peaches, nectarines, grapes, whatever you like—for each serving. In addition to creating an elegant fresh fruit dessert, use this topping on anything from frozen yogurt to a slice of angel food cake.   *Serves 6*

½ cup heavy cream
1½ cups plain nonfat yogurt
1 tablespoon dark brown sugar
6 Amaretti cookies, crushed into fine crumbs

1. Have your mixing bowl and beaters well chilled. Beat the heavy cream, incorporating as much air as possible, beating it past the stage of whipped cream to a very thick, dense cream. Fold in the remaining ingredients gently, distributing the Amaretti throughout. Serve over fresh fruit, frozen yogurt, or cake.

NOTE: The topping can be made up to two days in advance and kept refrigerated, tightly covered with plastic wrap. It may need a gentle refolding if any liquid has accumulated at the bottom of the bowl.

Lemon Cheese Mousse

Eating this light mousse creates the same rich sensation as eating a lemon-scented cheesecake.   *Serves 6*

1 tablespoon unflavored gelatin
2 tablespoons cold water
4 tablespoons freshly squeezed lemon juice
8 ounces part skim milk ricotta cheese
1 egg
¼ cup sugar
½ cup plain nonfat yogurt
2 tablespoons grated lemon zest
4 egg whites
¼ teaspoon cream of tartar

TOTAL TIME
4 to 6 hours, including chilling
WORK TIME
15 minutes

PER SERVING
127 calories
58 mg cholesterol
4 g fat
108 mg sodium

1. Sprinkle the gelatin over the water to soften for 10 minutes. Combine with the lemon juice in a small saucepan and stir over low heat until the gelatin is dissolved and no granules remain.

2. In a mixing bowl, beat the ricotta with the egg and sugar until light and fluffy. Beat in the yogurt, lemon zest, and gelatin mixture and set aside.

3. In a grease-free bowl, beat the egg whites until frothy at medium speed. Beat in the cream of tartar, raise the speed to high, and beat until stiff peaks form. Gently fold the ricotta mixture into the egg whites and pour the mousse into individual dishes or a serving bowl. Chill until set, about 4 to 6 hours.

NOTE: The mousse can be made up to two days in advance and refrigerated, tightly covered with plastic wrap.

Peach Melba Mousse

TOTAL TIME
4 to 6 hours, including
chilling
WORK TIME
20 minutes

PER SERVING
218 calories
28 mg cholesterol
8 g fat
63 mg sodium

The creamy, pale, fresh peach mousse with a drizzling of vividly toned raspberries is a dramatic and elegant dessert. It is cooling on a hot summer evening, when peaches are at their best and most reasonably priced.   *Serves 6*

1 tablespoon unflavored gelatin
2 tablespoons cold water
4 ripe fresh peaches
⅓ cup sugar
1 tablespoon freshly squeezed lemon juice
1 cup plain nonfat yogurt
½ cup heavy cream, whipped until stiff
3 egg whites, whipped until stiff

FOR THE SAUCE

1 pint fresh raspberries
2 tablespoons sugar
1 tablespoon *framboise* (optional)

1. Sprinkle the gelatin over the water to soften for 10 minutes. Bring a large pot of water to a boil and blanch the peaches for 30 seconds, removing them with a slotted spoon. Peel the peaches, discard the pits, and finely dice. Bring the peaches, sugar, and lemon juice to a boil over medium heat. Simmer 4 to 6 minutes, until the peaches are soft, then stir in the gelatin, stirring until dissolved and no granules remain. Puree in a blender or food processor fitted with the steel blade and refrigerate.

2. When the mixture is at room temperature, beat in the yogurt and gently fold in the whipped cream and beaten egg whites. Pour into a serving bowl and chill until set, about 4 to 6 hours.

3. For the sauce, puree the raspberries with the sugar and *framboise*, if used, in a blender or food processor fitted with the steel blade. Pass the mixture through a sieve to remove the seeds. To serve, spoon the mousse onto serving plates and drizzle some of the sauce over the top.

NOTE: The mousse can be made up to two days in advance and refrigerated, tightly covered with plastic wrap. The sauce will keep for up to four days, refrigerated and tightly covered.

Mocha Mousse

Coffee and chocolate are an unbeatable combination. With this mousse, add the cinnamon if you want to replicate the flavor of *cappuccino*, the rich Italian breakfast drink. *Serves 6*

TOTAL TIME
4 hours, including chilling
WORK TIME
15 minutes

PER SERVING
108 calories
2 mg cholesterol
2 g fat
86 mg sodium

1 tablespoon unflavored gelatin
2 cups skim milk
¼ cup sugar
1½ teaspoons instant espresso coffee powder
1 tablespoon Tia Maria
3 tablespoons finely chopped semisweet chocolate
¼ teaspoon ground cinnamon (optional)
5 egg whites, at room temperature
Pinch of cream of tartar

1. Sprinkle the gelatin over the skim milk to soften for 10 minutes. Stir in the sugar, instant espresso, Tia Maria, chocolate, and cinnamon. Heat, stirring constantly, over medium-high heat until the gelatin, coffee, and chocolate are dissolved and the mixture is dark. Pour the mixture into a mixing bowl and refrigerate until the mixture is at least room temperature or slightly chilled. If the mixture has begun to set, beat with a whisk until smooth.

2. Place the egg whites in a grease-free bowl and beat at medium speed until frothy. Add the cream of tartar, raise the speed to high, and beat until stiff peaks form. Gently fold the egg whites into the mocha mixture and chill for at least 2½ hours, until the mousse is set.

NOTE: The mousse can be prepared up to two days in advance and refrigerated, tightly covered with plastic wrap.

Bananas Baked with Rum

TOTAL TIME
30 minutes
WORK TIME
10 minutes

PER SERVING
162 calories
5 mg cholesterol
3 g fat
4 mg sodium

Breakfast at Brennan's in New Orleans—which may be where brunch was invented—frequently ends with flaming Bananas Foster flambéed tableside. This is a healthier—not to mention safer—version of the dish. Serve it over Maple Bourbon Frozen Yogurt (page 258) if desired.   *Serves 6*

6 bananas
2 tablespoons freshly squeezed lemon juice
¼ cup dark brown sugar
¼ cup dark rum, such as Myer's
1 tablespoon Grand Marnier or Cointreau
1 tablespoon unsalted butter
2 tablespoons grated orange zest

1. Preheat the oven to 350 degrees. Peel and halve the bananas and immediately roll in the lemon juice to prevent discoloration. Arrange the bananas in an ovenproof baking dish just large enough to hold them.

2. Combine the remaining ingredients in a small saucepan and bring to a boil over medium heat. Simmer for 2 minutes, then pour the syrup evenly over the bananas. Bake in the center of the oven for 15 minutes or until the bananas are soft. Serve warm or at room temperature.

NOTE: The bananas can be prepared up to two days in advance and refrigerated, tightly covered with plastic wrap. Allow them to reach room temperature before serving.

Strawberry Rhubarb Soufflé

You'll never miss the cholesterol-laden egg yolks in this *soufflé*. It's as light and delicious as any classic model, and the soft pink color is as delicate as the flavor. Although the egg whites have to be beaten at the last minute, the majority of the work can be done in advance.   *Serves 6*

TOTAL TIME
2 hours
WORK TIME
30 minutes

PER SERVING
70 calories
0 cholesterol
.3 g fat
52 mg sodium

2 cups finely diced fresh rhubarb
1 pint fresh strawberries, hulled
⅓ cup *crème de cassis*
2 tablespoons fruit-only strawberry jam
Vegetable oil and sugar for *soufflé* dish
6 egg whites, at room temperature

1. Combine the rhubarb, strawberries, *crème de cassis,* and jam in a small, heavy-bottomed saucepan. Bring to a boil over medium heat and simmer, stirring frequently, for 20 minutes or until the mixture has reduced and thickened. Puree the mixture in a blender or food processor fitted with the steel blade and refrigerate until chilled, about 1 hour.

2. Preheat the oven to 400 degrees. Oil a 2-quart *soufflé* dish and coat the interior with sugar, shaking over the sink to remove any excess.

3. Place the egg whites in a copper bowl (or use a pinch of cream of tartar if you're using a stainless-steel or glass bowl) and start beating at medium speed until light and frothy. Raise the speed to high and beat the egg whites until stiff peaks form.

4. Beat one third of the egg whites into the fruit mixture to lighten it and then gently fold in the remaining egg whites. Pour into the *soufflé* dish and place in the center of the oven.

5. Immediately turn the heat down to 375 degrees and bake for 25 to 35 minutes. The *soufflé* will have puffed, and the top will be brown. Serve immediately.

NOTE: The baking time varies according to your personal *soufflé* preference. If you like *soufflés* soft, take it out sooner. If you like them firm, you can leave it in longer. The fruit base also makes a wonderful fruit sauce or compote, either hot or cold.

Apricot Soufflé

TOTAL TIME
2 hours
WORK TIME
30 minutes

PER SERVING
123 calories
0 cholesterol
.4 g fat
54 sodium

The dried apricots combined with the fresh give this almost guiltless dessert a mellow, fruity flavor heightened by the orange liqueur.   *Serves 6*

6 ounces dried apricots
1 pound ripe fresh apricots
2 tablespoons Triple Sec or Cointreau
Butter and sugar for the *soufflé* dish
6 egg whites, at room temperature

1. Place the dried apricots in a mixing bowl and cover with boiling water. Let them soak for 15 to 20 minutes or until soft. Drain in a colander, squeezing with the back of a spoon to extract as much liquid as possible.

2. While the apricots are soaking, bring a large pot of water to a boil. Place the fresh apricots in a colander, and place in the boiling water for 1 minute. Remove and run under cold water until cool enough to handle. Peel, stone, and dice the apricots.

3. Combine the dried apricots, fresh apricots, and liqueur in a blender or food processor fitted with the steel blade. Puree until smooth, scraping down the sides a few times. Refrigerate until well chilled, at least 1 hour.

4. Preheat the oven to 400 degrees. Grease a 2-quart *soufflé* dish with butter and dust interior with sugar, shaking over the sink to eliminate the excess.

5. Place the egg whites in a copper bowl (or in a stainless-steel or glass bowl with a pinch of cream of tartar) and beat until stiff peaks form. Beat one fourth of the egg whites into the apricot mixture to lighten it and then gently fold in the remaining egg whites.

6. Scrape into the *soufflé* dish, place it in the center of the oven, and immediately reduce the heat to 375 degrees. Bake for 25 to 35 minutes, depending on whether you like *soufflés* wet or dry. The *soufflé* will have puffed, and the top will be brown. Serve immediately.

NOTE: The apricot mixture can be made up to three days in advance and kept refrigerated, covered with plastic wrap.

Rhubarb Custard

Rhubarb was cultivated by the New England colonists in the eighteenth century, and although it's a vegetable, it's been used for desserts since that time. This creamy custard is a vividly colored, delicious way to enjoy this sign of spring.   *Serves 6*

TOTAL TIME
2 hours
WORK TIME
20 minutes

PER SERVING
120 calories
93 mg cholesterol
2 g fat
48 mg sodium

1½ **pounds fresh rhubarb, washed, trimmed, and finely diced (4 cups)**
⅓ **cup sugar**
⅔ **cup freshly squeezed orange juice**
1 **tablespoon finely grated orange zest**
2 **tablespoons flour**
2 **eggs**
2 **egg whites**
¼ **cup milk**
Vegetable oil for *soufflé* **dish**

1. Preheat the oven to 350 degrees. Place the rhubarb, sugar, orange juice, and orange zest in a saucepan and bring to a boil over medium heat. Cook, stirring occasionally, for 20 minutes or until the rhubarb is soft. Stir in the flour and whisk until smooth.

2. Scrape the mixture into a mixing bowl and allow to cool, stirring occasionally to speed the process, for 15 minutes. Whisk the eggs, egg whites, and milk together in a mixing bowl and then beat into the rhubarb.

3. Oil the interior of a 6-cup *soufflé* dish and pour in the custard mixture. Place the dish in a baking pan in the center of the oven and pour boiling water halfway up the sides of the *soufflé* dish. Bake for 45 minutes or until a knife inserted in the center comes out wet but not dripping. Serve warm or at room temperature.

NOTE: The custard can be prepared up to a day in advance and kept refrigerated, tightly covered with plastic wrap. Allow it to reach room temperature before serving.

Apple Strudel Pie

TOTAL TIME
1½ hours
WORK TIME
20 minutes

PER SERVING
193 calories
8 mg cholesterol
3 g fat
4 mg sodium

This dish is included as much to demonstrate the method of pie making as for the finished product. Any fruit pie can be prepared in the same manner, and you will always achieve a crispy, golden crust with a succulent filling.   *Serves 6*

Butter for pie plate
6 sheets phyllo dough, totally defrosted
1½ tablespoons unsalted butter, melted
3 Granny Smith apples
2 tablespoons freshly squeezed lemon juice
¼ cup dark brown sugar
2 tablespoons flour
1 teaspoon grated lemon zest
½ teaspoon ground cinnamon
Pinch of freshly grated nutmeg
1 tablespoon brandy or Cognac
2 tablespoons fruit-only apricot jam

1. Preheat the oven to 350 degrees. Using a pastry brush, lightly butter a 9-inch pie plate. Working quickly since the phyllo dries out very rapidly, center 1 slice of phyllo over the round pie plate and then, working clockwise, place the others so that the sheets create a circle much larger than the plate. Brush with butter and then roll the phyllo up, forming a crown around the rim of the pie plate. Brush with butter again and set aside.

2. Peel, core, and thinly slice the apples. Toss immediately with the lemon juice to prevent discoloration and then add the sugar, flour, lemon zest, cinnamon, nutmeg, and brandy. Toss to coat evenly, then pack into the pie plate and bake in the center of the oven for 50 minutes, brushing the pastry with butter a few times during the cooking process, or until the apples are tender and the pastry is brown. While the pie is still hot, heat the jam in a small saucepan and paint it over the top of the pie with a pastry brush. Serve warm or at room temperature.

NOTE: The pie can be prepared up to six hours in advance and kept at room temperature.

Strawberry Frozen Yogurt

Commercial frozen yogurts are one of the deceptive products on the market. Most of them contain large amounts of sugar and are almost equivalent to ice cream in calories. This light and tangy alternative is a blush pink color and allows the flavor of the fresh fruit to emerge.   *Serves 6*

1 pint strawberries, washed and hulled
2 tablespoons *crème de cassis*
2 tablespoons sugar
1 pint plain nonfat yogurt
2 egg whites

TOTAL TIME
30 minutes to 2 hours (depending on freezing method)
WORK TIME
5 minutes

PER SERVING
100 calories
2 mg cholesterol
.3 g fat
75 mg sodium

1. Combine all ingredients in a blender or food processor fitted with the steel blade and puree until smooth. Freeze in an ice cream freezer according to manufacturer's instructions or using the method on page 275.

2. Allow to sit at room temperature for 20 minutes before serving if it's frozen very solid.

NOTE: The frozen yogurt will keep for up to a week in the freezer. Frozen berries packed without sugar can be substituted for the fresh, and the yogurt will freeze faster if you puree them frozen. Fresh or frozen raspberries or blackberries can be substituted for the strawberries.

Maple Bourbon Frozen Yogurt

TOTAL TIME
30 minutes to 3 hours
(depending on freezing
method)
WORK TIME
15 minutes

PER SERVING
111 calories
2 mg cholesterol
.3 g fat
60 mg sodium

This is a wonderful winter dessert, when apples are clearly the best fruit on the market. The fruit blends well with the distinctive taste of maple, and the hint of bourbon adds interest.   *Serves 6*

2 red delicious or McIntosh apples, peeled and grated
⅓ cup pure maple syrup
2 tablespoons water
¼ teaspoon maple extract
2 tablespoons bourbon
2 cups plain nonfat yogurt
2 teaspoons freshly squeezed lemon juice

1. Place the apples in a small saucepan along with the syrup, water, maple extract, and bourbon. Bring to a boil and simmer over low heat for 5 to 7 minutes or until the apples are tender.

2. Place the apple mixture in a blender or food processor fitted with the steel blade and puree until smooth. Stir in the yogurt and lemon juice and freeze in an ice cream maker according to manufacturer's instructions or using the method on page 275.

NOTE: The yogurt keeps for up to a week in the freezer, tightly covered. Allow it to sit at room temperature for 20 minutes before serving.

Champagne Orange Sorbet

There is no commercially available product similar to this tangy, citrusy *sorbet*. It ends a meal on an elegant note, and it can also be served as an intermezzo for a very formal dinner. It is also an inspired way to use up flat Champagne.   *Serves 6*

TOTAL TIME
30 minutes to 3 hours
(depending on freezing method)
WORK TIME
10 minutes

PER SERVING
150 calories
0 cholesterol
.2 g fat
23 mg sodium

1 tablespoon unflavored gelatin
¼ cup cold water
2 cups freshly squeezed orange juice
¼ cup sugar
2 cups Champagne or sparkling wine
1 tablespoon freshly squeezed lemon juice
2 tablespoons Grand Marnier
3 tablespoons grated orange zest
2 egg whites, lightly beaten
Fresh mint sprigs or Champagne for garnish (optional)

1. Sprinkle the gelatin over the water to soften for 10 minutes. Combine the orange juice and sugar in a small saucepan and bring to a boil over high heat. Simmer for 10 minutes or until the mixture is reduced by one third. Stir in the gelatin and stir until no granules remain.

2. Combine the orange gelatin mixture with remaining ingredients (except garnish) and whisk lightly. Freeze in an ice cream freezer according to manufacturer's instructions or using the method on page 275. Allow to sit at room temperature for 20 minutes before serving, garnishing with a sprig of mint or a few tablespoons of Champagne if desired.

NOTE: The sorbet stays fresh up to a week in the freezer, tightly covered.

Kiwi Sorbet with Aquavit

TOTAL TIME
30 minutes to 3 hours,
(depending on freezing
method)
WORK TIME
10 minutes

PER SERVING
119 calories
0 cholesterol
.1 g fat
24 mg sodium

While we are accustomed to spices such as cinnamon in desserts, the complex flavor of this bright green *sorbet* is derived from the hint of caraway in Danish Aquavit and the fresh flavor of ginger.   *Serves 6*

8 large (about 3½-ounce) ripe kiwifruit, peeled and thinly sliced
⅓ cup Aquavit
2 tablespoons ginger marmalade
2 egg whites
½ cup water

1. Combine all ingredients in a food processor fitted with the steel blade and puree. (Do not use a blender, or it will crush the seeds and give the *sorbet* a grayish tinge.) Freeze in an ice cream freezer according to manufacturer's instructions or using the method on page 275. If it's solidly frozen, allow it to sit at room temperature for 20 minutes before serving.

NOTE: If Aquavit is not available, marinate ½ teaspoon of caraway seeds in vodka overnight and drain before using. The *sorbet* keeps for up to a week in the refrigerator, tightly covered.

Techniques

The repertoire of culinary skills needed to complete any recipe in this book successfully is not extensive, and since many of them appear frequently, they are explained fully in this chapter. Happily, many of the complex techniques that accompany classic French cooking—such as constructing butter-laden puff pastry or emulsifying egg yolk and butter for a hollandaise—hold no position in this new style of healthful eating.

Most Gourmet Gazelle dishes have as their foundation the use of fresh vegetables, herbs, and spices. Learning to handle these ingredients properly, and "prep" them for cooking, is both quick and easy. Not only do these foods form the basis of the dishes, but the blending of their flavors—rather than time-consuming presentation—is what makes the foods memorable.

SMART SHOPPING AND PLANNING YOUR COOKING

None of the dishes in *The Gourmet Gazelle Cookbook* take more than 30 minutes of hands-on preparation time. In many cases, you can complete a three-course meal in less than an hour, provided you plan your time economically.

After you have selected your menu (see "Menus for Entertaining" for suggestions), take a few minutes to sit down with a notebook. The first way to save time is to compile a unified shopping list. Once you've started using this technique, it will be apparent how quickly a trip to the supermarket can be completed.

Make separate columns for produce; meat, poultry, and seafood; dairy products; and general grocery. If you always shop in the same supermarket, you can speed things up even more by listing the grocery items in the general order of the aisles.

Supermarkets are generally planned to channel you first into the produce department. However, this should be your last stop. Start first with the proteins, since they will determine many of your other purchases. Nothing wastes more time than returning vegetables when you discover that the fish they were complementing is out of season. Also, since vegetables are the most fragile items placed in the basket, you are not in danger of crushing a tender papaya with a six-pack of Perrier.

On the second page of your notebook, list the dishes you are cooking and the total time they require. Read the recipes carefully and work backward from the time you want to serve dinner, adding time for phone calls and other interruptions that will cause delays. You can then determine what dish you should start when and what steps of each recipe should be completed in what order. After a while, this becomes second nature, but in the beginning, actually make a list. For example: (1) Begin soup, (2) roast peppers, (3) bone chicken.

Another time-saving technique, based on the system used in commercial kitchens, is to start by slicing and dicing ingredients common to many recipes. Add up the number of cups of chopped onion, the number of cloves of garlic, or the number of peeled tomatoes required for the total meal. Do these tasks at one time, dividing the total amount as needed. After completing these tasks, you can speedily cook the dishes.

STOCKS

There's no secret to the depth of flavor of soups and sauces in restaurants. It's the result of long-simmered stocks that add richness without calories, requiring only the culinary skill of knowing how to boil water.

Stocks are also less expensive than buying the inferior canned products if you save up a cache of the necessary ingredients. I keep plastic bags in my freezer and fill them with poultry bones and skin for chicken stock, meat bones and trimmings for meat stock, fish skeletons and shellfish shells for fish stock, and vegetables that are slightly past their prime. When the bags are full, and I'm going to be at home for the day, it's time to make stock.

The stock specified most often in the recipes is chicken stock. If you don't have the necessary trimmings, the most economical way to make it is by purchasing chicken backs. The few pounds needed will cost less than $2 and will make 3 quarts of finished stock.

In the old days, butchers would just give you meat bones. Today you'll probably have to buy them; however, they are very inexpensive. If possible, have them cut into lengths of no more than four inches so they will fit more compactly into your stockpot.

Both chicken and meat stocks should always be made in advance and chilled so that the layer of fat—all saturated—can be removed from the top. I freeze a portion of the stock batch in ice cube trays and learned the capacity of a cube by measuring with a tablespoon. They will keep in a tightly sealed bag in the freezer for up to six months. Freeze the remainder of the batch in 1-cup measures.

If you're using canned stock, unless it's unsalted (which is tasteless) omit even the small amount of salt called for in the recipes in this book. You can also decrease the salt level and improve the flavor by simmering canned stock for 15 to 20 minutes with vegetables, a *bouquet garni,* and a sliced potato. The potato will draw out a bit of the salt, and the herbs and vegetables will boost what is, unfortunately, the flat flavor of canned stocks.

The third alternative, and clearly the least preferable, is powdered bouillon. I have never found any with an acceptable flavor.

Chicken Stock

TOTAL TIME
3½ hours
WORK TIME
15 minutes

Makes 3 quarts

6 quarts water
5 pounds chicken bones, skin, and trimmings
2 carrots
1 large onion
3 garlic cloves
3 celery stalks
3 fresh thyme sprigs *or* 1 teaspoon dried
6 fresh parsley sprigs
3 bay leaves
12 black peppercorns

1. Bring the water to a boil with the chicken over medium-high heat. When it starts to boil, turn down the heat so it is simmering and skim the scum that will rise for the first 10 or 15 minutes.

2. While the stock is coming to a boil, scrub and slice the carrots. Peel and quarter the onion. Halve the garlic cloves. Wash and slice the celery.

3. Add the vegetables, along with the thyme, parsley, bay leaves, and peppercorns, to the pot and raise the heat until it begins to boil again. Reduce the heat again and simmer the stock for 3 hours.

4. Strain the stock, pressing to extract as much liquid as possible from the solids, and discard the solids.

5. Let the stock sit undisturbed at room temperature until cool, then refrigerate until the stock is cold and the fat has congealed into a hard layer. Discard that layer.

NOTE: The stock can be refrigerated for up to five days, covered with plastic wrap, and can be frozen for up to six months.

Meat Stock

Makes 3 quarts

TOTAL TIME
6 hours
WORK TIME
20 minutes

8 pounds meat bones, preferably veal, and trimmings
2 onions
2 carrots
2 celery stalks
3 garlic cloves
8 quarts water
3 fresh thyme sprigs *or* 1 teaspoon dried
6 fresh parsley sprigs
2 bay leaves
12 peppercorns

1. Preheat the oven to 400 degrees. Place the bones and trimmings in a roasting pan and roast in the center of the oven for 45 minutes, turning occasionally and regulating the heat so they do not burn.

2. While the bones are browning, peel and quarter the onions. Scrub the carrots, trim the ends, and cut into chunks. Wash and cut the celery into 3-inch lengths. Cut the garlic cloves in half.

3. Add the vegetables to the pan and continue to roast for 20 minutes.

4. Place the bones and vegetables in a deep stockpot and pour off any accumulated fat. Add 1 quart of the water to the pan and place on the stove over high heat. Stir until the brown bits clinging to the bottom of the pan are incorporated into the water. Pour into the stockpot with the remaining 7 quarts of water and bring to a boil over high heat.

5. When the stock begins to boil, reduce the heat so that it is barely simmering and skim the surface of the scum that will rise for the first 10 or 15 minutes.

6. Simmer the stock for 5 to 6 hours; strain out the solids and discard. Let the stock sit undisturbed at room temperature until cool, then refrigerate until the stock is cold and the fat has congealed into a hard layer. Discard that layer.

NOTE: The stock can be refrigerated for up to four days, covered with plastic wrap, and can be frozen for up to six months.

Fish Stock

TOTAL TIME
3½ hours
WORK TIME
15 minutes

Makes 3 quarts

4 quarts water
1 cup dry white wine
4 pounds fish trimmings, including skin, skeletons, shellfish shells, lobster bodies broken apart, heads
1 onion
2 celery stalks
2 tablespoons lemon juice
4 fresh parsley sprigs
2 fresh thyme sprigs *or* ½ teaspoon dried
6 peppercorns

1. Bring the water and wine to a boil over high heat. Wash all the fish trimmings. Peel and slice the onion. Wash and slice the celery.

2. Add all the remaining ingredients to the pot. When the water returns to a boil, reduce the heat so that it is barely simmering and simmer for 2½ to 3 hours.

3. Strain the stock, extracting as much liquid as possible from the solids. Discard the solids and allow the stock to reach room temperature before refrigerating or freezing.

NOTE: The stock can be refrigerated for up to five days, covered with plastic wrap, and can be frozen for up to six months.

CUTTING BELL PEPPERS

There is a quick and easy method for removing the seeds and ribs from bell peppers, one of the ingredients for which I have the most enthusiasm.

It is similar to an artist working in relief, since what you will actually do is cut away the flesh of the pepper, leaving a skeleton of seeds and ribs.

Cut a slice from the bottom of the pepper so it will stand firmly on the cutting board. Hold the cap of the pepper in your free hand and carve down the natural curvature of the sections with a small, sharp paring knife. You will be left with the skeleton to discard, and the pepper will be ready for further cutting as indicated in the recipe.

ROASTING AND PEELING BELL PEPPERS AND CHILI PEPPERS

There are as many ways to accomplish the roasting and peeling of peppers as there are species of capsicum—including ones I don't recommend, such as holding a blowtorch to them. The two universal elements of the approaches are some form of heat to blister or char the skin and some steaming or cooling process to facilitate peeling it away.

For the first part, always make a few incisions around the cap of the pepper with a small paring knife to ensure that the peppers don't explode. Here are some options:

1. *Broiling.* Preheat a broiler and place the peppers on a baking sheet as close to the heat element as possible. Keep the oven door open, since you want them to broil not bake, and turn frequently, using tongs, until the skins are uniformly black. You may have to adjust the position of the broiler rack to char the bottoms of the peppers.

2. *Stove-top.* If you're using a gas stove, remove the metal grid. Place a metal cake rack over the burner and turn the heat on high. Place the peppers directly in the flame. This is one of the fastest methods, since more surface is charred at once. Turn as necessary.

3. *Grilling*. This is essentially broiling them; however, the heating element is below rather than above.

Regardless of how the peppers are roasted, there are two basic methods of peeling them:

1. Plunge the peppers into a bowl of ice water. Within a few minutes they will be cool enough to handle. Rub the charred skin with your fingers, and the peel will dislodge easily.

2. Place them in a heavy plastic bag and seal it airtight with a twist tie or rubber band. Allow the peppers to steam for at least 20 minutes or until cool enough to handle. Hold the peppers under cold running water and rub off the skin.

The disadvantages of the second method are not only the elapsed time but that the peppers also continue to cook and lose texture.

Roasted, peeled peppers keep up to three days refrigerated (covered with plastic wrap). It makes sense, therefore, to do a large number if you think you will use them within the allotted time.

HANDLING HOT CHILIES

The burning sensation in your mouth when eating hot chilies comes from the potent oils. These oils must be handled with respect when cooking with the chilies.

Most old-fashioned cookbooks say to wear rubber gloves; however, I find them clumsy to wear when using knives. The best kind are very thin surgeon's gloves, purchased at hospital supply stores. If you're wearing rubber gloves, remember to wash them with soap after chopping the chilies, or you'll transfer the oils to your hands while removing them.

An alternative is to lightly oil your hands, work with the chilies, and then wash your hands with strong soap. Remember not to touch your skin with your hands until they have been washed.

Don't handle the chilies under running water, since the water will release vapors that carry the oils to your face. It is also wise to cut chilies on a plate rather than a cutting board. The oils can be lodged in wood fibers or in the cuts on a plastic board.

PEELING AND SEEDING TOMATOES

Many recipes call for the pulp of fresh tomatoes that have been peeled, seeded, and diced. Since the peeled and seeded tomatoes can be kept for up to three days refrigerated, this is a task I do every few days.

Bring water to a boil in a Dutch oven or stockpot. Add a few tomatoes at a time, retrieving them after 30 seconds with a slotted spoon. Place them in a bowl of ice water and proceed until all tomatoes are blanched.

The skins should slip off easily when rubbed with your fingers. Then cut the core out with a sharp paring knife and hold the tomato over the sink or a garbage can. Squeeze gently, holding the tomato in the palm of your hand with the core end down. The seeds will emerge, and then you can dice or slice the tomato as specified in the recipe.

CLEANING LEEKS

While I love the delicate flavor leeks give dishes, they are all extremely dirty when you buy them, even if they look pristine and the root has been trimmed.

If you're using the leek whole, trim the base and remove any leaves that are not bright green, always discarding all but 2 inches of the green leaves. Slice the leek lengthwise to within 1 inch of the base and soak the leeks for 15 minutes in cold water. That should soften the grit so that when you wash it under cold water, turning the faucet on medium, the dirt will wash away.

If a recipe lists chopped leeks, your job is much easier. Trim the root end, slice the leek in half, and separate the leaves. Run each under cold water and then chop the leeks.

BONING CHICKEN OR TURKEY BREASTS

While boneless, skinless chicken breasts and turkey breasts are now available in almost all supermarkets, the price per pound for the edible meat is still less if you bone them yourself. In addition, your cache of bones and skin for making poultry stock is always replenished.

If possible, buy the chicken breasts whole rather than split. Pull the skin off with your fingers and then make an incision on either side of the breast bone, cutting down until you feel the bone resisting the knife.

Treating one side at a time, place the blade of your boning knife against the carcass and scrape away the meat. You will then have two pieces—the large fillet and the small tenderloin.

To trim the fillet, cut away any fat. Some recipes will tell you to pound the breast to an even thickness so it will cook evenly and quickly. Place the breast between two sheets of wax paper and pound with the bottom of a small heavy skillet or saucepan.

To trim the tenderloin, secure the tip of the tendon that will be visible with your free hand. Using a paring knife, scrape down the tendon, and the meat will push away.

If you buy boneless, skinless breasts, go over them carefully. Since they are boned by machine, chances are that stray bones or part of the breastbone will still be attached. You will also have to trim the tenderloin as detailed.

SKINNING FISH FILLETS

Fillets of fish such as salmon and snapper are usually purchased with the skin still attached. Wash the fillet and hold it with the tail end in your free hand. Using a boning knife, push the knife away from you, toward where the head of the fish would be, scraping it along the skin. The fillet will slide easily away from the skin. Keep the skin for making fish stock; there is no need to remove the scales since the stock is strained.

GRILLING

Entire books are devoted to proper grilling techniques, and I do not presume to cover the subject in a few short paragraphs. These notes are intended to give you some basic pointers, since many of the dishes in the book are grilled.

I have both a gas and charcoal grill and would not part with either one. You cannot beat a gas grill for convenience. It is as easy to start as turning the knob on the stove, and it preheats in 5 minutes. While it sears food acceptably, it doesn't impart the same grilled flavor as food cooked over charcoal. For smoking foods, such as the Smoked Tomato Sauce (page 203) or the chicken breasts in Smoked Chicken and Seafood Gumbo (page 35), I use the charcoal grill with wood chunks that have been soaked in water. I don't find that wood chunks work well on the gas grill.

If you're using a charcoal grill, the safest and easiest method of lighting it is with an electric starter placed under a bed of coals. Within 15 minutes the coals resting on the coil will be red hot, at which time it can be removed and the fire will grow. Another device is the chimney starter, in which charcoal covers a bottom layer of newspaper. Light the newspaper and the coals are ready in about 30 minutes.

With no other toys at your disposal, light a charcoal grill as you would the fire in a fireplace. Place a bed of newspapers on the bottom, with some dry kindling on top. Make a pyramid of charcoal in the center and then light the newspaper.

Why, you may wonder, have I not mentioned a charcoal lighter? Certainly it creates a roaring fire within minutes. However, I believe the petroleum taste is never completely burned off, and the food tastes like burning gasoline. This is especially true with the recipes in this book, since they are primarily delicate fish and poultry rather than heartier meats.

With the exception of boneless, skinless chicken breasts, which should be cooked on a very hot grill for a very short time, a grill is ready when the fire has burned to the point that the coals are uniformly covered with gray ash and you can hold your hand at grill level for five seconds.

FREEZING FRESH HERBS

Most of the dishes in this book rely on the use of a mixture of fresh herbs to achieve a satisfying, complex flavor. For people in warm climates, an herb garden is a year-round way of life. For others of us, however, herbs are purchased most of the year in the supermarket, and the bunches are frequently far larger than the amount listed in one recipe. Herbs can be frozen, however, for future use.

For parsley, cilantro, and dill, remove the tough stems, leaving only the usable portion of the herb. Wrap portions of herbs in a heavy layer of plastic wrap and store in the freezer. When ready to use the herb, hit the back of the package with the blunt side of a knife, and the herb will be chopped and ready for use.

For leafy herbs such as basil, oregano, and marjoram, chop the herb and mix it with a few tablespoons of vegetable oil. Pack the herb into ice cube trays and deduct ⅓ tablespoon oil and ⅔ tablespoon herb from recipes when calculating their use. You don't need to allow the herbs to defrost before using them if they are going to be heated in a sauce or soup.

FREEZING WINE

This is a surprising tip I learned from my trusted friend and wine consultant David Vaughan. If you have opened a wonderful bottle of red wine and failed to drink it all, replace the cork and put the bottle in the freezer. On another occasion when you'd love a glass of claret, for instance, to accompany your dinner, allow the wine to defrost at room temperature.

You will have to decant the wine carefully to avoid the sediment that will have formed during the freezing and defrosting process. Once you have decanted the wine, however, you'll discover that it's lost none of its bouquet and hasn't suffered the perils of oxidation.

THE GOURMET GAZELLE COOKBOOK

MAKING FROZEN YOGURTS AND SORBETS WITHOUT AN ICE CREAM MAKER

During the last few years there has been a renaissance in the popularity of ice cream making at home. This is due to both the new popularity of *sorbets* and the general growth of ice cream mania in the country. However, if you don't own one of these machines, ranging from the inexpensive Donvier recommended later in this chapter to the Rolls-Royce Gaggia, there is no reason to forgo delicious ice creams, *sorbets*, and frozen yogurts.

Food Processor Method: Complete the recipe through the step calling for freezing. If you own a food processor, freeze your mixture in ice cube trays for 45 minutes to 1 hour or until the cubes are almost frozen. Empty the ice cube trays into the work bowl fitted with the steel blade and process, using on-and-off pulsing motions, until smooth. Put the mixture back into the ice cube trays and freeze for another 30 minutes. At that point scrape out the contents of the work bowl into a plastic container or mixing bowl.

This first method will take little more time than freezing your *sorbet* or frozen yogurt mixture in an ice cream freezer. The second method, intended for those who don't own a food processor, will take a total of 4 to 5 hours.

Electric Mixer Method: Freeze the *sorbet* or frozen yogurt mixture in a mixing bowl until the outer 2 to 3 inches is frozen. Remove from the freezer and beat with an electric mixer until smooth. Repeat 2 more times, then allow to freeze totally.

With both of these methods, the *sorbet* or frozen yogurt will tend to be slightly more crystalline than if frozen in an ice cream freezer, constantly aerated and beaten. However, both are effective ways of creating luscious frozen treats without the benefit of the specialized machine.

STOCKING THE PANTRY

Most of us scan a recipe and purchase the main ingredients, pulling from the pantry a pinch of this and a tablespoon of that. While stocking the pantry is expensive initially, you'll learn to rely on the products and keep them stocked at all times.

Many of the recipes in this book call for common ingredients, and if you keep these in the house you'll be able to race through the completion of the dishes. To compile this list I surveyed my own kitchen and included brand names I think deliver the best flavor at the best price.

Vinegars. Many different vinegars are used in the recipes to heighten flavors without augmenting the salt. A number of boutique vinegars have been added to the shelves of specialty food stores during the last few years, and most of them are excellent. Crabtree & Evelyn vinegars are also available at the company's toiletry shops. In the supermarket, here are the brands to spot:

Wine vinegars (white wine, red wine, and tarragon): Paul Corcellet, Pouret, Berio.
Sherry vinegar: Gran Gusto
Balsamic vinegar: Fini, Monari
Raspberry vinegar: Paul Corcellet, Silver Palate
Rice wine vinegar: Kame or Ty Ling

Oils. Both olive oil and vegetable oil (a combination of mono- and polyunsaturates) are used extensively.

☐ *Olive oil,* like all fats in this book, is used in such small quantities that I always buy an expensive and fruity one that will deliver the flavor of the oil. This is a matter of personal preference, and you should try a number of different olive oils before brand loyalty sets in. As with vinegars, brands such as Miss Scarlett's, Santa Barbara Olive Oil, and Raineri are available at specialty stores. Some supermarket brands to consider are Old Monk, Colavita, Goya, and Bertolli Extra Virgin.

☐ *Vegetable oil* should have no flavor at all, especially since it is used in baked goods. Everyone has an opinion as to whether corn and peanut oils do or do not impart flavor. I use Puritan Oil, made from rapeseed, which has a light feel on the tongue.

❑ *Dark sesame oil.* This aromatic, full-flavored oil is used in most of the Asian-inspired recipes in this book. I love Asian markets, so I usually stock up on sesame oil imported from Taiwan or the PRC, as well as other condiments, on one of my treks to Chinatown. At the supermarket, options are few: China Bowl is widely available; however, I prefer Ty Ling for the nutty flavor and deeper color.

❑ *Nut oils.* Nut oils, like olive oil, are primarily monounsaturated. They are aromatic and full-flavored, and a tablespoon imparts the flavor of the nut. Nut oils are imported primarily from France; Pommery and Vivier are both excellent lines, reasonably priced. Buy the smallest quantity you can and store them in the refrigerator, since they quickly turn rancid.

Mustards. While I've never been a fan of mustards on sandwiches except for pastrami, I love the nuance of sharpness they impart to foods as an ingredient. A number of salt-free mustards are now on the market, if you must strictly reduce your sodium, and the best lines are Chalif and Meredith's. While flavored mustards have been a rage of the 1980s, I find their usefulness in cooking limited. There are only two mustards that are specified in this book:

Dijon: I use Balducci's; other brands to look for are Fauchon, Grey Poupon, Corcellet, Maille, and Old Monk.
Grainy: Moutarde de Maison, Chalif, Pommery, and Old Monk are excellent.

Dried pasta. Pasta should be bland; you're relying on the sauce for the flavor. Keep a supply of *orzo, vermicelli, spaghetti,* and small shells. The best ones I've tried, available in supermarkets and avoiding trekking to Little Italy, are San Giorgio, Fini, and De Cecco. In specialty stores, look for Martelli.

Fruit-only jams. These jams represent a considerable calorie savings—16 calories per teaspoon versus 54 calories for sweetened preserves. Better yet, they taste like real fruit and not like sugar. The best jams I've tried are the entire lines of Clearbrook Farms, Kozlowski Farms, American Spoon Foods, and Lost Acres.

Dried herbs and spices. To see for yourself what a difference quality spice makes, mix up three brands of cinnamon with a little sugar and butter and make cinnamon toast. It will range from aromatic and pungent to metallic and bitter. In general, the McCormick glass bottles are the best you'll find in the supermarket. At specialty stores, you can buy Select Origins, Dean & DeLuca, and McFadden Farm.

Store all dried herbs and spices in a dark closet to keep the color fresh, and when you open the jar, sniff it. It should smell like the herb or spice. When it loses aroma, it also loses flavor. At that point, throw the jar out.

Freshly grinding pepper makes even more of a difference than using fresh herbs. You do not have to grind it for each recipe, however. I grind a few teaspoons at a time while talking on the phone or waiting for a pot to come to a boil. Keep the pepper in an old spice bottle; it will keep its flavor for a few days. The same is true for freshly grated nutmeg.

For a huge quantity, you can use a coffee grinder. Just make sure you clean it out very thoroughly, or the next morning will start with an unwelcome shock.

The herbs and spices you should own are black peppercorns, white peppercorns, crushed red pepper, cinnamon, nutmeg, allspice, cloves, rosemary, oregano, basil, marjoram, bay leaves, thyme, cumin, chili powder, sage, and coriander.

While it's not a spice, Tabasco sauce is essential, and should always be bright red. If it starts to turn dark, toss it.

Reduced-sodium soy sauce. Not only is the sodium saving considerable—1,000 milligrams of sodium per tablespoon for regular and 600 for reduced—but the flavor is less harsh and more mellow than ordinary soy sauce. I use Kikkoman; it's right on the shelf next to the regular soy and has a green label.

Liqueurs. While I never cook with a wine I would hesitate to drink, I will not waste Jean Danflou *eau de vie* or VSOP Cognac in cooking. The top-of-the-line brands to stock for these recipes are Grand Marnier (or Cointreau) and Tia Maria. I use Jacquin's *crème de cassis*, which is imported from France. It's fruity and sweet and not expensive. Check the taste from time to time; unlike most spirits, it doesn't last forever.

Canned stock. If you're out of stock, the Campbell's low-sodium broths are the best alternative. The difference between this brand and Swanson's stock is 70 milligrams of sodium for a 10½-ounce can as compared with 1,300 for the Swanson's.

Canned tomato products. During winter, you can get more flavor in a dish using canned Italian plum tomatoes than from the pale, mealy fresh tomatoes in most supermarkets. Progresso packs an excellent tomato, and for salt-free products—tomatoes, tomato paste, and tomato sauce—Hunt's is the best I've encountered.

Dried fruit. Many of the recipes in this book rely on the succulent taste of dried fruits. Once the box is opened, store it in the refrigerator, tightly sealed in a plastic bag. Dried currants are occasionally hard to find during the summer months, so purchase a few boxes when you can find them. Keep a supply of currants, golden raisins, and raisins. The easiest brand to find is Sun-Maid, and the fruit is excellent. If your supermarket has dried fruits in bulk, it's better to purchase them that way and buy only a small amount at a time.

American Spoon Foods is the only company presently making dried cherries. The company also has an equally good dried blueberry. The address to receive their mail-order catalog is P.O. Box 523, Petoskey, MI 49770. Or, you can phone 800-222-5886 (in Michigan, 800-327-7984) for the names of markets in your city.

THE FOOD PROCESSOR AND OTHER COOKING EQUIPMENT

There are very few pieces of kitchen equipment that cannot be improvised, and since until recently my kitchen was the size of a doghouse for a Doberman, I pared down to the basics. For example, I long ago turned my fish poacher into a planter since a roasting pan not only held fish for poaching but also baked turkeys.

However, the one equipment addiction I have is the food processor, and you'll see that most recipes specify its use. The dishes in this book derive most of their volume, as well as texture and flavor, from vegetables. While you can endlessly dice onions or mince garlic by hand, using the pulsing key of a food processor turns laborious tasks into almost instantaneous accomplishments.

For pureed soups, a blender tends to aerate them into malt-eds, while the processor accomplishes this task with no side effects.

While I admit to purchasing every new blade when it first appeared, the only ones I use with any frequency are the steel blade for chopping and pureeing and a variety of slicing disks.

The collapsible metal vegetable steamer should be included in everyone's *batterie de cuisine*. It is invaluable and easy to retrieve from the steaming pot. Alternatives: if you don't have a steamer, or you want to steam large items, such as quartered spaghetti squash, which are cumbersome, either fit the pot in which you want to steam the food with a cake rack or colander or place an inverted custard cup in a pot and place the food to be steamed on a plate on top of it.

The other investment you might consider is nonstick pans. When they first appeared a few decades ago, the coating was so thin that a silver spoon could scrape it off the pan and into the food. This is not the case today, however, and even such august companies as Le Creuset have begun coating pans with SilverStone. This means you do not have to add as much fat, if any at all, in sautéing foods, nor do you have to oil baking pans. While the savings in calories and fat in one use may be negligible, when you add together how many times you use the pans in the course of a year, the savings in calories are substantial.

If you have a sweet tooth, a Donvier ice cream maker will revolutionize your life. It is an inexpensive machine, and it makes *sorbets* and frozen yogurts in a few minutes, with none of the ice and salt needed by conventional ice cream makers. In a pinch, it can also chill soups very quickly; the only trick is to remember the soup is in it so it does not turn into *gazpacho sorbet*.

Converting Your Favorite Recipes to Heathier Foods

As we're devoting more attention to a fundamental change in our eating habits, our cooking habits have to change, too, so that preparing healthier foods becomes second nature.

Although we're becoming more adventurous in the foods and flavors we enjoy eating, most of our food tastes are still rooted in the foods of our childhoods.

In the same way, our cooking habits exist on both conscious and unconscious levels. We began to absorb cooking techniques watching as children in the kitchen. Who doesn't remember the beating of butter and sugar together as the foundation of countless goodies? When cookbooks and cooking classes were virtually unknown, generations of cooks learned only by oral instruction, and passed on the basic techniques of cooking rich food suitable for farmers and laborers. Healthy cooking methods are a very recent phenomenon, and it's often difficult to reconcile them with our favorite traditional foods.

You may have an old recipe in your files—a family favorite—that you know is not healthful. Yet, it's like an old friend, whose flaws you overlook and whose delights you enjoy.

This chapter will help you modify your cooking habits as your eating habits are changing and will give you tips on how to continue enjoying favorite dishes by lowering their calories, cholesterol, fat, and sodium.

HEALTHY COOKING METHODS ARE A VERY RECENT PHENOMENON, AND IT'S OFTEN DIFFICULT TO RECONCILE THEM WITH OUR FAVORITE TRADITIONAL FOODS

BODY BASICS

It is difficult to determine how many calories each individual should eat in the course of a day to maintain weight and, therefore, determine what number is needed in order to lose weight. We have begun to consider calories only in terms of those we take in; however, calories are a measurement of energy and of potential output rather than intake.

Calories are burned by every human activity, including lying perfectly still and breathing. The number of calories that an individual will burn during any given task varies according to personal metabolism. When the body is using more calories than it is taking in, the necessary energy is taken from the storage of fat cells in our bodies. While that number is individually determined, a rule of thumb is that it takes 3,500 more calories of output than intake in order to lose 1 pound; eating 500 calories less a day or expending an extra 500 calories will subtract 1 pound a week, at least in theory.

There is no question that we have become a nation of diet fanatics. *Better Homes and Gardens* magazine reported in 1986 that 90 percent of all Americans think of themselves as overweight, and 35 percent want to lose at least 15 pounds. Additionally, a Gallup poll released in November 1986 stated that 31 percent of American women ages 19 to 39 diet at least once a month, and 16 percent consider themselves perpetual dieters.

It is a paradox that while concern about the shape of our shapes is at an all-time high, the American diet continues to be notoriously unhealthful and high in fat. It's not just how many calories we consume in a day but also which foods comprise those calories that determine whether or not our diet is healthful.

NUTRITIONAL SAVVY

Medical authorities now believe that no more than 30 percent of our caloric intake should come from fat. Only 10 percent of our calories should come from saturated fats—the fats in animal fats and dairy products. Lowering our saturated fat intake will significantly lower the chances of cardiovascular diseases—stroke, heart attack, and hardening of the arteries.

While everyone agrees that saturated fats are unhealthful, there is still considerable controversy in the scientific community concerning the relative merits of monounsaturated and polyunsaturated fats.

Recent studies have conjectured that polyunsaturated fat lowers both the low-density (bad) and high-density (good) cholesterol in the bloodstream in a manner that keeps them in the same damaging ratio. These studies propose that monounsaturated fats alone lower only the "bad" cholesterol (LDL), maintaining the level of "good" cholesterol (HDL), and thereby favorably affecting the all-important ratio between them.

Olive oil and nut oils (walnut and almond, for instance) contain the highest percentage of monounsaturated fat, more than three quarters. Of the vegetable oils, canola oil (marketed under the Puritan label), made from rapeseed, is the highest in monounsaturated fat, 58 percent. By contrast, safflower oil is only 13 percent monounsaturated, and peanut oil (peanuts are legumes, not nuts) is 48 percent monounsaturated.

Corn oil margarine, according to the USDA, is made up of 46 percent monounsaturated fat, 18 percent polyunsaturated fat, and 13 percent saturated fat. Butter, although it's 50 percent saturated fat, is used in this book in small quantities. The total fat content of both butter and margarine is 80 percent of the total weight. Whether to "bank" the saturated fat allowances and eat margarine or eat small quantities of butter for the taste it imparts is an individual decision. The calories and total fat intake are the same.

As the percentage of calories from fat in our diet remains constant, so do certain guidelines concerning intake of cholesterol and sodium.

In general, cholesterol should not exceed 250 to 300 milligrams per day. If you keep in mind that a single egg yolk contains 270 milligrams of cholesterol, and most processed meats are high in sodium, it is not surprising that the cover of *Time* magazine in 1986 showed a frowning face of bacon and eggs. That "All-American breakfast" has contributed significantly to the unhealthiness of the American diet. But cholesterol is manufactured in the body using any kind of fat available in the diet, so lowering the total fat intake will also affect the cholesterol count.

Sodium, according to the National Research Council, should be limited to from 1,100 to 3,000 milligrams per day for a healthy adult. Sodium is present in trace elements in almost every food we eat, and some foods, such as celery, are excellent sources of natural sodium. Table salt is a wonderful flavor enhancer; I'm not advocating that the saltshaker be banished forever. However, moderation is the key, as well as retraining the palate not to require the amount of salt once added automatically to recipes.

In converting your recipes to healthier foods, the two main areas of attack are substituting ingredients and modifying cooking methods.

MODIFYING YOUR COOKING METHODS

Learn to look before you cook, always keeping an eye to how you can cut back on the fat, sodium, or cholesterol in a dish. It's a good idea to read through a recipe in advance, rather than attempting to change it while concentrating on the mechanics of its successful completion. Annotate the recipe with the substitutions you plan to make and then make notes about the results.

SAUTÉING

Use only enough butter or oil to coat the bottom of a pan lightly. One or 2 tablespoons of fat is all that is necessary to prevent the foods from sticking to the pan when you're sautéing onions, garlic, or other vegetables. If a recipe calls for more, cut back.

MEAT AND POULTRY

Although it takes a few more minutes, get into the habit of grinding your own meats. The recipes in this book specifying ground meat or poultry include the instruction to grind it or chop it in a food processor. There is no ground meat commercially available as low in fat as the meat you grind yourself.

The ground turkey available in supermarkets, for example, may include cholesterol-laden bits of skin and other fatty tissue. Even Louis Rich, a very reputable brand, lists 46 calories and 2.84 grams of fat per ounce for ground turkey, as compared with the USDA's calculations of 32 calories and .45 gram of fat for light-meat turkey.

Ground meats offer the butchers a chance to use the fatty, gristly scraps of meat left over from leaner cuts. It is much healthier to trim a piece of inexpensive round steak of all visible fat and then grind it yourself. The USDA deems fat contents from 17 percent to 27 percent of total weight acceptable for ground beef. A piece of well-trimmed round steak has a fat content of less than 10 percent of total weight.

The leaner cuts of pork to grind are the tenderloin and the loin. Leg of lamb, not lamb shoulder, produces the leanest chopped lamb.

In addition to grinding your own meat, look at your recipe to determine whether ground turkey or chicken could be substituted for ground red meat. The fat savings are substantial, usually without jeopardizing the taste of the finished dish.

If you must buy preground meat, the best rule to follow is to let your eye choose. The lighter the tone of the ground beef, the more fat is present. Look for a package that is solidly bright red.

For red meat to be roasted or braised, the savvy cook can save money while reducing the level of fat. Part of what designates prime-grade meat is the marbling of fat within the tissue. While it's slightly tougher, choice or good meat is substantially leaner. For example, a 3-ounce piece of broiled prime beef tenderloin contains 270 calories and 20 grams of fat, while the same size piece of graded good contains 216 calories and 13 grams of fat. If you can't find the Good grade, ask your butcher to order it for you. Ethnic markets are often a good source.

Also keep in mind that while veal has a slightly lower calorie and fat content than beef, lamb, or pork, it is higher in cholesterol. Regardless of the cut, you should remove all visible fat from red meat prior to cooking.

The calories and fat saved by eating skinless poultry are equally impressive. A 3.5-ounce serving of chicken breast with the skin attached has 197 calories and 8 grams of fat, while the same meat with the skin removed has 165 calories and 4 grams of fat.

Removing the skin is also a way of eating a more healthful version of rich, succulent duck. The skin of a duck contains a thick layer of fat, while the breast meat (referred to as *magret* on many French menus) is rather lean.

If you want to prove to yourself how much saturated fat is contained in poultry skin, cut a piece of chicken skin into small pieces and render the fat in a small saucepan. The skin from just one chicken breast will render 2 to 3 tablespoons of saturated fat.

In general, 3 to 4 ounces of red meat or 6 ounces of poultry should be considered a serving. Fill out the remainder of your meal with vegetables, whole grains, and fruits.

For meat and poultry, try to use dry rather than wet cooking methods. Marinating foods and then grilling, broiling, or baking them allows much of the fat within the fiber to be released and drip into the cooking pan; the marinade ingredients also impart flavor with a fraction of the calories of a sauce.

On a cold winter night, however, there are few foods as comforting as a plate of steaming stew. Braised dishes should be made either the day before you want to serve them or in the morning of that day. Chill all braised meat dishes prior to serving, to remove any saturated fat that has seeped from the meat during the cooking process. It will have become a solid layer on the top of the casserole.

SALT

The source of much excess sodium in our diets is mindless shaking of the saltcellar. For example, don't add salt to the water in which pasta is cooked; the sauce topping the pasta will be enough to flavor it.

In the same way, salt should be added only after a dish has finished cooking or to a marinade. Rather than automatically grabbing your saltshaker, taste the dish first and then determine whether it needs salt. Then add ⅛ teaspoon and taste again, adding up to ¼ teaspoon in total for 6 servings. Should individuals require more salt, they can add it themselves.

The same principle for salting only after cooking applies to steamed or boiled vegetables. Sprinkle them with a little lemon or lime juice, and the acid will boost the flavor and perk the palate as well as a sprinkling of salt.

SUBSTITUTING INGREDIENTS

At first, your cream soup may taste "thin" made with whole milk instead of heavy cream, and your banana bread may not have the identical texture when it's made with one third of the amount of nuts specified in your grandmother's recipe.

But by learning how to substitute lower-fat, lower-cholesterol, and lower-sodium products for ones you have been using, you can preserve the basic nature of your old favorites. As your palate generally adjusts to lighter foods, these old favorites will still taste good to you—just slightly different from your childhood memories.

Don't expect your palate to adjust immediately to some of these suggested substitutions; take it a step at a time. Cut back on the cream by one third, for example, and the next time make it two thirds. Our palates have the infinite ability to appreciate flavors, but they take time to evolve.

DAIRY PRODUCTS

Dairy products are perhaps the largest category of foods open to substitutions. There are very few recipes that absolutely require the use of heavy cream in large amounts. The caloric and fat savings are incredible: heavy cream has 800 calories per cup, half-and-half has 300 calories per cup, and whole milk has 150 calories per cup.

In recipes such as cream soups, part of the classic French tradition, substitute whole milk for the cream specified. If you want the soup to have a "creamier" consistency, thicken it slightly with 1 teaspoon of arrowroot or cornstarch mixed with 2 tablespoons of cold water.

Another genre of recipes specifying heavy cream is mousses, which call for whipped cream either to make them light or to hold their shape. In place of pure heavy cream, use one third of the amount and whip it extremely stiff. Add two thirds nonfat yogurt and fold gently to replicate the texture of whipped cream. To mold a mousse with less cream, soften 1 tablespoon of unflavored gelatin in 2 tablespoons of water for 10 minutes and then heat this mixture over low heat until the granules have dissolved. Fold the gelatin into your mousse base.

Sour cream, as luscious as it may be, is another high-fat culprit, so whenever possible, substitute nonfat or low-fat yogurt. The difference per tablespoon is 31 calories and 3 grams of fat versus 8 calories and .3 gram of fat for nonfat yogurt.

The difference between whole buttermilk and 3.5 percent low-fat buttermilk is 464 versus 150 calories a cup, with a cholesterol count of 83 milligrams a cup as compared with 35.

Changing the cheeses you use and the amount of cheese can create foods with a creamy, cheesy taste and a fraction of the fat. In French cooking, the term *gratinée* is used to describe the process of sprinkling with cheese and then browning lightly just prior to serving. This method allows you to taste the wonderful flavor of cheese but saves hundreds of fat calories since the cheese is only on the surface. For example, 1 tablespoon of Parmesan cheese has only 23 calories, 4 milligrams of cholesterol, 2 grams of fat, and 93 milligrams of sodium. On top of pasta, a few tablespoons is all you need for flavor, while a recipe for classic Italian pesto sauce contains a few cups.

Use low-fat cottage cheese, part-skim ricotta and mozzarella cheeses, and use *Neufchâtel* in lieu of cream cheese. For cottage cheese, the fat and cholesterol content is half; for ricotta, mozzarella, and *Neufchâtel*, it is about one third less than the higher-fat products.

OTHER SOURCES OF CHOLESTEROL

In addition to dairy products, two leading sources of cholesterol are egg yolks and organ meats. Unfortunately, two scrambled eggs for breakfast should enter the culinary archives along with *hollandaise* sauce. If you feel the need for this sort of hearty breakfast, try cutting 1 whole egg with 3 egg whites and lightly scrambling them.

Thicken sauces with cornstarch or arrowroot instead of egg yolks.

Organ meats, while high in nutrients such as iron and low in calories, are very high in cholesterol. A 3.5-ounce serving of sweetbreads contains 294 milligrams, and the same size serving of kidneys contains 387 milligrams of cholesterol.

Most organ meat recipes will work equally well with tender cuts of veal or chicken breast. In the same way, either cut the amount of shrimp in half in a recipe, augmenting it with scallops or fish, or substitute another species of seafood altogether. Until recently it was thought that all shellfish are high in cholesterol, but testing methods have become more sophisticated, and we now know that only shrimp is moderately high in cholesterol, with 332 milligrams per 6-ounce serving.

BAKED GOODS

In sweets and baked goods, many of the modification rules for the courses that precede them apply. You can usually cut back by 1 whole egg in a cake and substitute 2 additional egg whites. You can also glaze baked goods with egg whites rather than whole eggs.

I've found that most baked goods will not suffer if the sugar and fat are reduced by 25 percent. While baking is more precise than most cooking, and there are certain chemistries involved, few recipes are intolerant of some reductions.

For creaming the butter and sugar for a cake, for example, a few tablespoons less will only subtly change the resulting product, while the savings in calories and fat are on the positive side.

Nuts, an ingredient in many baked goods, are very high in calories. Walnut pieces, for example, have 770 calories and 74 grams of fat per cup. While the texture might be slightly different, you will have the same nutty taste by cutting the amount of nuts in half, toasting them in a 350° oven for 5 minutes to release their flavor and crisp them, and then substituting 1 tablespoon of walnut oil for other fat in the recipe.

For pastries and pies, roll the dough as thinly as possible and bake it for a shorter period of time. A one-crust pie, rather than the standard double-crust pie, is a tremendous fat and calorie saver.

Another idea is using uncooked rolled oats with a small amount of butter to give baked desserts a crunchy topping instead of making the streusel crumbs with flour and a large amount of fat.

PROCESSED FOODS

While foods in their natural form create some health hazards, learning to read labels and carefully choosing processed ingredients is equally important to better cooking.

An increasing number of food producers are beginning to carry nutritional labeling on their products. What is important to notice, in addition to the counts, is what serving size is specified. If you estimate that you will be eating half a package, and calculate that the nutritional information is based on one fourth or one fifth of that package, multiply accordingly to calculate how much you will really be eating.

Examine processed foods carefully, especially meats. In the past few years a number of products have appeared that are healthier than the traditional cold cuts, although a reduction of fat and sodium in an essentially unhealthy product does not ameliorate its ills substantially. Look for the reduced-fat, reduced-sodium cold cuts—different companies now produce salami, bologna, and ham. Rather than purchasing turkey or chicken roll, which is injected with a high-sodium stock and contains fat, look in the delicatessen for roasted turkey breast, lean baked ham, or lean freshly roasted beef.

Water-packed tuna is another example of an easy way to cut back on fat. A 3.5-ounce portion of tuna packed in water and drained has 127 calories and less than 1 gram of fat, as compared with 197 calories and 8 grams of fat for the fish packed in oil. If oil-packed tuna is the only option, allow it to drain for several minutes and then pat it with paper towels to remove as much oil as possible.

In the same way, if you don't make your own salad dressings, drain some of the oil from commercial salad dressings (you'll find it floating on top) and dilute them with water or chicken stock.

Frozen fruits are another category in which a random choice can make a difference. Buy only fruits that are packed without sugar syrup, and the calorie counts will be almost equivalent to those of fresh fruit. For example, 1 cup of frozen strawberries has 52 calories, while the same amount packed in sugar syrup has 245 calories.

By watching your own cooking, you can significantly cut back on the fat, cholesterol, and sodium in your diet. While the savings may not be that great at any individual meal, the cumulative effect of altering your style of cooking can substantially improve your health.

Menus for Entertaining

Fall and Winter Entertaining
Spring and Summer Entertaining
Ethnic Dinners

t always puzzles me that people who eat sensibly when alone have come to equate calories and fat as synonymous with gracious entertaining. I think the contrary is true, and when you are giving a party, your guests' thank-you notes will be all the more sincere if they are not cursing you when they step on the scale the next morning.

Since this book is meant to be part of everyday life, there's no reason not to utilize its recipes for entertaining. This is especially true since one of my rules for parties is that all but some last-minute details should be done in advance, even a day head.

All of the recipes listed as part of party menus can be completed at least partially in advance so that you can be a guest at your own party rather than a galley slave.

Organization is the key to a good party. Tape a sheet of paper to the refrigerator listing what steps still need to be taken to complete the meal and at what time they should be accomplished. It might seem trivial, but include such tasks as "open wine to breathe" and "grind coffee." Also build into the schedule setting the table, arranging flowers, and allowing yourself enough time to shower and dress.

Also list the menu. The pressure of guests in the house and a glass of wine are enough to lead you to forget the dish you've already spent time and money to make. Next to the dishes, list what bowls or platters you plan to use and count them to be sure you have the serving pieces required.

Always begin a party with the dishwasher and sink empty, the counters clean, and enough time to put your feet up for 10 minutes before the first guest arrives.

I haven't used calories as a guide to these menus; they were chosen to represent a compatible array of flavors, colors, and textures. I have planned the menus seasonally, since not only fresh foods but also entertaining occasions are seasonal.

Buffet parties are planned so that guests need only a dinner fork. I've never been good at the octopus syndrome—juggling a knife and fork with a plate in my lap and a wineglass in the other hand.

YOUR GUESTS' THANK-YOU NOTES WILL BE ALL THE MORE SINCERE IF THEY ARE NOT CURSING YOU WHEN THEY STEP ON THE SCALE THE NEXT MORNING

FALL AND WINTER ENTERTAINING

TRADITIONAL THANKSGIVING OR CHRISTMAS DINNER

Holidays should be subtitled "national days of carbohydrates and fat." A few years ago I was horrified to realize I had used more than 4 pounds of butter in cooking Thanksgiving dinner for eight people. I do believe variety and a bountiful table are part of the holiday spirit, and that's why this dinner will amply feed eight people, although the recipes are written for six. I've added more dishes, so the portion size of each will be smaller.

Butternut Squash Soup, page 24
Roast Turkey (or Turkey Breast)
Cranberry Sauce, page 217
Pumpkin Muffins, page 226
Spaghetti Squash au Gratin, page 181
Sweet Potatoes with Apples, page 198
Gingered Red Cabbage, page 80
Apple Pear Cobbler, page 246

A HOLIDAY COCKTAIL PARTY

I plan cocktail parties as forkless buffets when the size of the guest list has surpassed any hope of seating them. However, I always serve enough food, both passed by servers and on the dining room table, so that no guest should end up wanting dinner, and there are small plates on the table to encourage eating a greater amount of finger foods. All of the recipes listed below can be multiplied easily. To calculate how much food you need, the total should equal ⅓ to ½ pound of food per person.

Phyllo Egg Rolls, page 42
Herbed Quesadillas, page 46
Chinese Eggplant Spread, page 49 (served with crackers)
Herbed Turkey Sausage, page 54 (made as miniatures)
Shrimp-Stuffed Wild Mushrooms, page 60
Salmon Tartare, page 63 (served with crackers or in canapé shells)
Japanese Pork Balls on Wilted Spinach, page 68

A WINTER VEGETARIAN MEAL

With the cornucopia of spring and summer vegetables, and weather that leads us to lighter eating, devising a vegetarian dinner is less of a concern than when it's cold and your guests are looking forward to hearty food. This vegetarian menu fits the bill.

Lemon Egg Soup, page 31
or
Mushrooms Stuffed with Spinach and Chèvre, page 50
Pasta with Onion Sauce, page 205
Gingered Red Cabbage, page 80
Chardonnay Baked Apples, page 244

A CASUAL SUPPER

Sweaters and comfortable clothes in front of the fireplace after a brisk walk in the crisp air dictate a menu of comforting, old-fashioned food. Beverages to start with could be hot mulled cider or Swedish *glögg*.

Herbed Quesadillas, page 46
Alfred's Meat Loaf, page 158, with Herbed Tomato Sauce, page 202
Stuffed Baked Potatoes, page 190
Creamed Spinach, page 184
Maple Bourbon Frozen Yogurt, page 258

A SUPER BOWL PARTY

It's amazing how quickly traditions catch on in our seemingly untraditional society. One of these, gathering a group of friends around the television to watch the yearly gridiron classic, is now as important to sports fans as long-standing events like the Kentucky Derby. No one seems to know how chili became an unofficial Super Bowl food; however, this menu follows suit with its own healthy version.

Grilled Vegetable Pizza, page 44
Turkey Chili, page 136
Mexican Cilantro Slaw, page 82
Potato Salad Vinaigrette, page 85
Chocolate Angel Food Cake, page 235

A ROMANTIC DINNER FOR VALENTINE'S DAY

Valentine's Day should be hearts and flowers, and I frequently concoct a Valentine's Day dinner around some sentimental theme. In this case, the foods are basically all red and white, the day's official colors. The Lemon Cheese Mousse could be molded in a heart-shaped mold and decorated with strawberries or raspberries. While a Valentine's Day dinner should be stimulating, it should never be so heavy as to dull other, more appropriate physical reactions.

Red Pepper Bisque with Seafood, page 32
Pasta with Fresh Tomato Sauce and Crab, page 156
Radicchio Salad with Balsamic Vinaigrette, page 75
Lemon Cheese Mousse, page 249

A FALL/WINTER BUFFET

Stews are perfect buffet party foods. They can be made well in advance and require only a fork to eat. This menu is based on subtly seasoned foods with glorious colors.

Curried Carrot Soup, page 25
Veal Stew in Mustard Sauce, page 165
Braised Wild Rice with Pine Nuts, page 197
Spaghetti Squash Primavera, page 181
Stuffed Zucchini, page 187
Apple Strudel Pie, page 256

A FALL/WINTER FORMAL DINNER

A cold winter day, with no outside activities competing for your attention, is a perfect time to prepare an elegant dinner for special friends. The following menu lists two entrees, so serve smaller portions of each in order to have the traditional passage of a fish to a meat course and a white wine to a red wine.

Seafood Sausages, page 146
Veal Scaloppine with Fresh Shiitake Mushroom Sauce, page 162
Potato Onion Pudding, page 189
Braised Endive, page 178
Green Bean and Tomato Salad, page 76
Mocha Mousse, page 251

SPRING AND SUMMER ENTERTAINING

A PICNIC

In a shaded knoll or on a sun-drenched beach, the following menu will be welcome for its bright refreshing flavors. Unlike traditional picnic foods, none of these dishes contains mayonnaise, which should be avoided for both its fat and cholesterol content.

Chicken Yakitori, page 57
Curried or Cajun Chicken Salad Stuffed in Pita Pockets, page 91 or page 97
Dilled Cucumbers, page 78
Wild Rice Salad, page 88
Chocolate Hazelnut Meringue Cookies, page 233

DINNER FROM THE GRILL

It's only in recent years that Americans have discovered that grills are not exclusively synonymous with hot dogs and hamburgers. The following menu is a sophisticated combination of dishes and tastes.

Grilled Vegetable Kabobs, page 47
Tuna Brochettes, page 148
Smoked Tomato Sauce, page 203
Mixed Grilled Vegetable Salad with Rosemary Vinaigrette, page 74
Grilled Polenta, page 194
Fresh Fruit with Gazelle Cream, page 248

A COLD ASIAN BUFFET

The clean, crisp flavors and textures of Asian food make the dishes perfect for warm weather, when cream and butter tend to feel heavier than usual. All of the slicing, dicing, and stir-frying for this menu can be done well in advance.

Chinese Eggplant Spread, page 49
Shrimp and Snow Pea Salad, page 100
Chinese Chicken and Pasta Salad, page 110
Asian Cabbage Salad, page 83
Citrus Angel Food Cake with Fresh Fruit, page 234

A CASUAL SPRING/SUMMER DINNER

Spring and summer meals should have as their base the bounty of nature. This menu combines many of the fresh flavors of the seasons, from minty coolness in the soup to vivid rhubarb in the dessert.

Honeydew Gazpacho, page 12
Turkey Tonnato, page 139
Pasta Salad Provençal, page 107
Mushrooms à la Grecque, page 86
Rhubarb Custard, page 255

A FORMAL SPRING/SUMMER DINNER

In addition to honoring parents, May and June are filled with other rites of passages—graduations, possibly weddings. At these sentimental times, a formal dinner with starched linens, polished silver, and a basket of baby's breath on the table notes the occasions with the proper respect.

Zucchini Mousse with Salsa, page 48
Fish Steamed in Napa Cabbage with Red Pepper Sauce, page 142
New Potatoes with Rosemary, page 192
Tossed Salad with Yogurt Dill Dressing, page 210
Apricot Soufflé, page 254

A FOURTH OF JULY BARBECUE

Just at the time when you want to wear a bathing suit proudly, baked beans, potato salad, and side dishes swimming in oil make the season of casual entertaining fraught with calories and fat. For example, my favorite baked bean recipe is calculated at 521 calories a serving. This barbecue menu combines the traditional with the innovative.

Golden Gazpacho, page 16
Grilled Chicken Kabobs, page 120
Potato Salad Vinaigrette, page 85
Pickled Celery Salad, page 77
Corn Muffins, page 223
Strawberry Frozen Yogurt, page 257

A SPRING/SUMMER BUFFET PARTY

The same role filled by stews in the winter is assumed by elegant, festive salads on a summer buffet table. This all-cold menu is extremely colorful, and while each dish has distinctive flavors, none overwhelms the others.

Spinach and Carrot Loaf, page 52
Salmon and Cucumber Salad, page 99
Grilled Chicken and Red Pepper Salad, page 90
Confetti Rice Salad, page 87
Apricot Ginger Muffins, page 222
Peach Melba Mousse, page 250

ETHNIC DINNERS

While none of the foods in this book are authentically part of an ethnic cuisine, menus that are inspired by various national and regional fare can be compiled.

AN ITALIAN DINNER

This is a hearty winter meal. The menu emphasizes the robust nature of Italian cookery and its reliance on fresh vegetables and the quality of the basic ingredients. Serve small portions of each dish, since in traditional Italian fashion a number of courses are served.

Italian Chicken Vegetable Soup, page 37
Pasta with Seafood Baked in Foil, page 154
Peppers Stuffed with Beef and *Orzo,* page 161
Radicchio Salad with Balsamic Vinaigrette, page 75
Almond Meringue Cookies, page 232
Figs Poached in Grand Marnier, page 247

AN ASIAN DINNER

Most Asian cultures have practiced for centuries what Americans are just learning—a little bit of protein goes a long way. Asian cuisines are essentially healthy, and this menu amplifies those aspects of the culture.

Phyllo Egg Rolls, page 42
Chinese Chicken Tacos, page 58
Asian Grouper, page 152
Steamed Rice
Tossed Salad with Ginger Dressing, page 214
Kiwi Sorbet with Aquavit, page 260

A SOUTHWESTERN DINNER

The increasing popularity of new southwestern cooking is hardly surprising. This recent offshoot of New American cuisine combines assertive flavors and bright colors. In this menu those flavors are vividly displayed, but without the high fat content of many southwestern dishes.

Southwestern Vegetable Soup, page 28
Seviche Salad, page 103
Southwestern Halibut, page 149
Red Pepper Pasta, page 106
Southwestern Salad, page 84
Chocolate Pudding, page 241

A CAJUN DINNER

The cuisine indigenous to the remote bayous of Louisiana has ignited our national palate as much as cayenne pepper. This is a traditional Cajun menu, intended for cool rather than hot weather.

Smoked Chicken and Seafood Gumbo, page 35
Jambalaya, page 133
Tossed Salad with Celery Seed Dressing, page 215
Bananas Baked with Rum, page 252
or
Rice Pudding, page 242

A FRENCH DINNER

To many people, French food remains synonymous with ele-
gance. It has been only during the last decade that the country's
finest restaurants were not all French in derivation. Classic
French cookery is based on extensive use of butter, heavy cream,
and egg yolks. This menu contains the restrained seasoning and
luxurious texture of French food and is deceptively healthy.

Vichyssoise, page 15
Salmon with Basil Cream Sauce, page 143
Parsley Rice Pilaf, page 196
Brussels Sprouts with Lemon and Parsley, page 175
Tossed Salad with Rosemary Vinaigrette, page 212
Champagne Orange Sorbet, page 259

The Spa at Home Diet

Fall and Winter Menus
Spring and Summer Menus

The
Spa at Home
Diet

Fall and Winter Menus
Spring and Summer Menus

magine dieting without ever seeing a bowl of low-fat cottage cheese or a salad bowl drizzled with only lemon juice for flavor.

There is no question that it's when you're dieting that the Gourmet Gazelle approach to cooking is most welcomed. Since the calories are not reduced by portion control, the meals are large and satisfying. And since the sodium content of the dishes is low, you will see a difference in your weight almost immediately as the body is purged of retained fluids.

And there is also no question that if you follow the menu programs in this chapter, you'll lose weight. In fact, I lost 4 pounds the week I devised the program.

The diet is designed to keep a daily intake of calories to less than 1,000. Weight loss, as usual, depends on individual metabolism and how many calories are burned through exercise. For weight maintenance, add 50 percent to the portion size for lunch and dinner.

THERE IS NO QUESTION THAT IF YOU FOLLOW THE MENU PROGRAMS IN THIS CHAPTER, YOU'LL LOSE WEIGHT

The idea for the Spa-at-Home Diet occurred to me on New Year's Day, 1988, when my yearly weight loss resolution had yet to experience its inevitable goal modification from 20 pounds to 5. I was adamant with myself: I would eat only the food sold at the shop for a month. I wrote down a daily menu, calculating serving sizes and creating total variety.

In my second week it occurred to me that this was an idea that could be shared with our customers. The shop delivered shopping bags loaded with a day's meal each morning, and during the first six months of the program, more than 400 people dieted successfully.

For a business, it was possible not to repeat a dish for an entire week, since the kitchen prepares a constantly changing repertoire. For this book, however, I have repeated dishes, since I doubt anyone really wants to cook 40 to 50 recipes a week. Lunches are all cold, so they can easily be transported to the office.

You'll find yourself full at the end of these meals. Eating slowly will allow you to enjoy the combination of textures and flavors that are part of each meal. If you wish to supplement these foods, add some vegetable crudités to lunch and dinner and some fresh fruit to breakfast.

The menus are selected seasonally and are arranged in a two-week cycle. For the purposes of dieting, the portion size is listed. The portions correspond to approximately one sixth of a recipe. I suggest that you purchase a kitchen scale and actually weigh out the meals, especially until you begin to have the ability to judge portion size visually.

In addition to the food prepared from this book, purchase some fruit-only jams (page 277) for your breakfast breads and muffins and whatever noncaloric beverages you like to drink.

If you want to enjoy a glass of wine with dinner, remember to factor those calories into your day or cut back on the size of your dessert.

As with any weight reduction program, you should contact your physician before beginning.

FALL AND WINTER MENUS

BREAKFAST: Cherry Muffin, page 225 (freeze the extra muffins in an airtight plastic bag), with 2 teaspoons of jam

LUNCH: Asian Chicken Salad, page 93 (8 ounces)

DINNER: Scallion Soup, page 23 (8 ounces)
Roasted Monkfish in Plum Wine Sauce, page 140 (6 ounces)
Parsley Rice Pilaf, page 196 (4 ounces)
Tossed Salad with Blue Cheese Dressing, page 211 (3 tablespoons)
Chardonnay Baked Apple, page 244 (1 medium)

DAY 2

BREAKFAST: Corn Muffin, page 223 (freeze the extra muffins in an airtight plastic bag), with 2 teaspoons of jam

LUNCH: Celery Root Rémoulade, page 81 (6 ounces)
Mixed Grilled Vegetable Salad with Rosemary Vinaigrette, page 74 (6 ounces)

DINNER: Butternut Squash Soup, page 24 (8 ounces)
Chicken Loaf with Watercress, page 121 (6 ounces)
Stuffed Baked Potato, page 190 (1 serving)
Spaghetti Squash au Gratin, page 181 (6 ounces)
Zinfandel Poached Pear, page 245 (1 medium)

DAY 3

BREAKFAST: Cherry Muffin, page 225, with 2 teaspoons of jam

LUNCH: Salmon and Cucumber Salad, page 99 (6 ounces)
Tossed Salad with Blue Cheese Dressing, page 211 (2 tablespoons)

DINNER: Scallion Soup, page 23 (8 ounces)
Beef Braised in Stout Beer, page 160 (6 ounces)
Potato Onion Pudding, page 189 (4 ounces)
Celery Root Rémoulade, page 81 (4 ounces)
Chardonnay Baked Apple, page 244 (1 medium)

DAY 4

BREAKFAST: Corn Muffin, page 223, with 2 teaspoons of jam

LUNCH: Asian Chicken Salad, page 93 (8 ounces)

DINNER: Mushrooms Stuffed with Spinach and Chèvre, page 50 (2 large caps)
Chicken Loaf with Watercress, page 121 (6 ounces)
Parsley Rice Pilaf, page 196 (4 ounces)
Mixed Grilled Vegetable Salad with Rosemary Vinaigrette, page 74 (6 ounces)
Apricot Soufflé, page 254 (one sixth of recipe)

DAY 5

BREAKFAST: Carrot Bread, page 230 (1 slice; freeze the extra slices individually, wrapped in aluminum foil), with 2 teaspoons of jam

LUNCH: Salmon and Cucumber Salad, page 99 (6 ounces)
Spaghetti Squash au Gratin, page 181 (4 ounces)

DINNER: Butternut Squash Soup, page 24 (8 ounces)
Turkey Chili, page 136 (6 ounces)
Stuffed Baked Potato, page 190 (1 serving)
Tossed Salad with Blue Cheese Dressing, page 211 (3 tablespoons)
Zinfandel Poached Pear, page 245 (1 medium)

DAY 6

BREAKFAST: Cherry Muffin, page 225, with 2 teaspoons of jam

LUNCH: Pasta Salad Provençal, page 107 (6 ounces)

DINNER: Mushrooms Stuffed with Spinach and Chèvre, page 50 (2 large caps)
Fish Steamed in Napa Cabbage with Red Pepper Sauce, page 142 (6 ounces)
New Potatoes with Rosemary, page 192 (4 ounces)
Celery Root Rémoulade, page 81 (4 ounces)
Fresh Fruit with Gazelle Cream, page 248 (3 tablespoons)

DAY 7

BREAKFAST: Carrot Bread, page 230 (1 slice), with 2 teaspoons of jam

LUNCH: Curried Chicken Salad, page 91 (8 ounces)

DINNER: Pasta Salad Provençal, page 107 (4 ounces)
Beef Braised in Stout Beer, page 160 (6 ounces)
Stuffed Baked Potato, page 190 (1 serving)
Mixed Grilled Vegetable Salad with Rosemary Vinaigrette, page 74 (6 ounces)
Chardonnay Baked Apple, page 244 (1 medium)

WEEK 2   **DAY 1**

BREAKFAST: Pumpkin Muffin, page 226 (freeze the extra muffins in an airtight plastic bag), with 2 teaspoons of jam

LUNCH: Cajun Chicken Salad, page 97 (6 ounces)
Dilled Cucumbers, page 177 (4 ounces)

DINNER: Cream of Celery Soup with Tarragon, page 30 (8 ounces)
Turkey Stew with Marsala and Sage, page 135 (6 ounces)
Radicchio Salad with Balsamic Vinaigrette, page 75 (3 tablespoons)
New Potatoes with Rosemary, page 192 (3 ounces)
Apple Strudel Pie, page 256 (one sixth of recipe)

DAY 2

BREAKFAST: Apricot Ginger Muffin, page 222 (freeze the extra muffins in an airtight plastic bag), with 2 teaspoons of jam

LUNCH: Shrimp and Snow Pea Salad, page 100 (6 ounces)
Radicchio Salad with Balsamic Vinaigrette, page 75 (2 tablespoons)

DINNER: Grilled Vegetable Kabobs, page 47 (1 kabob)
Southwestern Halibut, page 149 (6 ounces)
Mushrooms à la Grecque, page 86 (4 ounces)
Steamed Rice (3 ounces)
Mocha Mousse, page 251 (one sixth of recipe)

DAY 3

BREAKFAST: Pumpkin Muffin, page 226, with 2 teaspoons of jam

LUNCH: Cajun Chicken Salad, page 97 (6 ounces)
Cold Grilled Vegetable Kabobs, page 47 (1 skewer)

DINNER: Cream of Celery Soup with Tarragon, page 30 (8 ounces)
Alfred's Meat Loaf with Herbed Tomato Sauce, page 158 (6 ounces)
Mushroom Barley Casserole, page 195 (3 ounces)
Radicchio Salad with Balsamic Vinaigrette, page 75 (3 tablespoons)
Apple Strudel Pie, page 256 (one sixth of recipe)

DAY 4

BREAKFAST: Banana Bread, page 229 (1 slice; freeze the extra slices individually, wrapped in aluminum foil), with 2 teaspoons of jam

LUNCH: Shrimp and Snow Pea Salad, page 100 (6 ounces)
Mushrooms à la Grecque, page 86 (4 ounces)

DINNER: Red Pepper Bisque with Seafood, page 32 (8 ounces)
Turkey Stew with Marsala and Sage, page 135 (6 ounces)
Mushroom Barley Casserole, page 195 (3 ounces)
Pickled Celery Salad, page 77 (6 ounces)
Apple Pear Cobbler, page 246 (one sixth of recipe)

DAY 5

BREAKFAST: Apricot Ginger Muffin, page 222, with 2 teaspoons of jam

LUNCH: Mediterranean Lamb Salad with Barley, page 111 (6 ounces)
Pickled Celery Salad, page 77 (4 ounces)

DINNER: Grilled Vegetable Kabobs, page 47 (1 skewer)
Creole Swordfish, page 150 (6 ounces)
Steamed Rice (3 ounces)
Deviled Leeks, page 179 (2 leeks)
Mocha Mousse, page 251 (one sixth of recipe)

DAY 6

BREAKFAST: Banana Bread, page 229 (1 slice), with 2 teaspoons of jam

LUNCH: Cold Creole Swordfish, page 150 (6 ounces)
Radicchio Salad with Balsamic Vinaigrette, page 75 (2 tablespoons)

DINNER: Red Pepper Bisque with Seafood, page 32 (8 ounces)
Alfred's Meat Loaf with Herbed Tomato Sauce, page 158 (6 ounces)
Garlic Roasted Potatoes, page 193 (4 ounces)
Gingered Red Cabbage, page 80 (4 ounces)
Apple Pear Cobbler, page 246 (one sixth of recipe)

DAY 7

BREAKFAST: Apricot Ginger Muffin, page 222, with 2 teaspoons of jam

LUNCH: Mediterranean Lamb Salad with Barley, page 111 (6 ounces)
Gingered Red Cabbage, page 80 (4 ounces)

DINNER: Spinach Soufflé, page 185 (one sixth of recipe)
Herbed Chicken Legs, page 129 (one sixth of recipe)
Mushroom Barley Casserole, page 195 (3 ounces)
Deviled Leeks, page 179 (2 leeks)
Mocha Mousse, page 251 (one sixth of recipe)

SPRING AND SUMMER MENUS

WEEK 1 **DAY 1**

BREAKFAST: Cherry Muffin, page 225 (freeze extra muffins in an airtight plastic bag), with 2 teaspoons of jam

LUNCH: Seviche Salad, page 103 (6 ounces)
Mexican Cilantro Slaw, page 82 (4 ounces)

DINNER: Honeydew Gazpacho, page 12 (8 ounces)
Turkey Tonnato, page 139 (6 ounces)
Mixed Grilled Vegetable Salad with Rosemary Vinaigrette, page 74 (4 ounces)
Confetti Rice Salad, page 87 (3 ounces)
Strawberry Frozen Yogurt, page 257 (one sixth of recipe)

DAY 2

BREAKFAST: Carrot Bread, page 230 (1 slice; freeze the extra slices individually, wrapped in aluminum foil), with 2 teaspoons of jam

LUNCH: Curried Chicken Salad, page 91 (6 ounces)
Southwestern Salad, page 84 (4 ounces)

DINNER: Chinese Eggplant Spread, page 49 (4 ounces)
Grilled Chicken Kabob, page 120 (1 skewer)
Grilled Polenta, page 194 (1 serving)
Tossed Salad with Celery Seed Dressing, page 215 (3 tablespoons)
Citrus Angel Food Cake, page 234 (1 serving)

DAY 3

BREAKFAST: Cherry Muffin, page 225, with 2 teaspoons of jam

LUNCH: Seviche Salad, page 103 (6 ounces)
Mixed Grilled Vegetable Salad with Rosemary Vinaigrette, page 74 (4 ounces)

DINNER: Honeydew Gazpacho, page 12 (8 ounces)
Caribbean Grouper, page 145 (6 ounces)
Parsley Rice Pilaf, page 196 (3 ounces)
Southwestern Salad, page 84 (4 ounces)
Strawberry Frozen Yogurt, page 257 (one sixth of recipe)

DAY 4

BREAKFAST: Carrot Bread, page 230 (1 slice), with 2 teaspoons of
jam

LUNCH: Curried Chicken Salad, page 91 (6 ounces)
Mexican Cilantro Slaw, page 82 (4 ounces)

DINNER: Salsa Soup with Seafood, page 18 (8 ounces)
Turkey Tonnato, page 139 (6 ounces)
Confetti Rice Salad, page 87 (3 ounces)
Tossed Salad with Celery Seed Dressing, page 215
(3 tablespoons)
Citrus Angel Food Cake, page 234 (1 slice)

DAY 5

BREAKFAST: Corn Muffin, page 223 (freeze the extra muffins in an
airtight plastic bag), with 2 teaspoons of jam

LUNCH: Cold Grilled Chicken Kabob, page 120 (1 skewer)
Mixed Grilled Vegetable Salad with Rosemary Vinaigrette, page 74 (4 ounces)

DINNER: Chinese Eggplant Spread, page 49 (4 ounces)
Stuffed Flank Steak, page 167 (6 ounces)
Grilled Polenta, page 194 (1 serving)
Southwestern Salad, page 84 (4 ounces)
Fresh Fruit with Gazelle Cream, page 248 (1 serving)

DAY 6

BREAKFAST: Cherry Muffin, page 225, with 2 teaspoons of jam

LUNCH: Scallop and Asparagus Salad, page 101 (6 ounces)

DINNER: Salsa Soup with Seafood, page 18 (8 ounces)
Pasta with Seafood Baked in Foil, page 154 (one sixth of recipe)
Tossed Salad with Balsamic Vinaigrette, page 213 (3 tablespoons)
Strawberry Frozen Yogurt, page 257 (one sixth of recipe)

DAY 7

BREAKFAST: Corn Muffin, page 223, with 2 teaspoons of jam

LUNCH: Scallop and Asparagus Salad, page 101 (6 ounces)
Tossed Salad with Balsamic Vinaigrette, page 213 (2 tablespoons)

DINNER: Chinese Eggplant Spread, page 49 (4 ounces)
Stuffed Flank Steak, page 167 (6 ounces)
Grilled Polenta, page 194 (1 serving)
Gingered Red Cabbage, page 80 (4 ounces)
Fresh Fruit with Gazelle Cream, page 248 (1 serving)

BREAKFAST: Banana Bread, page 229 (1 slice; freeze the extra slices individually, wrapped in aluminum foil), with 2 teaspoons of jam

LUNCH: Grilled Chicken and Red Pepper Salad, page 90 (6 ounces)
Tossed Salad with Blue Cheese Dressing, page 211 (2 tablespoons)

DINNER: Golden Gazpacho, page 16 (8 ounces)
Asian Grouper, page 152 (6 ounces)
Steamed Rice, (3 ounces)
Asian Cabbage Salad, page 83 (4 ounces)
Kiwi Sorbet with Aquavit, page 260 (one sixth of recipe)

DAY 2

BREAKFAST: Bran Muffin, page 224 (freeze the extra muffins in an airtight plastic bag), with 2 teaspoons of jam

LUNCH: Tuna Salad Niçoise, page 104 (6 ounces)
Three-Pepper Gazpacho Salad, page 79 (4 ounces)

DINNER: Dilled Cucumber Soup, page 20 (8 ounces)
Cold Poached Chicken Breast with Spicy Melon Relish, page 123 (6 ounces)
Confetti Rice Salad, page 87 (3 ounces)
Tossed Salad with Pear Dressing, page 210 (3 tablespoons)
Zinfandel Poached Pear, page 245 (1 pear)

DAY 3

BREAKFAST: Banana Bread, page 229 (1 slice), with 2 teaspoons of jam

LUNCH: Grilled Chicken and Red Pepper Salad, page 90 (6 ounces)
Three-Pepper Gazpacho Salad, page 79 (4 ounces)

DINNER: Golden Gazpacho, page 16 (8 ounces)
Alfred's Meat Loaf with Herbed Tomato Sauce, page 158 (6 ounces)
Asian Cabbage Salad, page 83 (4 ounces)
Potato Salad Vinaigrette, page 85 (3 ounces)
Kiwi Sorbet with Aquavit, page 260 (one sixth of recipe)

DAY 4

BREAKFAST: Bran Muffin, page 224, with 2 teaspoons of jam

LUNCH: Tuna Salad Niçoise, page 104 (6 ounces)
Asian Cabbage Salad, page 83 (4 ounces)

DINNER: Vichyssoise, page 15 (8 ounces)
Cold Poached Chicken Breast with Spicy Melon Relish, page 123 (6 ounces)
Tossed Salad with Balsamic Vinaigrette, page 213 (3 tablespoons)
Potato Salad Vinaigrette, page 85 (3 ounces)
Strawberry Rhubarb Soufflé, page 253 (one sixth of recipe)

DAY 5

BREAKFAST: Banana Bread, page 229 (1 slice), with 2 teaspoons of jam

LUNCH: Asian Chicken Salad, page 93 (8 ounces)

DINNER: Dilled Cucumber Soup, page 20 (8 ounces)
Tuna Brochettes in Red Wine with Smoked Tomato Sauce, page 148 (6 ounces)
Confetti Rice Salad, page 87 (3 ounces)
Tossed Salad with Pear Dressing, page 210 (3 tablespoons)
Zinfandel Poached Pear, page 245 (1 pear)

DAY 6

BREAKFAST: Bran Muffin, page 224, with 2 teaspoons of jam

LUNCH: Cold Tuna Brochette, page 148 (6 ounces)
Tossed Salad with Balsamic Vinaigrette, page 213 (2 tablespoons)

DINNER: Vichyssoise, page 15 (8 ounces)
Alfred's Meat Loaf with Herbed Tomato Sauce, page 158 (6 ounces)
Spinach Soufflé, page 185 (one sixth of recipe)
Garlic Roasted Potatoes, page 193 (3 ounces)
Kiwi Sorbet with Aquavit, page 260 (one sixth of recipe)

DAY 7

BREAKFAST: Banana Bread, page 229 (1 slice), with 2 teaspoons of jam

LUNCH: Asian Chicken Salad, page 93 (8 ounces)

DINNER: Garlic Steamed Clams, page 65 (one sixth of recipe)
Pasta with Fresh Tomato Sauce and Crab, page 156 (one sixth of recipe)
Tossed Salad with Blue Cheese Dressing, page 211 (3 tablespoons)
Zinfandel Poached Pear, page 245 (1 pear)

Metric Conversion Chart

Ounces (oz)	Grams (g)
1 oz	30g*
2 oz	60g
3 oz	85g
4 oz	115g
5 oz	140g
6 oz	180g
7 oz	200 g
8 oz	225g
9 oz	250g
10 oz	285g
11 oz	300g
12 oz	340g
13 oz	370g
14 oz	400g
15 oz	425g
16 oz	450g
20 oz	570g
24 oz	680g
28 oz	790g
32 oz	900g

*Approximate. To convert ounces to grams multiply number of ounces by 28.35.

CONVERSIONS OF QUARTS TO LITERS

Quarts (qt)	Liters (L)
1 qt	1 L*
1½ qt	1½ L
2 qt	2 L
2½ qt	2½ L
3 qt	2¾ L
4 qt	3¾ L
5 qt	4¾ L
6 qt	5½ L
7 qt	6½ L
8 qt	7½ L
9 qt	8½ L
10 qt	9½ L

*Approximate. To convert quarts to liters, multiply number of quarts by 0.95.

CONVERSIONS OF POUNDS
TO GRAMS AND KILOGRAMS

Pounds (lb)	Grams (g); kilograms (kg)
1 lb	450 g*
1¼ lb	565 g
1½ lb	675 g
1¾ lb	800 g
2 lb	900 g
2½ lb	1,125 g; 1¼ kg
3 lb	1,350 g
3½ lb	1,500 g; 1½ kg
4 lb	1,800 g
4½ lb	2 kg
5 lb	2¼ kg
5½ lb	2½ kg
6 lb	2¾ kg
6½ lb	3 kg
7 lb	3¼ kg
7½ lb	3½ kg
8 lb	3¾ kg
9 lb	4 kg
10 lb	4½ kg

*Approximate. To convert pounds into kilograms, multiply number of pounds by 453.6

CONVERSIONS OF FAHRENHEIT
TO CELSIUS

Fahrenheit	Celsius
170°F	77°C
180°F	82°C
190°F	88°C
200°F	95°C
225°F	110°C
250°F	120°C
300°F	150°C
325°F	165°C
350°F	180°C
375°F	190°C
400°F	205°C
425°F	220°C
450°F	230°C
475°F	245°C
500°F	260°C
525°F	275°C
550°F	290°C

*Approximate. To convert Fahrenheit to Celsius, subtract 32, multiply by 5 then divide by 9.

CONVERSION OF INCHES
TO CENTIMETERS

Inches (in)	Centimeters (cm)
⅙ in	¼ cm*
⅛ in	½ cm
½ in	1½ cm
¾ in	2 cm
1 in	2½ cm
1½ in	4 cm
2 in	5 cm
2½ in	6½ cm
3 in	8 cm
3½ in	9 cm
4 in	10 cm
4¼ in	11½ cm
5 in	13 cm
5½ in	14 cm
6 in	15 cm
6½ in	16½ cm
7 in	18 cm
7½ in	19 cm
8 in	20 cm
8½ in	21½ cm
9 in	23 cm
9½ in	24 cm
10 in	25 cm
11 in	28 cm
12 in	30 cm
13 in	33 cm
14 in	35 cm
15 in	38 cm
16 in	41 cm
17 in	43 cm
18 in	46 cm
19 in	48 cm
20 in	51 cm
21 in	53 cm
22 in	56 cm
23 in	58 cm
24 in	61 cm
25 in	63½ cm
30 in	76 cm
35 in	89 cm
40 in	102 cm
45 in	114 cm
50 in	127 cm

*Approximate. To convert inches to centimeters, multiply number of inches by 2.54.

Index

INDEX